Property Office Economy

Dr Robert Harris

2005

EG BOOKS

A division of Reed Business Information

Estates Gazette
1 Procter Street, London WC1V 6EU

ISBN 0 7282 0476 2

Typeset in Palatino 10/12 by Amy Boyle, Rochester, Kent
Printed by Bell & Bain Ltd., Glasgow

Contents

Foreword

The importance of this book is directly correlated with the enormous changes that have reshaped London in the past two decades, reinforcing the city's position as one of the three global centres for financial and professional services and, perhaps more importantly, for the growing network of businesses that make up the knowledge economy. Dr Rob Harris is unique in that he is the first commentator to have been an eye witness with the depth of practical experience to describe the role that the property industry has played in these changes as well as having the breadth of vision to explain the historical background and the economic, technological and social drivers of change. He does all this with the confidence of having been an active participant in the process of change both at DEGW, an international architectural practice specialising in office design, and at Stanhope, the most innovative of all the London office developers. He is also an extremely well read, thoughtful and disciplined intellectual, well formed in that most physical and integrative of all disciplines, geography.

The great thing about the book is that Rob Harris not only explains what has happened, and is happening, in the property market but that he always has a point of view. Perhaps the most important of his points of view, all too rare in the property industry, is to be continually sensitive to the importance of the needs of office space users. Office buildings, in his opinion, are not just a commodity to be traded but are essential tools to facilitate the conduct of business. In this he follows the pioneering work of Peter Cowan and his colleagues whose book, *The Office: a Facet of Urban Growth*, as early as 1969, firmly established the ever-changing patterns of office use as one of the most important aspects of urban structure.

Not that it was a book much read by institutions, developers or letting agents. In fact, throughout *Property and the Office Economy*, Rob Harris is a stern critic of the supply-led thinking of the property industry — if thinking is not too honourable a word to be used to describe the visceral and backward-looking responses to market forces of the vast majority of London developers and letting agents. He mocks their fascination with economic cycles as an alleged predictor of change, pointing out that they would do better to try to understand the huge changes that information technology is making in modern business practice, leading to greater mobility, new timetables, and increasingly distributed work.

Nor does Rob Harris spare the planners. His devastating analysis shows that practically every post-war planning policy intended to control and direct the contribution of offices to the future of London that has been promoted by either central or local government has turned out not only to be half-baked and wrong-headed but also, in every case and on the whole fortunately, a failure.

However, a record of incompetence by great parts of the property industry and by many planners is no guarantee of continuing future success. The miracle is that London, despite these failures, has succeeded, particularly in the past two decades, in rebuilding the infrastructure that supports its role as a centre for global business. Particularly in the City and at Canary Wharf, but also increasingly on the South Bank and in suburbs such as Chiswick, the city has better and more intelligently designed office buildings than ever before. Clients and users today have become much more discriminating. Perhaps pressure from these intelligent and demanding tenants living on the edge, in a violently changing economy, with the constant imminence of catastrophic failure has been the factor that has brought out the best in certain developers and in not a few architects, giving London today far better and much more innovative office buildings than, for example, New York where, in a bigger, more robust and much more secure economy, innovation in office design for developers means one thing and one thing only: cost cutting.

Rob Harris is right to remind us in this fascinating, well-timed and clearly written book that the key to future success for London, and indeed for all cities, as we enter the knowledge economy is, first, to understand the complex forces and processes that have shaped cities in the past and, second, to have an imaginative appreciation of the opportunities for better ways of living and working that information technology is bringing us. Bill Mitchell, director of the Media Lab at MIT, has pointed out the likely demise of the two conditions that have shaped all cities for the past two centuries, the predominant need for work to be both co-located and synchronous. Given robust, reliable and ubiquitous technologies, neither condition is necessary for 21st century office work.

The obvious conclusion is that the office building, and consequently the property market, are both likely to change more in the next decade than ever before. This book provides the rationale for two dimensions of change: changes in the fabric of office buildings and changes in the processes by which they are financed, developed, marketed and, above all, used.

Francis Duffy

Acknowledgements

This book is a history of the modern office, reflecting the thoughts and ideas of scores of people who have written and spoken on the subject during the past century or so. It is also the outcome of my direct involvement in the office market over the past two decades, during which I have benefited from sharing countless ideas about office buildings, the organisations that occupy them and the people and institutions who define the property-supply process. The book therefore reflects much more than my own thoughts: it could not have been written without this sharing of knowledge through personal experience and dialogue.

For the experience, an enormous debt of gratitude is owed to Frank Duffy and John Worthington, founding partners of DEGW, and to Stuart Lipton, chairman of Stanhope Properties. Frank and John provided the original inspiration for an interest in offices, and all three provided the perfect platform on which to consider the nature of offices unencumbered by the drag of traditional thinking. The positive results of working with all three are reflected throughout the book.

The large number of friends and colleagues whose thoughts and ideas are bound up in the heart of this history are too many to mention by name, but my thanks are extended to them all. I hope that the text reflects the quality of the shared ideas. Particular thanks should be extended to a number of friends who have helped in the later stages of the book, acting as sounding boards, challenging ideas and providing creative input. They include: Erik Brown, Ian Cundell, Christopher Hedley, Sandra Jones, Peter McLennan and Geoff Woodling.

Finally, and very importantly, thanks are due to the patient and forgiving Kerry, Megan and Nathalie.

Introduction 1

The transformation of work

The world of work has been transformed during the past three decades. In the 1970s, one-third of the UK's workforce had a job in manufacturing; today, this has shrunk to less than one-sixth. Instead, three-quarters of the workforce are in service-based jobs. Many of the new jobs are in finance and insurance, where total employment has risen from 1m to 1.8m jobs. And, if you think there are more managers and administrators than in the past you are right — their numbers have risen by 54%. Conversely, the number of craftsmen has halved. Call centres, the new factories of the technology age, employ nearly 800,000 people in the UK — more than in coal, steel and car manufacturing combined. However, we remain a nation of shopkeepers — although not always in a form we would recognise from our childhoods. A massive 2.8m people now work in retailing. But the greatest employer of them all is government. Despite widespread outsourcing of jobs to the private sector, the number of people employed by the state stands at over five million, roughly one in five of all jobs in the economy. There are over half a million civil servants alone, which is equivalent to the population of Sheffield.

These broad employment figures are indicative of a social and economic change that is every bit as profound as the transition from agrarian to industrial economy in the 18th and 19th centuries. In the Industrial Revolution, machinery and mechanisation turned the worker "into a manipulator of machines worked by inanimate energy",[1] thereby enabling the replacement of a society based on working the land with one based on commerce, manufacturing and the professions.[2] It was truly revolutionary, changing much more than modes of production. The new world required different ways of thinking to support entirely new social and economic structures.

The current revolution is just as profound, and technological advancement is, once again, implicated in enabling a new world to emerge. It is, of course, progressing much faster than the earlier revolution. It is also a global phenomenon. Perhaps, more significantly, it is not over. Change continues, opening up an unending spectrum of new opportunities, bringing with it social, environmental, economic and ethical implications that stretch the minds of the greatest philosophers. The spectacular growth of the US economy over the past two decades is due, in large measure, to advances in information and communications technologies (ICT). Since IBM launched the personal computer in 1981, a screen and keyboard have appeared on almost every desk, and "computer aided" is a term now applied to thousands of daily work processes. And the consequent rise of "weightless" companies — where weightless knowledge replaces tangible goods — has led some to suggest that information and knowledge are the defining characteristics of the new revolution, as we move from a service economy to a knowledge economy, the so-called quaternary economy.

It is not only the jobs that we do, but also the way in which we engage with work that has changed. The notion of the nine-to-five, Monday-to-Friday week, and virtually everything closed on Sundays has become a distant memory. While half of the private sector companies in the UK still employ fewer than 10 people, over half of us work in businesses with more than 500 staff. As this consolidation has taken place, we have seen the introduction of flexitime, the enormous spread of part-time work, short-term contracts and self-employment. In the past 30 years, part-time employment has doubled to 30% of the workforce. Working from home, at least on a part-time basis, has become commonplace. New corporate structures, new ways of working, emerging markets and new technologies are all harbingers of a new era in which our accepted norms of what white-collar work is, and how it is undertaken, are being turned upside down.

Much has been written in recent years about the changing nature of

---

1 Cippola C (1973) *The Industrial Revolution* Fontana, Glasgow p7.

2 Cippola (1973) *op cit* p9.

work. The 1990s generated a plethora of management books in which the disciples of a new age management ethos spread the gospel of downsizing, outsourcing, delayering, re-engineering: methods for becoming leaner, more efficient, more flexible and more competitive. We were told that as these efficiency measures took hold they would lead, for example, to horizontal networks replacing vertical hierarchies, and highly skilled, group-based knowledge workers replacing clerical, departmentalised information processors. But what has all of this change meant for the individual? Has work become easier? Are we happier? Are we more productive? Are we to believe that, 30 years on, conditions have changed in any major respect for the individual? If social commentators are to be believed, long hours, stress and work-related illnesses are more common today than they have ever been. Life moves at a faster pace. The great productivity paradox continues to mystify economic observers. And for large sections of the workforce, the grim reality remains a daily, difficult commute to a workplace some distance from home. In other words, work continues to dominate our lives. The rise of the long-promised leisure economy remains as elusive as ever, and there is every indication — not least in demographics and the pension time bomb — that we will continue to work hard for some time to come. In short, the jobs have changed; our commitment to work has not.

Given the degree of change in work and its continuing dominance of our lives, it is perhaps a little puzzling that so little attention has been devoted to one of the more enduring aspects of the workplace: the workplace itself. While the economy evolves, management fads come and go, and technology radically alters our accepted norms about the nature of work, the buildings within which we work remain relatively unchanging. We readily accept that the activities that take place inside offices, shops, schools, universities, hospitals, factories and warehouses are all subject to change, yet our thinking about the physical environments within which they occur has changed relatively little. It is this relationship between built space and the activities that it accommodates, which provides the raw material for this book.

Offices and the activities they accommodate

Our understanding of the role of real estate in cities and the modern economy, the people who build and own it, the organisations that occupy and manage it and the nature of the space itself are the areas that the book tackles. In doing so, it provides an insight into the otherwise relatively little-known world of the commercial property market. There have been many books produced on real estate but, with notable exceptions, almost all have viewed the property process from the perspective of the property supply industry. Oliver Marriott's classic *The Property Boom*[3] and Edward Erdman's *Property and People*,[4] for example, both focused on the characters in the industry. Other texts have taken particular slices of the supply process as their focus. Marian Bowley's *The British Building Industry*[5] and Christopher Powell's *The British Building Industry Since 1800*[6] are set texts for anyone interested in the history of construction; while Michael Thompson's *Chartered Surveyors*[7] traced the evolution of the middle-man profession. Several have taken a more institutional perspective, particularly of the development process: Michael Bateman,[8] Patsy Healey and Rupert Nabarro[9] and Jack Rose[10] are all notable examples. Yet others have taken a more academic perspective, with a focus on spatial outcomes: Peter Daniels,[11] John Goddard,[12] Raymond Murphy[13] and, more recently, Simon Guy and John Henneberry[14] are all good examples of such work, with that of Peter Cowan and colleagues[15] perhaps one of the most significant ever written in this area.

---

3 Marriott O (1967) *The Property Boom* Pan Books Ltd, London.

4 Erdman E (1982) *People and Property* Batsford, London.

5 Bowley M (1966) *The British Building Industry: Four Studies in Response and Resistance to Change* Cambridge University Press, Cambridge.

6 Powell C (1996) *The British Building Industry Since 1800: an Economic History* (2nd Edition) E&FN Spon, London.

7 Thompson F M L (1968) *Chartered Surveyors: The Growth of a Profession* Routledge & Kegan Paul, London.

8 Bateman M (1985) *Office Development: A Geographical Analysis* Croom Helm, London.

9 Healey P and Nabarro R (1990) *Land and Property Development in a Changing Context* Gower Publishing, Aldershot.

10 Rose J (1985) *The Dynamics of Urban Property Development* E&FN Spon, London.

11 Daniels P W (1975) *Office Location: An Urban and Regional Study* G Bell, London.

12 Goddard J B (1968) Multivariate Analysis of Office Location Patterns in the City Centre: A London Example *Regional Studies* Vol 2 pp69–85; and Goddard J B (1970) Functional Regions within the City Centre: A Study by Factor Analysis of Taxi Flows in Central London *Trans. Inst. Brit. Geogr.* Vol 49 pp161–182.

13 Murphy R E (1972) *The Central Business District* Longman, London.

14 Guy S and Henneberry J (2002) *Development and Developers* Macmillan, London.

15 Cowan P, Fine D, Ireland J, Jordan C, Mercer D and Sears A (1969) *The Office: A Facet of Urban Growth* Heinemann Educational Books Ltd, London.

By contrast, the underlying theme of this book is to view real estate from the perspective of the organisations that occupy the space, rather than those who supply it. In tackling the subject in this way emphasis is placed upon an *activity-based* approach to understanding real estate and the market within which it is set. In taking this approach, the book sets out to provide an alternative perspective on why the property market lunges from boom to bust with such alarming regularity; why the quality of new buildings for much of the post-war period was so poor, and why it is that the customer of the property development process is not the "end user" but rather the institution that owns and leases the end product. All of these factors are explained largely by the fact that the supply process has not taken a more activity-based approach. Arguably, these factors are also most acute in the office sector, and it is within this sub-sector of the property market that the book is rooted.

It is implicit in the activity-based approach that buildings are not inert and passive, but an integral part of the rich dynamic between settings and activities, and the recent history of this relationship provides the material for a fascinating story. At the very least, buildings provide weatherproof environments within which activities take place. Whether those activities perform an economic function, such as offices, or whether they perform a more social function, such as schools, they provide the setting within which work activities occur. But buildings are more than weatherproof environments. Buildings can enable activity, or they can hinder it. They can have a positive effect on the people working within them, or a negative one. They can be enabling or intrusive. They can respond to change, or they can become obsolete. In these ways and more, buildings are the skeletons onto which all the muscular, neurotic and circulatory systems of organisations are hung. Described in this way, the demand for buildings is derived from the production, organisation and delivery of goods and services. And as those goods and services change, so the environments in which they are produced need to change.

Occasionally, change to activities is so profound that it becomes impossible to adapt the existing buildings to the new work practices. This happened during Big Bang in the City of London in 1986, when newly formed finance houses demanded large, intensively serviced buildings, with dealing floors the size of football pitches. The same has occurred in logistics in recent years: here demand has driven the appearance of vast distribution centres, some the size of small farms, where robotic machinery whirs and clunks in total darkness without the assistance of human input. In both cases, it was the nature of change within the businesses, or activities that drove a demand for a new kind of space to accommodate different work processes.

The original inspiration for an activity-based perspective on real estate, and on offices in particular, was provided by a text written half a century ago. In his 1956 masterpiece *The Core of the City*, John Rannells[16] placed the spotlight on an activity-based approach to understanding buildings, arguing that the renewal of the built environment should be driven by the changing demands of its users:

> It is necessary to take in somewhat more than relates directly to land use, since changes in demand for space or location may come about as secondary results of business decisions or consumer preferences which, in themselves, have no concern with questions of land use.[17]

And he emphasised the fact that the nature of activities within buildings undergoes a perpetual process of change, as new assortments of occupiers "are always being formed by the continually changing ways of doing business which are characteristic of commercial enterprise."[18] In other words, there is a direct relationship between the changing nature of work and the settings needed to support that work, leading to a constant process of obsolescence and replacement. Yet, for much of the post-war period the property-supply industry was disconnected from its market, cushioned from the need to address the changing needs of occupiers by a set of rules the like of which was to be found nowhere else in the economy, and nowhere else on the planet. In the aftermath of the Second World War, it devised its own set of rules that remains largely intact to the present time. For example, until the 1990s, the UK was the only place in the world where occupiers of commercial buildings were expected to sign leases that bound them by contract to their landlords for no less than 25 years, made them responsible for maintaining and repairing the internal environment, and committed them to a rent review every five years that could only see the rent rising, irrespective of what was happening in the economy generally.

The commercial property market, and the industry that is identified with it, are in some ways the antithesis of the fast-changing,

---

16 Rannells J (1956) *The Core of the City* Institute of Urban Land Use and Housing Studies, Columbia University Press.

17 Rannells (1956) *op cit* pp5–6.

18 Rannells (1956) *op cit* p42.

unpredictable world of work described earlier. It is relatively slow-moving, rigid, reactive and long term. Some of its practices, such as valuation and construction, have barely changed in decades. A workman on the construction site of the new Wembley Stadium emerging in London today could probably find his way around the site of the old stadium 70 years ago. Kipling's *A Truthful Song* was not so very wide of the mark:

> I tell this tale, which is strictly true,
>   Just by way of convincing you
> How very little, since things were made,
>   Things have altered in the building trade.

Contrary to the demand-driven concept of buildings as settings for economic activity described above, the property market has in fact been a supply-driven one, in which the priorities of the property *industry* are the key drivers. Some properties are owner-occupied and some are bespoke to the requirements of specific occupiers but, in the main, commercial property is delivered speculatively, and rented by businesses on long-term arrangements. It is perhaps this speculative aspect of the industry that has created the rather negative image of the property developer in the minds of the general public. For over half a century, commercial buildings have been built primarily to meet the needs of the organisations that own them, rather than those that occupy them. In this way, the pension funds and insurance companies have been the clients of the developers who deliver product, not the businesses that lease and occupy their buildings. This distancing of suppliers from customers has had a harmful effect on the real estate process because, for many years, it led to the delivery of mediocre buildings with negligible architectural merit, built to crushingly tight budgets and to the highest possible density. Many of the ugliest and most dysfunctional contributions to the urban landscape over the past 50 years are the direct outcome of this separation of interests between delivery, ownership and occupation. The situation has begun to change in recent times, and the story of how this change has come about forms an integral theme of this book.

Contrary to this rather gloomy perspective, it could also be argued that London, and the UK generally, have reaped the benefits of one of the most liquid and successful property investment markets in the world, and over a long period of time. Direct investment by UK institutions and overseas investors, attracted by the long leases and secure income, have poured huge amounts of money into commercial property, and the market has provided an enormously valuable alternative to gilts and equities. However, while the interests of owners and investors are explored in chapter 5, the dynamics of the commercial property investment market have been covered in numerous texts over recent years and are not the focus of this book. The focus of this book is on the activities that take place within offices, and how various actors — owners, developers, policy makers, occupiers and so on — have responded to the changing dynamics of those activities.

The relationships between the various actors in the property-supply process are highly fragmented. The core of the industry comprises a triumvirate of interests, encompassing the developer who spots opportunities and takes the necessary risks, the financial institution who buys the end product, and the broker who arranges the deals. In this sense, the industry is deal-driven: it behaves in a herd-like way as sentiment rides the ups and downs of changing economic circumstances. Around these key players there floats a whole host of professional advisors — architects, engineers, cost consultants, planners and so on. It is in no sense an integrated industry or process, and is very opaque. Investors, constructors, building managers and architects all operate in parallel but separate universes. The scope for inefficiency, for mismatch between supply and demand and for inappropriate product, is awesome. There is little collective knowledge about the market, and the industry has, over the second half of the 20th century, lurched between bouts of gorging on freely available finance to build speculatively, and famines of activity during periods of oversupply. This fragmentation and its implications are explored in detail.

On the one hand, the world of work is changing perhaps more radically than at any time since the Industrial Revolution, with fundamental questions being raised over the way in which work is done. On the other hand, there is a market for real estate that obeys its own rules, and has been cushioned from the changing fortunes of its "customers" for decades. It is this tense and often adversarial dynamic between the needs of the businesses and organisations that occupy buildings, and the desires of those who plan, deliver, trade and manage them, that lies at the core of the book. There are particular reasons for considering this relationship now; not least the fact that changes in the office economy might be in the process of forcing the supply industry into an historic period of change. It is easy to forget that the current structure of the real estate market is a relatively recent phenomenon. And this becomes particularly important when considering the future: it is easy to take the present for granted and to underestimate the potential for change. More particularly, it is relatively simple to hide in the present and deny the unknown. For this reason, the book's subject matter is placed in a broader historical context. While the focus is on the post-Second World War era, a picture of the way in which real estate itself, and those involved in its delivery and use have changed over a longer time frame is used to illustrate the constancy of change.

The book seeks to explain how real estate, from the level of the city to the level of the workplace, has come to be understood. Until recently, real estate has been regarded as a necessary by-product of other activities, or something to be tolerated by those who use it, and something to be justified by those who pay for it. For many years, the role of offices as a fundamental driver of city economies was virtually ignored. In public policy terms, offices were more frequently seen as a problem than as an economic benefit. At the macro level, the unfolding understanding of its key role in urban transformation has only relatively recently been fully appreciated and addressed in the academic environment. At the micro level, we have only just begun to scratch the surface of understanding how real estate affects the performance of organisations and individuals in the workplace.

In taking an activity-based approach, it has been necessary to make constant reference to "the occupier", "occupancy", "occupational issues" and so forth. Most organisations and individuals working in office buildings do not perceive themselves as "occupiers", and the term itself might be seen by some as jargon. However, the range of alternative collective nouns for those who use offices is limited. For reasons that will become clear, the term "tenant" has been deliberately avoided. One of the benefits of the use of the term occupier is that it reminds us what office buildings are for: they provide a physical resource to support economic and other activity. Secondarily, they might be architectural masterpieces or highly successful in providing income return; but their primary function is to support work activities.

A further character of the study is the use of London as the backdrop. It might be argued that a more international perspective could have been taken, but the story as told is so rich and full of interesting, thought-provoking material, that the temptation to take in even more has been resisted. It is recognised, however, that an international perspective remains a task that has yet to be undertaken. Using London as a backdrop, every attempt has been made to write a narrative that is grounded in reality rather than the realm of theory, and to this end the story describes real events and the people involved in them in order to convey the richness of a fascinating story. London as a backdrop serves this purpose well. Emerging in the 19th century as a world city based on its trading position in the Empire, London, over the past 100 years, has continually reinvented itself, becoming today a principal model of the office economy. This continuous reinvention provides a fabulous laboratory for the study of the changing nature of real estate, the office, and the ever-evolving nature of the activities that it accommodates. While the role of the City of London in world financial markets brings with it some peculiarities to the London office market, the sheer scale of the market makes it a viable case study. At around 25 million sq m (270 million sq ft), around 25% of all office space in the UK, and some 35% of the value of all institutional property, Greater London offers an enormously useful case study. Many of the issues explored and the lessons will resonate throughout the national and international markets.

In his analysis of the Enlightenment, the great naturalist Edward O Wilson observed that the main branches of learning emerged in their present form — natural sciences, social sciences and the humanities — out of a unified Enlightenment vision that searched for an ordered, intelligible universe. However, as scientific knowledge expanded exponentially, reductionism, its key method, pushed thinking in the opposite direction. Consequently, scientists have become so professionally focused that it is "not surprising to find physicists who do not know what a gene is, and biologists who guess that string theory has something to do with violins."[19] Similarly, within the property industry, there are many specialists whose interests and expertise are minutely focused. Wilson's lesson has been absorbed here, and a wide perspective on real estate is taken by placing the subject matter into a broader socio-economic context. The book's preparation has involved drawing upon a wealth of ideas, information and data from many, diverse sources. This has been a conscious attempt to write a text that can both inform and entertain. Furthermore, it has been an objective to narrate an interesting story while at the same time providing readers with the ability and means to follow-up particular lines of enquiry or interest.

For all these reasons, the book is aimed at both informed and lay readers. For those informed about the dynamics of the built

---

19 Wilson E O (1998) *Consilience: The Unity of Knowledge* Little, Brown & Company, London p41.

environment, whether as practitioners, students or teachers, the book will provide a deeper understanding of a neglected part of the built environment, the office economy. Such readers will find much material linking fields that are normally treated in isolation, in a story that weaves together the pressures exerting change on those who occupy office space with the activities and motives of those who supply and manage it. The book also gives directions to sources for more specialised writings. For those readers who are less directly involved in practice or study in the built environment, the book provides an insight into what is now a hugely important aspect of our economy, and also explains the history, workings and future of the built spaces in which almost half the working population spend their daily lives. The story of our unfolding understanding of offices, the changes through which they have passed, and the nature of office work itself and its continuing evolution is a fascinating one, and should appeal to anyone with an interest in contemporary society and its systems and structures.

The structure of the book

The material in the book breaks down into four parts. The first part describes the emergence and rise of the office economy. While chapter 2 provides a contextual description of the origins of the office economy in the latter part of the 19th century, chapter 3 explains how offices and our understanding of them have evolved, particularly since the Second World War. It demonstrates how, until relatively recently, offices were a poorly understood phenomenon, and yet have been the outward manifestation of a profound shift in the national and international economy.

The second part deals with the office supply process — development, investment and public policy. Chapter 4 asks whether the boom-bust pattern that has been a central feature of post-war property development is inevitable or avoidable, and suggests that supply-side inefficiencies are more important than any intrinsic cyclical characteristics. The post-war speculative property industry is placed in the broader context of the restructuring of the UK economy, and the chapter asks whether the predominant pattern of development is now changing.

In chapter 5, the story switches to the property industry itself and the actors within it. The frontier nature of development in the aftermath of the Second World War when individuals amassed great fortunes doing deals on war-damaged sites is examined, and the changing fortunes of property companies and financial institutions are outlined. The chapter examines the paradox whereby the real customer of the development process is the industry itself rather than those who rent and occupy its buildings, and it describes how the property industry has struggled to reinvent itself in recent years in response to profound changes in the demand for space.

The policy frameworks that successive governments and local authorities have directed at offices, ranging from indifference to outright hostility, are the subjects of chapter 6. What emerges is a lack of understanding of the role of offices in the modern economy. Policy measures that sought to deal with the "office problem" failed to anticipate, research, understand or plan for the office economy. The chapter concludes by asking whether, after so many decades of neglect, public policy seems to be swinging in favour of a major expansion of the office economy just at a time when the office economy itself might be starting to demand something different.

The third part of the book turns the spotlight on office buildings themselves, and shows how our understanding of office buildings during recent decades has changed from seeing them as inert and passive, to a much more sophisticated understanding of how they can act as a resource to the organisations that use them. Chapter 7 examines the role and scope of research in addressing the mismatch between supply and demand, a mismatch that has been exacerbated in recent times by the changing and more demanding nature of occupiers' operations; the revolution in ICT and the growing importance attached by occupiers and employees towards their place of work. The chapter outlines three themes in the development of a more sophisticated understanding of offices: refining the physical parameters of the product, improving the quality of market, intelligence and feedback, and developing rigorous approaches to understanding how to measure the performance of buildings.

Chapter 8 examines how office buildings have come to be regarded as a business resource in their own right. The chapter outlines the emergence of an entirely new profession — people whose core skill and training relate to the management of real estate. The management of real estate in the UK cost around £77bn in 2002,[20] twice as much as

---

20 Tenon Livingstone Guarantee (2002) *Facilities Management Sector Review* 2002 TLG, London.

all the tourist expenditure in the UK. But until the 1980s it did not exist as a recognised profession, since when it has organised and professionalised. The chapter traces the development of new approaches to real estate management, including outsourcing and the commoditisation of space, before concluding with thoughts on the growing trend towards integrated business resource management.

The final part of the book focuses on recent changes in the office economy, and looks to the future. Chapter 9 examines how working life and work processes have changed within office buildings during recent times, and the impact that this is having on the way in which offices are organised and planned. Trends as diverse as global competition and demand for more work-life balance from stressed office workers are leading to new approaches to the occupation of office space. This, inevitably, is changing the nature of demand for real estate. The key question, of course, is how profound will this change be?

Chapter 10 addresses this question head-on. Traditionalists within the supply process see the potential changes as marginal: certainly not sufficiently profound to radically alter the nature of buildings. However, the conclusion from the research that forms this book is less constrained by history and comes to a different view. After five to six decades of almost continuous growth, the office economy is maturing, and this process of maturation is being enabled by new technologies that will lead to wholesale change in the nature of demand for space, rendering much of our existing stock, and certainly the arrangements and contracts under which it is procured, obsolete within the next 20 years. A supply process that is predicated on the growth pattern of history is likely to result in further dysfunctions of the type that have dogged the history of the office economy in modern times.

2 The Origins of the Office Economy

Office pre-history

Each of the chapters in this book examines the office from a distinctive perspective. In this sense, the book is organised not into a single chronological story, but rather into a series of short stories, each with their own internal chronology, thereby allowing the complexities and subtleties of each perspective to be examined to an appropriate depth and without interruption. However, such an approach demands a contextual setting within which to place the major themes that are examined and this chapter sets out a historical context for those themes. While the main focus of the book is on the latter half of the 20th century, many of the issues dealt with can be traced farther back in time. This chapter provides the necessary linkages to this longer historical perspective by tracing the history of the office from its very early beginnings, through to the birth of the modern office in the late-19th century and up to the Second World War. It provides an insight into the structure of the property industry and some of the key actors in the property process. It also provides the opportunity to describe some of the major changes that have occurred to London and the economy during the history of the office and that provides the backdrop to many of the events described in the book.

The history of the office and of office activity has been traced back into the depths of time. Its earliest manifestation might have been the scribes of ancient Egypt in around 3000BC. Certainly they recorded transactions and prepared documents, inventories and accounts, but they cannot be described as office workers in any recognisably modern sense. Perhaps, more realistically, we can point to the adoption by Italian merchants of double entry bookkeeping as the origin of offices. Pacioli's *Summa* codified double entry bookkeeping as the "Venice system" towards the end of the 15th century. Using new printing technology, the system spread quickly through Europe. Consequently, accounting took a major step forward and began to form the administrative backbone of commerce.

But, of course, offices perform not only a commercial function but also one of civil governance. Some of the earliest buildings that can be called offices were built for the government of cities. Again, the earliest examples were in Italy: in the mid-16th century, the Uffizi were built in Florence to house the administrative offices of Cosimo de Medici. As international trade became more important, the development of banking and modern capitalism sparked the development of business capitals, such as Amsterdam, Florence, London and Venice. London, in particular, grew quickly and early. During the bulk of the great Tudor dynasty (1485–1603), London witnessed unprecedented growth. People flocked there from around the country and from Europe and beyond in search of work and opportunity. Between 1500 and 1600, the population almost tripled, from 75,000 to 220,000. But along with the growth came poverty and squalor. Overcrowding was acute; sanitation and housing conditions were appalling. In an attempt to alleviate the problems, Queen Elizabeth proclaimed in 1580 that one house should belong to one family, and she later took the apparently desperate step of prohibiting the further growth of London, which, at the time, meant the area bounded by the walls of the City of London. However, rather than being an early example of urban planning, this was more likely a gesture towards protecting the trading interests of the people of London against the proliferation of traders beyond the city walls. In any case, it was an empty gesture: London continued to grow.

Conditions were barely any better during most of the 17th century. Indeed, the plagues of 1603, 1625 and 1665, and the Great Fire in 1666 (that led John Evelyn famously to declare: "London was, but is no more") were all worsened by the sheer density of humanity and the poor building and sanitary conditions. But, despite these tumultuous events, London continued to expand.

The Great Fire saw the end of timber construction in London; land speculation began in earnest and the West End was developed as the better off sought calm and dignity away from the intensity of the City. Piccadilly was begun in the early 1600s, and in the 1630s the Earl of

Bedford began to develop Covent Garden. Nicholas Barbon, most noted for the building of Downing Street, undertook major developments in Red Lion Square, Bedford Row, New Square, Lincoln's Inn and Buckingham Street. The intense level of building activity prompted one anonymous writer to complain about the effects of land speculation:

> The desire of profit greatly increaseth buildings and so much the more, for that this great concourse of all sorts of people drawing near unto the City, every man seeketh out places, highways, lanes and covert corners to build upon ... These sort of covetous builders exact great rents, and daily do increase them in so much that a poor handscraftman is not able by his painful labours to pay the rent of a small tenement and feed his family.[1]

Plus ça change, plus c'est la même chose. But despite the increasing rents, growing numbers of people did afford to pay, and by mid-century the population of London had reached nearly half a million. However, despite the best endeavours of the new developers, much of the physical fabric of London remained medieval in appearance.

The 18th century witnessed boom periods following the Treaty of Utrecht in 1713 and the Peace of Paris in 1763. The period gave us Mayfair, Hanover Square, Portman Square and Russell Square and its surroundings. By the end of the century, London had a population of over 900,000 — twice the size of Paris. Banking and insurance services were developing to provide credit and cover for the expanding trade passing through the port of London. And London's skyline was continuously changing as the city grew into one of the most vibrant and cosmopolitan in the world. During this period, small, opulent offices, normally related to the burgeoning industrial businesses and commercial enterprises of the time, emerged in London and Europe to reflect the new-found wealth of their owners. Even so, during much of this time, many of the banks and other businesses occupied private houses: the symbols of the city prior to the mid-18th century remained the castle, the cathedral, the palace and the market place, and the place of the office was very small indeed.[2]

Gradually, however, permanent exchanges were established and paper became a means of conveying security. The Bank of England moved into its George Sampson-designed building in Threadneedle

---

1 Gray R (1978) *A History of London* Hutchinson & Co, London p151.

2 Cowan P, Fine D, Ireland J, Jordan C, Mercer D and Sears A (1969) *The Office: A Facet of Urban Growth* Heinemann Educational Books Ltd, London p28.

Street in 1734, and the Corn Exchange was established in 1751. Such institutions reflected broader changes and, in particular, the maturing of international trade and commerce. During the mid-1700s to the mid-1800s, the economic and social landscape of Europe began to alter dramatically. In Britain and elsewhere in Europe, a rigid and relatively unchanging landscape began to industrialise: small villages and farms with an aristocracy and local craftsmen yielded to larger towns and cities as the Industrial Revolution gained momentum and as manufacturing industries expanded rapidly. A new class of industrialist emerged and the population spiralled.

The origins of modern, speculative property development can be traced back to this time. Funding arrangements; construction contracting and intermediation all evolved quickly, and the West End and the City began to take on their modern shape in distinctive bubbles of property development. Some of these bubbles created entire new districts, and they were distinctive not only in a temporal sense, but also in the architectural footprint they left behind. The emergence of Regent's Street and Regent's Park, with the architecture of John Nash and the patronage of the Prince Regent, is perhaps one of the most distinctive. John Blashfield built Kensington Palace Gardens in the mid-1840s, and John Duncan and Jacob Connop transformed the area that became Ladbroke Grove.

The tentacles of European trade stretched out across the globe. London's international role, and the country's transformation into the greatest trading block the world had ever seen, is exemplified by the development of the docks. Although they had been expanding for several decades, it was during the 19th century that the docks' full commercial potential was realised, with the opening of purpose-built, enclosed docks. The West India Company opened the first large enclosed dock in 1802; followed in quick succession by the East India (1805); the London (1805); and the Surrey (1807); and then later by St Katherine's (1828); Royal Victoria (1855) and Royal Albert (1880). By mid-century, half of Britain's trade passed through the port of London. The rapid expansion of the docks was driven by Britain's growing global influence, and the relationship between the two is suggested by the various specialities of the docks: softwood at Surrey; grain at Millwall; wool, sugar and rubber at St Katherine's; ivory, spices, coffee and cocoa at London, and rum and hardwood at West India dock.

The administrative institutions necessary to oversee this increasingly complex web of commercial activity matured and began to cluster, thereby becoming a physical presence as well as a commercial one. In

Paris, for example, the financial district began to take shape, literally, between the Bourse and the Opera. Elisabeth Pelegrin-Genel cites the example of the architect Hector Horeau who proposed, in 1871, the construction of an office building entirely without living accommodation. Then in 1876, Henri Germain, the founding president of Credit Lyonnais, decided to house his Paris headquarters on the Boulevard des Italiens, "a building that was destined to become a model for banking headquarters of the future" and featuring a large central atrium, glazed skylight, mezzanine with reception rooms and a first floor reserved for senior management.[3] Paris' development, however, was eclipsed by the growth and change taking place in London.

Although London was emerging as the financial capital of Europe and the centre of world trade by the early-19th century, as mid-century was reached, its pre-eminence was unchallenged. One of the most visible symbols of its international role at this time was the Great Exhibition in 1851. Designed by Joseph Paxton, and built in the centre of Hyde Park to a programme and budget that puts the London Dome of 150 years later into an embarrassing perspective, the Exhibition can only be described in superlatives. Its 100,000 exhibits from the farthest reaches of Empire, as well as examples of technological advancement much closer to home, attracted 6 million visitors in its short five-month life. London was booming. Between the Great Exhibition and the eve of the First World War, the population of London doubled from 2.4 million to around 4.5 million. This growth in people saw the physical fabric of the city expand to cover a larger area and to intensify in the central area.

The growth of London during the 19th century was genuinely international from very early on. Its future was shaped — physically and economically — by a generation of international financiers many of whose great names in banking live on into the 21st century. One of the most influential of these was Nathan Rothschild, a young German immigrant who, following a run on gold and an economic crisis in London in 1825, saved the Bank of England by organising a £10m shipment of gold to shore up the Bank's reserves. Rothschild was followed by a number of other immigrants, whose names came to symbolise merchant banking in the UK and whose work and reputations established the City as a truly global financial centre. Many came from Europe, including Hambro, Kleinwort, Lazard, Schroder

3 Pelegrin-Genel E (1996) *The Office* Flammarion, Paris pp27–28.

and Seligman, while others came from the US. One such was Peabody, who emigrated from Baltimore in 1831 to found the firm that was to grow and split into JP Morgan and Morgan Grenfell. Such individuals helped to transform London into a truly global city.

The birth of the office economy

The expansion and growing complexity of commercial activity had to be supported by increasingly sophisticated trading. By 1875, Britain was supplying not only between one-third and one-half of the world's trade in manufactures, but also the facilities that made possible most of the rest of trade and investment.[4]

> City banks advanced large sums of short-term credit to importers and exporters and arranged the finance of long-term investments overseas. The Stock Exchange was the centre of the world's capital market; and London's insurance companies had no serious international competitors.[5]

By the 1870s, London was the world's principle money market, and it further consolidated its position through the expansion of foreign issues. For example, by 1890, some 30% of the capital stock of American railways, and an even larger percentage of the Argentine and Indian railways, were held in Britain.

The public transport infrastructure that struggles to cope with London's daily tidal wave of commuters today is constrained by this heritage of unplanned Victorian expansion. There was no strategic plan and virtually no public planning: the development of London took place in a truly *ad hoc* manner, and entirely as the result of private capital and private enterprise. The overriding and continuing influence of the private sector is shown by the fact that the opening of Kingsway and Aldwych remained virtually the only major 20th century public improvement in central London until the Hyde Park Corner underpass was built in 1962.[6] London's first directly elected government, the London County Council, was not to appear until 1889. Even then, although the Council presided over the whole urban area, except for

---

4 Dunning J H and Morgan E V (1971) *An Economic Study of the City of London* Economists Advisory Group George Allen and Unwin, London p33.

5 *Ibid.*

6 Gray (1978) *op cit* pp295–296.

the City of London, it lacked the strategic powers to have any great impact on the *laissez-faire* development of the city. It had no strategic planning powers; it had no social welfare responsibilities, and its housing responsibilities were limited to slum clearance.

In the absence of any formal planning framework, the powerful forces of international trade were, in the latter part of the 19th century, driving the physical growth of the city. London responded to the growing volume of trade in products and commodities with increasingly complex trading arrangements and it began to provide a sophisticated infrastructure for trade. This took the form of financial, insurance, accountancy, legal and other professional services. Very quickly, clerical and administrative activities expanded in the City to support the growing diversity of markets and trades in manufactures and services:

> It was the City's ability to supply such a comprehensive range of financial and trading services which was largely responsible for its emergence as a centre of international repute. No other city could offer such a "package deal" of interrelated activities.[7]

Thus it was that in this firmament of change from, roughly, the 1870s through to the zenith of Britain's colonial expansion during the Edwardian period that the office economy was born. The structure and distribution of office activity in central London today is largely the result of the city's expansion and evolving role during this period. The emerging importance of office activity in the national economy is seen directly in the growth of white-collar work during the latter half of the 19th century (table 2.1). The figures show that the transformation that led to the dominance of the office economy in the 20th century had been gradually gathering pace during the latter half of the 19th. In 1841, there were fewer than 50,000 clerical workers in England and Wales (this figure refers to commercial clerks only and excludes clerks working in industrial establishments). By 1871, this number had risen to over 90,000; and by the turn of the century to 362,710. The remarkable increases in the 1860s and 1870s are coincident with the introduction of office automation in the form of typewriters, telegraphy and telephony.

---

7 Dunning and Morgan *op cit* pp34–35.

Table 2.1 Growth in clerical employment in England and Wales, 1841–1901

Year	*No of clerks*	*% of total labour force*
1841	46,689	0.6
1851	60,353	1.0
1861	56,132	1.5
1871	91,475	1.9
1881	182,457	2.6
1891	246,761	3.4
1901	362,710	3.9

Source: Daniels[8]

Throughout the period up to the First World War, the City remained primarily a centre of commerce and trading. As late as 1911, banking and finance (excluding insurance) accounted for only 9% of City employment, while manufacturing and commodity businesses accounted for 46%.[9] Office activity, as we understand it today, was very limited: much of it was ancillary to commercial and trading enterprises, and much occupied buildings that had previously been in residential and light industrial uses. However, offices were beginning to spread. The growing importance of office activity in the City during the latter half of the 19th century and the early years of the 20th century is reflected in the relative decline in the residential population as commercial uses gradually displaced residential uses. Table 2.2 shows how the population in the City of London fell by nearly 80% in the latter half of the 19th century. As the City was shrinking in population terms, so London generally was expanding. Over the same period, London's total population multiplied two-and-a-half times.

The growing dominance of office activities was therefore not a sudden phenomenon, but a slow-burning process, with office activity, industry and trade, through the docks that remained close to the heart of the City, co-existing for a long period of time. As late as 1907, there

8 Daniels P W (1975) *Office Location: An Urban and Regional Study* G Bell & Sons, London p33.

9 Rose H (1994) *London as an International Financial Centre: A Narrative History* The City Research Project, Corporation of London p6.

Table 2.2 Population trends in London, 1851–1931

Year	*Greater London (000s)*	*City of London (000s)*
1851	2681	128
1861	3223	112
1871	3886	75
1881	4767	51
1891	5634	38
1901	6581	27
1911	7251	20
1921	7480	14
1931	8204	11

Source: Dunning and Morgan[10]

remained 39,524 people employed in 1058 factories in the City.[11] However, with the gathering pace of change in the main business activities of the central London area, manufacturing gradually yielded to the expansion of office activity, reflecting the more general restructuring of the national economy. The physical fabric of the City, and London generally, responded and evolved to accommodate the changing nature of economic activity.

By contrast, the physical fabric of many North American cities was being made for the very first time. It was here that the office building took on its distinctive modern form, with regular internal space, repetitive façades, with a specialisation in control and administration, together with the characteristic spread of paper. While Britain and Europe were reaching their maximal global expansion, the American economy switched structural models from an entrepreneurial, owner-managed form characterised by many layers of production and distribution, to a model dominated by large, vertically integrated companies that gained significant economies of scale and stripped out the add-on costs of intermediaries, brokers and distributors. The modern corporation was born. As with Europe, up to this period office activity was accommodated typically, although not exclusively, in

10 Dunning and Morgan *op cit* p34.
11 Dunning and Morgan *op cit* p37.

buildings that had been created for other purposes, in which the office activity was an ancillary use. After this period, purpose-built, large, centrally located offices buildings became the norm. This was the period in which office activity became a distinct urban function:

> The office function was clearly due to grow, and to grow quickly. And in addition it would need to separate off from other facets of urban activity, because of the growing complexity and intricacy of organisation needed to finance, administer and support the industrial revolution.[12]

The specific characteristics of London's evolving office economy left a physical legacy, the ghostly pattern of which survives to the present day. It was by no means the same for all cities. For example, as the 19th century drew to a close, and the 20th got under way, the huge American economy was thundering along at great speed, and undergoing a different experience. The famous grid iron pattern of urban development in the US, reflective of its later development and great differences in scale, was spreading. The fundamental changes in the economy gave rise to a fundamentally new building form: the skyscraper. Tall office buildings have an iconic power. They symbolise wealth and economic success, as well as cultural and technological advancement. And they can express the self-confidence of a city, or even of a nation. Nowhere has this iconic significance been greater than in the skylines of Boston, Chicago, New York, Philadelphia and the other great American cities. The American nation embraced the tall office building and celebrated its central role in the daily heartbeat of the nation from the very beginnings of the office economy in the 1870s and 1880s. The differences with European cities were stark, although most cities shared the effects of greatly increased densities in their core areas as well as the growing dominance of the office economy.

Curiously, it is in the conflagration that engulfed Chicago in 1871 that the origins of tall office buildings are to be found. After the devastation of the fire, the demand for new buildings was intense, sending land prices to all-time highs: if only "some means of piling up accommodation in the centre were to be found, the profits of the owners of real estate would multiply."[13] The solution was found by the wonderfully named William LeBaron Jenney, who designed the first

---

12 Cowan *et al* (1969) *Ibid.*

13 Bowley M (1966) *The British Building Industry: Four Studies in Response and Resistance to Change* Cambridge University Press, Cambridge p9.

high-rise building in which an iron skeleton of vertical columns and horizontal beams carried the whole load of the building, and in which the external walls were reduced to panel infillings between the members of the frame. Built between 1883 and 1885, the 42m (138ft), 10-storey building (later extended by two floors) became famous as the Home Insurance Building. The savings on expensive foundations, owing to the reduced weight of the building, and "the commercial possibility of buildings with more than 12 storeys, owing to the saving of space and increase of light on the lower floors, which went with the elimination of load-bearing masonry, provided the economic basis for the skyscraper."[14] As new technologies, including lifts, lighting, telephones and sanitation, made great strides, so the buildings could become larger and taller still.

Skyscrapers spread rapidly in the latter part of the 19th century. They came to celebrate the new corporatism that was sweeping through the reorganising American economy, and many became synonymous with the corporations that occupied them. In New York, for example, there were the Singer Building (sewing machines); the Metropolitan Life Building (insurance); the Woolworth Tower (retailing) and the Chrysler Building (cars). In some areas, concentrations of skyscrapers jostled with each other as corporations sought to stand out from their competitors. New York's famous "Newspaper Row" contained the Pulitzer Building (aka the World Building) that housed the New York World; the Tribune Building; the Times Building and the Potter Building (home to the New York Press).

The buildings' patrons were themselves often exuberant, larger-than-life characters. Frank W Woolworth teamed up with architect Cass Gilbert to create the Woolworth Tower. Its opening ceremony created a little history. President Woodrow Wilson pressed a button in the White House to activate 80,000 light bulbs in front of 900 assembled guests. One of them, the redoubtable Samuel Parkes Cadman, a prominent clergyman, was said to have cried out "the cathedral of commerce!" A few years later, Walter P Chrysler set his architect a very simple brief for his own tower: make it taller than the Eiffel Tower. William Van Alen's design typified many buildings of the period with its ornate design, intricate patterns, mixing of materials and complex structural style. As time passed, the buildings became much simpler, and more economic and utilitarian in their design, but their iconic status simply grew.

---

14 Bowley (1966) *op cit* p10.

It is an interesting footnote of history that the quintessentially American term "skyscraper" is neither American in origin nor originally a reference to tall buildings. Its etymological origins are traced back not to an office building at all, but a horse. Specifically, Skyscraper was the name of the winner of the 1789 Epsom Derby. Slipping into everyday usage as a term for high-standing horses and for tall men, by the beginning of the 19th century the term also referred to tall hats and bonnets, and later to tall stories. By the mid-19th century, the term was applied to the small triangular sail set above the skysail on sailing ships in order to maximise the effect of a light wind in calm latitudes. The first use of the term skyscraper in the context of high-rise buildings was in 1883, and was made in reference to the tall buildings being erected in Chicago.

Europe's relationship with tall office buildings has been very different to that of the US. Europe did not, and has not, embraced the tall office building with such enthusiasm. London had to wait until 1967 for Richard Seifert's 111m (365ft) Centre Point; until 1981 for his 183m (600ft) Nat West Tower (since renamed Tower 42), and until 1991 for I M Pei's 235m (771ft) One Canada Square in Canary Wharf. Mainland Europe also shunned tall buildings until recently — the 257m (843ft) Messeturm was completed in Frankfurt in 1990. The proliferation of tall buildings in the Far East in recent times perhaps underscores their iconic status as these emergent economies compete to express their positions in the world economy. Table 2.3 shows the rise of the skyscraper with a selection of iconic buildings, culminating in the Freedom Tower that will replace the Twin Towers in New York.

The muted response to tall buildings in the UK and Europe is deeply rooted in economic and cultural factors, not to mention the physical constraints imposed by the complex and aged nature of its city centres. The US, free from such constraints, embraced the new office economy and drove many of the technological innovations that were to create the modern office.

While the arrival of the skyscraper was necessitated by the reorganisation of business, it was enabled by new technologies, not the least of which included lifts, telephony, steel frame construction and new sanitation techniques. In a process not dissimilar to that which is changing the office environment today, the birth of the modern office in the late-19th century was enabled and driven by a number of technological innovations. The impact of these innovations was so profound that it might be argued that the subsequent 100 years of office development were mere refinements on this early model. The

Table 2.3 The rise of the skyscraper

Year	*Building*	*City*	*Height*	
			m	*(ft)*
2008	Freedom Tower	New York	541	(1775)
2004	Taipei 101	Taipei	509	(1670)
1998	Petronas Towers	Kuala Lumpur	452	(1483)
1974	Sears Tower	Chicago	442	(1450)
1973	World Trade Centre	New York	419	(1375)
2003	Two International Finance	Hong Kong	415	(1361)
1997	CITIC Plaza	Guangzhou	391	(1283)
1931	Empire State Building	New York	381	(1250)
1992	Central Plaza	Hong Kong	374	(1227)
1990	Bank of China	Hong Kong	367	(1204)
1930	Chrysler Building	New York	319	(1046)
1997	Commerz Bank Tower	Frankfurt	259	(850)
1990	Messeturm	Frankfurt	257	(843)
1991	1 Canada Square	London	235	(771)
1913	Woolworth Building	New York	232	(761)
1909	Metropolitan Life Insurance	New York	213	(699)
1984	AT&T Building	New York	197	(646)
1908	Singer Building	New York	189	(620)
1980	Nat West Tower	London	183	(600)
1985	Hong Kong & Shanghai Bank	Hong Kong	158	(518)
1958	Seagram Building	New York	152	(500)
1890	Pulitzer Building	New York	94	(308)
1902	Flatiron Building	New York	87	(285)
1885	Home Insurance Building	Chicago	52	(171)

same degree of change was not to occur again until the late-1980s and into the 1990s. The Atlantic cable linked the US and Europe in 1866, thereby enabling inter-continental telegraph messaging. In 1868, Sholes, Glidden & Soule patented the first typewriter — an invention that spread quickly. Sales figures for the Remington 2 grew from "146 in 1879 and rose to an annual figure of 65,000 in 1890".[15] In 1876, Bell patented the telephone, and there were more than one million "phones in the US by the end of the century".[16] World-changing innovations

15 Daniels (1975) *op cit* p10.
16 Daniels (1975) *op cit* p11.

were not confined to the US. For example, in 1861 Gestetner started his own duplicating business in the City of London. And not all innovations were technological wonders: the first stapler was patented in 1878, and the humble paper clip was invented by Norwegian Johan Vaaler in 1899.

As well as the tools of office work, the buildings themselves were changing. For example, larger, taller buildings were enabled through advances in elevator technology: the first passenger elevator was installed by Elisha Graves Otis in New York in 1857. The incandescent electric lamp was invented around 1870. Sanitation too was critical to the development of the modern office buildings. Alexander Cummings' 1875 patent for a toilet with a "stink trap" that prevented sewer gases from backing up through drains was an important development. And as we have already seen, steel frame construction was born, enabling the spread of tall buildings free from the limitations of load-bearing concrete structures.

These technological innovations within office buildings were simply part of a wider process of change that was a having fundamental impact on the organisation of the economy and that brought with it massive social change. Thus, while the technological advances of the age were shaping the development of the office building, they were also changing the nature of work and of social relations. The importance of these advancements therefore also lay in their ability to make obsolete previously dominant forms of organisational structure and, as Cowan and colleagues observed, help create an office economy that was no longer simply part of other facets of urban life but a facet in its own right. Thus:

> The telephone changed office activities in a similar fashion to the telegraph a few decades earlier. Not only did the ability to speak directly with people at a distance affect the dispersal of office functions, but within the office itself the telephone changed things and increased the workload ...[17]
>
> But if we look back to the end of the 19th century we can see that the office function had become well established as a separate entity in the city: new buildings were being constructed to house it; more and more of the labour force were working in offices, and women especially were beginning to go into office work in large numbers. The outlines of the office as we know it were laid down.[18]

---

17 Cowan *et al* (1969) *op cit* pp32–33.

18 Cowan *et al* (1969) *op cit* p34.

As the new century dawned, the office economy as a distinct facet of urban life was firmly established. New building forms had evolved to accommodate its activities, and the property supply industry necessary to its continuing development was largely in place.

The emergence of a property industry

As London was developing rapidly as the centre of commerce in Europe through the 19th century, so supporting professions also began to flourish. Not least of these was the property industry that began to organise and professionalise. Builders, for example, became more sophisticated and responded to new building techniques and materials. While many remained as specialist craftsmen a growing cohort evolved into general contractors, undertaking both contracted and speculative projects: they became what would be recognised today as developers.

One of the earlier and most successful and influential developer-builders was Thomas Cubitt. Born in 1788, the son of a Norfolk farmer, Cubitt learned his trade as a ship's carpenter, before setting up business in Holborn in 1811. He applied his considerable organisational skills to building a business that was one of the first to employ the full range of skilled building craftsmen on a permanent basis. Within four years of setting up in business, Cubitt was laying out the Calthorpe Estate, near Gray's Inn Road. He had become a skilled developer and urban designer. The Cubitt phenomenon was also something of a family affair. By 1825, he had been joined by his brothers: Lewis, who built parts of Eaton Place and Lowndes Square, and William, who developed Cubitt Town on the Isle of Dogs in the 1840s and 1850s to house the rapidly growing numbers of workers in the nearby docks and shipyards. Cubitt's large, permanent staff required a constant flow of work, and this necessity led to a number of large-scale agreements with the Grosvenor Estate.

In 1826, Lord Grosvenor obtained an Act of Parliament enabling him to build on the land that is now Belgravia, an area that takes its name from a village that is now a district on the northern outskirts of Leicester, where the Grosvenor family once owned an estate. Up to this point, the land was extensively used for market gardens and frequent duck shooting and cock fighting. Cubitt successfully applied his business and financial acumen to securing an agreement with Lord Grosvenor in which he gained virtually exclusive rights to build on the land, and found financial backing from the City to fund his work.

Between 1826 and the mid-1830s, Cubitt bought building leases on adjacent plots, building as market conditions allowed. Cubitt based his plan on four squares — Belgrave, Eaton, Chester and Lowndes, which were linked by wide roads and crescents. "The expert can detect subtle differences in each block as fashions in architecture changed from classical to Italianate. But the remarkable thing is that the extraordinary unity of the whole scheme was maintained over a period of some 10 years of development."[19] Cubitt started Belgrave Square in 1826. In an example of literal interdependence between the growth of the docks and the expansion of homes in the west, Cubitt used earth excavated from the new St Katherine's Dock (also a Cubitt family scheme) to raise the land level above its marshy surroundings.

Cubitt's skills as a builder, designer and businessman are shown by the fact that Seth Smith, who worked on the north side of Belgrave Square, sank rapidly into debt, and Joseph Cundy, who took on Chester Square, went bankrupt. Neither was able to replicate the grandiose vision and bold spirit of the master builder Cubitt. As well as Belgravia, Cubitt also worked on Gordon Square and Tavistock Square between 1820 and 1826, large parts of Pimlico during the 1830s and Victoria in the 1840s and 1850s. This huge output made Cubitt fabulously wealthy, but he never lost his zeal and vision for London. As well as a builder, Cubitt considered himself what we would call today an urban planner and he made several contributions to reforms aimed at improving living conditions. But it was with his craft that he established his strongest reputation:

> He made his name, and kept it, by the excellence of his workmanship and the quality of his finishes. It was a reputation achieved only by the most painstaking attention to detail and by his innovation of building up a strong workforce — numbering 1000 men at its height — to whom he assured continuous employment and from whom he secured a high degree of loyalty.[20]

At the time of his death in 1855, Cubitt had done more than any other individual to change the London skyline. Reflecting on his life, Queen Victoria (for whom Cubitt had built Osborne House on the Isle of Wight) wrote sombrely in her diary: "a better, kinder-hearted or more simple, unassuming man never breathed".

---

19 Jenkins S (1975) *Landlords to London: The Story of a Capital and its Growth* Book Club Associates, London p81.

20 Jenkins (1975) *op cit* p84.

Cubitt was a 19th century phenomenon. His vision was awesome, his business skills extraordinary and his technical understanding of development probably second to none. He had "commercialised" development and defined a new approach that was to be the forerunner of today's development industry. Cubitt's work, and that of others, was providing homes for the growing population of increasingly affluent people engaged in the city's commerce. During his working life, London had become "the workplace of the new 'professions', as engineers and accountants and architects and lawyers moved ineluctably towards the city of empire",[21] and apart from sowing the seeds of the office economy, these "affluent 'consumers' created a market for new 'department stores' and new restaurants" and "there arose a revived and more salubrious 'West End' of theatres under such actor-managers as Irving and Beerbohm Tree."[22] But in the time after his death property development and construction changed fundamentally, partly in response to the increasingly complex nature and scale of buildings, but also in response to changing social structures and professional specialisation.

In 1887, the roles of architect and builder were formally split in the charter of the Royal Institution of British Architects (RIBA). This was a critical moment because it separated two skills that up to this point had gained mutual benefit from close association. The split reduced communication between design and delivery, and ultimately led to a separation of interests and a deep-rooted suspicion of motives on both sides. From this point on the client or building owner chose an architect and an outline design was agreed. A bill of quantities would be drawn up by a quantity surveyor, and then the contract would be put out to competitive tender to builders who would seek to undercut each others' prices to win the work. This new arrangement stratified responsibilities and led to social and professional niches. Marion Bowley argued that the architectural profession was "moulded on the social and aesthetic pattern of the 18th century" when it was considered that "buildings were of interest to an architect primarily as the vehicles of his [sic] art, the purpose of the building being secondary".[23] Bowley is forthright in her analysis:

---

21 Ackroyd P (2000) *London: The Biography* Vintage, London pp718-719.

22 *Ibid*.

23 Bowley (1966) *op cit* p348.

It can be regarded as one of the accidental tragedies of history that the architectural profession crystallised at this time, just as a new era of building for an industrial society started. By the outbreak of the First World War the industry had assumed its modern pattern of contractors and subcontractors, estate developers and speculative builders, and of distinct and separated designing professions. This was part of a process of adaptation and resistance to economic expansion and technical change.[24]

The long-term effects of the emergent structure were profound: the replication of English social stratification in the structure of the property process, with the client and architect forming the uppermost tier, propped up by the professions with the lowly builders at the base of the pile has worked to the detriment of the industry and the consumers of its products ever since. The mass provision of speculative offices and other buildings during the 1960s and 1970s that lacked any architectural merit or client-side interest in functionality were a direct outcome of this structure. So too is the ongoing separation of interests between the ownership and management of buildings where the client-side roles of ownership and building design are distant from the ongoing occupation of buildings. The lack of feedback between the two sides has been largely responsible for the supply-led culture of the industry and almost complete disconnect between supplier and customer.

As the property profession evolved in the later years of the 19th century, so it began to deliver new forms of buildings. Most businesses in the early years of the office economy occupied buildings that had been built for functions other than offices: residential buildings, industrial buildings, warehouses and so on. But the increasingly complex nature of the emerging organisations demanded a more sophisticated and fitting kind of physical environment. Again, Marian Bowley captured the essence of the situation:

The significance of such investment is not always appreciated. Buildings required for industry and trade are as much part of the basic capital investment required for the effective functioning of the economic system as machinery, railways, etc. In the 19th century it was necessary to provide the buildings for an expanding economy changing from an agricultural to an industrial basis.[25]

---

24 *Ibid.*

25 Bowley (1966) *op cit* p326.

So it was that the number of purpose-built offices began to proliferate. For example, in 1867, a new head office was built for National Provincial Bank (later National Westminster) on Bishopsgate and, in 1881, Barings Bank rebuilt its headquarters, also on Bishopsgate. Also, in 1879, the first stage of Prudential's iconic head office on Holborn was completed to architect Alfred Waterhouse's design. These new buildings were far more complex than their predecessors and new skills were evolving to deal with increasingly complex physical infrastructure. One of the key professions, itself made up of numerous specialist skills, was the surveying profession. Today, there are around 95,000 people registered as professional surveyors in the UK. Their advice spans a bewildering array of specialist areas grouped into areas including agency, building surveying, construction, facilities management, minerals, planning and development, project management, quantity surveying, rural land management, valuation and waste management. Their most high-profile role with respect to the story being told in this book is their transactional, or agency, role. This encompasses either buying or selling office buildings as standing investments, primarily for property companies and investment institutions, or transacting leasing deals, working either on behalf of the lessor (owner) or lessee (occupier). For both these roles, surveyors are widely referred to in the market either as "agents" or "brokers".

Surveying has a long history, and as such it has gone through many transformations as the economy has changed to present new challenges and areas of work. The original growth of the surveying profession can be traced back to the land reforms of the 16th century. Changes to agricultural tenure and management led to the demand for measuring, surveying and valuation.[26] Population growth, together with economic changes and a more intense use of land, led to a demand for more sophisticated approaches to the measurement and valuation of land. Ownership rights, for example, which were often bitterly contested over many years, could be resolved or avoided with accurate, measured records. As the land market matured during the 17th century, surveyors became more involved in transactional activity. Land supply was being bolstered as monastic, crown and church estates were being broken up,[27] and demand for measuring and valuing grew as a result.

---

26 Thompson F M L (1968) *Chartered Surveyors: The Growth of a Profession* Routledge & Kegan Paul, London.

27 Thompson (1968) *op cit* p25.

However, the role of the surveyor really got under way during the 18th century when landlords began to appoint estate managers to improve the efficiency and productivity of their land.[28]

Although recent mergers and acquisitions, combined with internationalisation of the profession, have changed the structure of the industry, it is possible to trace the origins of many of the firms in existence today back to this time. For example, Cluttons was founded in 1765; Richard Ellis (now part of CBRE) was founded in 1773, and Jones Lang Wootton (now Jones Lang LaSalle) dates back to 1783. Table 2.4 shows a selection of the oldest firms, many bearing the names of their founding partners. Until relatively recently, they were all partnerships, in which the equity partners shared the profits of the business and took an equal share of responsibility for the performance of their firms.

Table 2.4 Some of the oldest names in surveying

Historic name	*Most recent name*	*Year founded*
Cluttons	Cluttons	1765
Richard Ellis	CBRE	1773
Jones Lang Wootton	Jones Lang LaSalle	1783
Chestertons	Chestertons	1805
Healey & Baker	Cushman & Wakefield Healey and Baker	1820
Grimley & Son	GVA Grimley	1830
St Quintin	CBRE	1831
Wetherall Green and Smith	ATIS Real Wetherall	1860
Fuller Peiser	Fuller Peiser	1883
Strutt & Parker	Strutt & Parker	1885

Source: RICS[29] Reproduced with permission of the Royal Institution of Chartered Surveyors, which owns the copyright.

During the 19th century, as the industrial revolution reached its zenith, the demand for surveyors grew stronger, and their roles diversified

28 Leyshon A, Thrift N J and Daniels P W (1987) *Large Commercial Property Firms in the UK: The Operational Development and Spatial Expansion of General Practice Firms of Chartered Surveyors* Working Papers on Producer Services Series No 5 University of Bristol and University of Liverpool.

29 Royal Institution of Chartered Surveyors (1987) *Yearbook 1987* RICS, London.

further. The huge expansion of the railway network, the digging of canals, the building of sewers and drainage, and expansion of factories all demanded surveying skills. While, on the one hand, surveyors responded by providing the by now traditional skills of measuring and valuing, they also developed into an advisory capacity by acting for principals involved in the acquisition of land by public utilities.[30] This latter activity set the tone for the development of surveying practices because it was those firms that "steered clear of the measuring side and concentrated on the negotiating and valuing who made good, and established themselves as the commanding figures of the mid-Victorian years."[31]

As the number of surveyors grew, so they began to professionalise. In 1834, the Land Surveyors Club was formed, and in 1868 the Institution of Surveyors was established. Chartered status and qualifying examinations were introduced in 1881, and the profession grew rapidly. The 1871 Census of Population recorded 15,598 people engaged in surveying-related work. The industrialisation of the economy during this time and the immense transformation of land into buildings to accommodate the new economy created a vast workload and enabled the profession to mature quickly. The profession was awarded "Royal" status in 1946 in appreciation of the work undertaken by surveyors during the war.

By the end of the 19th century, the key built environment professions — construction, design and surveying — were organised along lines that are familiar today. The intense period of economic and social reorganisation during the Victorian period involved fundamental changes to the nature of work, and the built environment professions organised themselves and delivered the structures required to accommodate its new processes, as well as the infrastructure needed to transport raw materials and finished goods. Peter Cowan and colleagues described how this period saw the industrial revolution reach its climax, and how "the role of the city changed utterly."[32] As the industrial processes evolved and changed, so too did their administration and governance. Office activities grew in importance and began to assume their own, distinct identity in the urban environment. Again, Cowan and colleagues identified the link between changing economic relations and the rise of the office:

---

30 Leyshon *et al* (1987) *op cit* p5.

31 Thompson (1968) *op cit* p109.

32 Cowan *et al* (1969) *op cit* p26.

> We have seen that, until the industrial revolution, the office function was generally an integral part of other facets of urban life. But it is a commonplace that, as an organisation or an organism grows in complexity, certain parts or functions become separate from others. The office function of communication and control is just such a case. When an organisation is fairly simple, as in a cottage industry or a small workshop, the office function is integral with the production process itself. But as the enterprise grows and increases in complexity ... so the office function begins to separate off.[33]

By the turn of the century, the office economy had become a distinct facet of the urban environment. It had gained a momentum of its own and it was driving a new period of growth in London. Despite the growing international crisis that would erupt in 1914, by 1910, around 30% of all quoted securities in the world were listed on the London Stock Exchange.[34] By 1914, 80% of all issues on the London market were for overseas borrowers.[35] Improvements in communic-ations reinforced London's role as the leading centre in an increasingly integrated world securities market. Its growth as a commercial and international trading centre, together with its position as the hub of world communications, led inevitably to it becoming the world's foremost shipping market. Before 1914, the British merchant fleet accounted for around half the world's tonnage, and one-third of the fleet was then engaged in trade that never touched Britain's shores at all.[36]

Despite the appalling losses and huge cost of the First World War, London's inexorable growth resumed quite quickly in its aftermath. During the inter-war years, the working population of the City of London grew by more than a quarter, and many new landmarks appeared on the London skyline that reflected the growing sophistication of the property-supply industry. For example, a rebuilt Waterloo Station opened in 1922, Wembley Stadium opened in 1923, and a remodelled Regent Street opened in 1927. The growing impact of transport was having a profound effect on the long-term shape of London. Electrification and upgrading of the Underground together with the expanding road network were pushing London ever outwards. In 1925, the first stretch of the Great West Road (the A4) was opened, between what is now Chiswick roundabout and Hounslow.

---

33 Cowan *et al* (1969) *op cit* p28.

34 Rose (1994) *op cit* p21.

35 Rose (1994) *op cit* p20.

36 Rose (1994) *op cit* p22.

This was to establish a major artery of growth westwards, leading to the development of other iconic buildings such as those of Beechams, Firestone and Gillette. The dynamism of this particular growth corridor was to be felt throughout the 20th century and was epitomised by the influx of the computer industry in the 1980s.

However, it was in the centre where the growing impact of the burgeoning office economy was most obvious. Many signature buildings were created during this time, some reflecting Britain's continuing influence in the world through its Empire. At the Aldwych, Australia House for the Australia High Commission (designed by A Marshall Mackenzie and A G R Mackenzie, and opened in 1918) and India House for the High Commissioner (Sir Herbert Baker and A T Scott; 1930) are both superlative examples. There were several buildings that came to be synonymous with their famous and long-term occupants: the London County Council's (later GLC) County Hall on the South Bank (1922), the London Passenger Transport Building (1929) occupied by the forerunner of London Underground in Victoria, the BBC's Langham Place (1932), and the University of London's Senate House (1936) are a few notable examples. Many corporate office buildings were also completed. For example, the Midland Bank building in Poultry (1924); the distinctive Daily Express building (Ellis and Clarke with Sir Owen Williams; 1931), the first example of a curtain wall office building in Britain; and Unilever House (1931) on the Thames at Blackfriars, designed by J Lomax-Simpson with Sir John Burnet, Tait and Lorne.

A similar process, though on a larger scale, was under way in the US. Of course the late-1920s and early-1930s were overshadowed by the Stock Market crash, and the subsequent Depression. Nevertheless, by the year of the crash, there were nearly 5000 buildings of 10 stories or more in the US, with half of them in New York.[37] The office economy was vibrant and dominant; it was absorbing large numbers of workers, and it was generating vigorous economic growth. However, its impact on the urban environment was not welcomed by everyone. American sociologist Lewis Mumford (see chapter 3) was forthright in his description of the office economy in North America:

---

37 White J R (1993) *The Office Building: From Concept to Investment Reality* Counsellors of Real Estate, Chicago p14.

Plainly, no great corporate enterprise with a worldwide network of agents, correspondents, market outlets, factories, and investors could exist without relying upon the services of an army of ... stenographers, filing clerks, and bookkeepers, office managers, sales managers ... right up to the fifth vice-president whose name or o.k. sets the final seal of responsibility upon an action.[38]

He went on describe the form of the office economy and the buildings that were springing up to house its processes:

... files, vaults, places for live storage and dead storage, parade grounds of documents, where the records of business were alphabetically kept, with an eye to the possibility of future exploitation, future reference, future lawsuits, future contracts. This age found its form in a new type of office building: a sort of human filing case, whose occupants spent their days in the circumspect care of paper: numbering, ticketing, assorting, routing, recording, manifolding, filing, to the end that the commodities and services thus controlled could be sold to the profit of the absentee owners of the corporation.[39]

In the US and Europe, rapid developments in motor transport, particularly cars, trams and trains, acted as a spur to suburbanisation of populations and increased densities in city centres. More dense, higher rise and more chaotic, American and European cities were becoming increasingly dominated by the economic activity that was evolving particularly at their centres. As their central areas intensified, so cities spread rapidly outwards, encouraged by ever-denser networks of rail and tram transport, and the growing impact of the motor car. Cities began to take on a whole new level of complexity, with increasingly large and anonymous corporate offices at their centres. By the outbreak of the Second World War, the office economy had, in many respects, come to define downtown.

---

38 Mumford L (1938) *The Culture of Cities* Secker and Warburg, London p227.
39 *Ibid.*

The Modern Office Economy

3

Patterns in office activity

It is a curious fact of history that even as office buildings came to dominate city centres there remained only the crudest understanding of the internal dynamics of the office economy. For decades, academic analysis of cities barely recognised offices as a distinct facet of urban structure, and when they did the work was largely descriptive rather than analytical. This neglect of offices in academic endeavour was reflected in public policy and in the supply process, as both struggled to keep up with the changing dynamics of the office economy. The situation has changed in more recent times as studies have begun to explain the role of office activities in the changing structure of cities. This chapter explains how our understanding of cities, and particularly the role of the office economy within them, has evolved. There are a number of ways in which this story could be told; the approach taken here is to trace the major changes in thinking largely through academic work.

The frenetic economic activity of the latter three decades of the 19th century, which led to the birth of the modern office, and the consequent increases in building densities and equally inflated land prices at the core of most cities, attracted the attention of economists curious to explain the forces at work. Early on, as the growing number of tall buildings reached ever higher, the economists turned to the question of how land values were determined. One of the earliest in the field was British economist Alfred Marshall, who, in 1890, argued that the land use that captures a particular site is the one "from which the most profitable results are anticipated."[1] This concept of price bidding came to dominate urban land economics, resulting in "a voluminous literature."[2]

Basically, urban land economics suggest that land prices are determined by the interactions of the owners of real estate and those who wish to rent or buy buildings for transacting their business or as living space. This pricing mechanism reflects perceived levels and sources of demand. As demand for land intensifies, so less intense land uses and less profitable uses are displaced to fringe or transitional areas where the cost of centrality is less onerous. The classical explanations for these processes that cause activities to be tightly clustered around urban centres are traced back through inelegantly named theories, such as agglomeration economics and bid rent theory. The explanations typically involve individual enterprises in decisions to maximise the benefits of a convergent public transport system; exploit access to labour, gain a competitive position and so on. In so doing, they suggest an explanation for the tendency of central areas to rise vertically.

Perhaps the most significant work from these early years, and certainly the one that cast the longest shadow, was *Principles of City Land Values*, first published in 1903 by Richard Hurd.[3] One of the earliest proponents of urban modelling, Hurd suggested that a cursory glance revealed similarities among cities, and that closer analysis revealed that their structural characteristics responded to definite principles. The key principle that he identified, adopted and adapted from Ricardian theories of agricultural land value theory, was that economic rent in cities was based on locational advantage:

> Since value depends on economic rent and rent on location, and location on convenience, and convenience on nearness, we may eliminate the intermediate steps and say that value depends on nearness.[4]

In other words, a desire for businesses to be close together forced land values upwards: good old-fashioned supply and demand. Hurd developed this thinking, going on to propose a more general citywide model of structural form, in which he argued that cities grew outwards in a sectoral pattern:

---

1 Marshall A (1890) *Principles of Economics* Macmillan, London p445.
2 Alonso W (1964) *Location and Land Use* Harvard University Press, Mass.
3 Hurd R M (1903) *Principles of City Land Values* Arno Press, New York.
4 Hurd (1903) *op cit* p13.

> Cities originate at their most convenient point of contact with the outside world and grow in the lines of least resistance or greatest attraction ... Growth in cities consists of movement away from the point of origin in all directions, except as topographically hindered ... Central growth takes place both from the heart of the city and from each subcentre of attraction, and axial growth pushes into the outlying territory by means of railroad, turnpikes and street railroads.[5]

Hurd's was the first comprehensive model of urban structure and he set the agenda for the next 40 years as urban geographers, economists and others strove to find and explain pattern in urban structure. Indeed, so seminal was his work considered by some that Paul Wendt was moved to comment half a century later: "No more comprehensive analysis of the dynamics of city growth has appeared since his work."[6] Praise indeed but, although comprehensive in its context, Hurd's analysis left much detail to be elaborated upon. Not least Hurd, like all his contemporaries, failed to give any separate treatment of offices. Yet, as the spectre of the First World War loomed over Europe, purpose-built offices were already an established feature of the American urban landscape, and were becoming established in European cities. The massive economic expansion of the Victorian period had culminated in the establishment of the office economy as a distinctive feature of the urban landscape: by the early years of 20th century.

The pattern of development in cities did not meet with universal approval, and one of its severest critics was Lewis Mumford. Born in 1895, Mumford was one of the greatest observers of urbanism that ever lived, his long working life coinciding with the maximal period of growth in the office economy. He was also a great humanist. Leaving college early due to tuberculosis, Mumford spent enormous amounts of time studying, sketching and simply watching New York. What he saw was the dehumanising effect of modern urban life, its stultifying impact on the human soul, ultimately its denuding of human purpose. Mumford regarded medieval cities as having been built on a human scale and balancing human needs, whereas to him the general advent of modernity signalled not emancipation and progress but a deterioration of community. This might be seen as just part of the long goodbye given to the mythical idyll of rural life that accompanied the

---

5 Hurd (1903) *op cit* p14.

6 Wendt P F (1956) *Real Estate Appraisal* New York p107.

industrialisation of western economies. A century before, William Wordsworth was mourning the passing of rural innocence and virtue in England in *The Prelude*: "Cities where the human heart is sick." But Mumford was no iconoclast. He balanced his withering criticism with active participation in urban planning (in 1923 he co-founded the Regional Planning Association of America) and pursued a lifetime of writing on cities, architecture, environmentalism, technology and literature. Mumford argued passionately for a more integrated, more human urban landscape that performed a complex balance of roles:

> The city in its complete sense, then, is a geographic plexus, an economic organisation, an institutional process, a theater of social action, and an esthetic symbol of collective unity. On the one hand it is a physical frame for the common place domestic and economic activities; on the other, it is a consciously dramatic setting for the more sublimated urges of a human culture.[7]

Mumford's humanistic approach to urban planning was reflected in the study of urban morphology as the limitations of urban land economics yielded to a sociological approach that was more sensitive to the differences between urban areas. In particular, there was the work of a group of scholars collectively referred to as the Chicago School, after the city in which they worked. During the 1920s and 1930s, these early theorists generated a number of models of urban morphology that are taught to undergraduates of geography to this day. They were ecologists and sociologists, and for them the urban system was a metaphor for an organism in which they were trying to understand emergent processes. Perhaps the most famous of the models, known as the concentric zone theory, was put forward by Ernest Burgess in 1923.[8] The model is based on the notion that urban growth is a centripetal force, expanding outwards in a series of concentric zones, each with their own characteristics. The central area is surrounded by a zone in transition where high value uses are pushing outwards. And this zone yields to residential uses, and gradually to less intensive land uses.

---

7 Mumford L (1938) *The Culture of Cities* (2nd Edition) Secker and Warburg, London p480.

8 Burgess E W The Growth of the City: An Introduction to a Research Project In: Park R E, Burgess E W and McKenzie R D (1925) *The City* University of Chicago Press, Chicago.

Recognising the growing influence of the motor car, in 1932 Frederick Babcock proposed a modification to the model, suggesting that the concentric ring theory would be affected by the sub-optimal distribution of route ways.[9] This would result in sites a given distance from the centre being either more or less accessible to the centre. This led to the axial theory, where development away from the centre grows outward further along major transport routes than in the interstices. A third model, proposed by Homer Hoyt in 1939,[10] was also strongly influenced by the road infrastructure. His proposal was that differences in land use near the centre would be perpetuated as the city expanded, thereby creating distinctive wedges of activity stretching from the centre, often along route ways. This gave rise to the sector theory of urban growth. In all three of these models, the close relationship between motorised transport and urban growth that has been such as feature of most US cities can be clearly detected.

The final classical model was that proposed by Chauncy Harris and Edward Ullman. Theirs was the multiple nuclei theory,[11] a model that proposed a cellular structure for cities in which distinctive clusters of land use developed around specific points, or nuclei. The model recognised that most cities do not originate from a single central area but evolve, rather, by the gradual coalescence of a number of separate nodes into a single urban mass.

A common characteristic of many of the models of urban morphology up to this point was their two-dimensional representation of the dynamics of urban change over time. Furthermore, they remained focused on residential and industrial activity, saying very little about the growing influence of the office economy. Nowhere was this truer than in the area that lay at the centre of each of the models: what had become known as downtown, the central business district, or CBD. The lack of any real understanding of the CBD up to this point possibly reflects the fact that the CBD sat at the centre of each of the models, with all the change, development and growth taking place around, for example in the zones of transition. Ironically, the CBD was isolated by its own centrality, and not regarded as needing any

---

9 Babcock F M (1932) *The Valuation of Real Estate* McGraw-Hill New York.

10 Hoyt H (1939) *The Structure and Growth of Residential Neighbourhoods in American Cities* FHA, Washington.

11 Harris C D and Ullman E L (1945) The Nature of Cities *Annals of the American Academy of Political Science* Vol 242 pp7–17.

particular explanation. Yet it was here that the office economy was emerging as the dominant land use.

The CBD represents the theoretical point of maximum accessibility in the urban system. It is the focus for the public transport system, both intra- and inter-urban systems. It is home, generally, to those activities that require the highest levels of contact, whether business-to-consumer or business-to-business, and companies arrange themselves in order to minimise the friction of distance. As we have seen, the intensity of land use has historically led to an interpretation of urban morphology that focuses on competition, and therefore price, for land. The classic bid-rent curve — so beloved of urban geographers and a set piece on all first-degree courses for over 40 years — sits at the heart of this analysis.

The first major work to recognise that the CBD was not a homogeneous lump of economic activity but rather a complex interplay of relationships and activities feeding off each other and the benefits of centrality was by Robert Haig.[12] This famous urban geographer observed that through a process of competition for space, the CBD becomes divided into functional sub-areas where strongly linked economic activities agglomerate. This complexity can be easily seen in central London. For many years, London comprised a rich mosaic of "sub-markets" of economic activity that clung together in their historic clusters before being nudged out by the higher rent-paying, white-collar activities. Of course, the City itself was a cluster, albeit one broken down into a number of concentrations of distinctive business activity, including banking, stock broking and jobbing, insurance, shipping, fur trades, publishing and commodities. To this day, the insurance sector remains tightly packed into the EC3 postal district in the south-east corner of the City. Such clusters were often associated with the historic centres, such as the Bank of England; Lloyd's insurance market; the wharfs of the fur trade or the Commodity Exchange. Apart from the City, there were many other sub-markets.

In the West End, government-related activities grouped around Whitehall and the civil engineering practices clustered close by to facilitate lobbying when Acts of Parliament, for example, had to be passed before constructing canals and railways. Similarly, large oil companies were clustered in the Victoria area; while private banks and

---

12 Haig R M (1926) Towards an Understanding of the Metropolis Parts 1 and 2 *Q. J. Econ.* Vol 40 pp179–208 and pp402–434.

small headquarters were predominantly in Mayfair and St James's — handy for the "gentlemen's clubs". Other examples of clustering included:

- Bethnall Green — clothing
- Clerkenwell — jewellery
- Fleet Street — printing
- Harley Street and Wimpole Street — medicine
- Inns of Court — solicitors and lawyers
- Mayfair — property companies and chartered surveyors
- north of Oxford Street — clothing
- Shoreditch — furniture and printing
- Victoria — government

Of course, not all of these clusters exist today — evidence that such clusters originate, evolve and die with notable regularity. One of the more interesting modern originations has occurred in the West End during the past few years. This cluster is focused on the area around Curzon Street in the West End, which has latterly become a focus of the hedge fund industry. Estimates suggest that between 2000 and 2003, some 250 hedge funds established offices in the neighbourhood.[13] In terms of evolution, one of the most dramatic phases of change in recent times was the mass exodus of the publishing industry from Fleet Street, a street that was once synonymous with the industry that it accommodated. Finally, the death of clusters occurs as the pressures on space and the progress of technology marginalise businesses, and as industries themselves undergo structural decline. One example is the furniture industry in Shoreditch that suffered the combined impact of the City creeping northwards and structural changes in its market.

While the urban ecologists had begun to peel back the layers of activities within cities to reveal dynamism and process, the models they worked with continued to operate at the city-wide level, rather than at the level of the activities therein. And they were predominantly descriptive rather than explanatory. Specifically, there remained a yawning gap in understanding the nature and role of the emerging office economy.

---

13 Marsh G, Chippendale D and Sadek F (2003) *London Offices Policy Review* London Property Research, London p52.

The corporate years

The Culture of Cities,[14] published on the eve of World War Two, was one of Lewis Mumford's finest works. The book is a history of urbanism, beginning with the medieval town — which Mumford viewed fondly as akin to the garden city. His biographer, Donald Miller, described the book as "a study of the erosion of a balanced, decentralised civilization and its replacement by one with an oppressive metropolitan centralization of power, people and culture."[15] *Culture* traces the history of urbanism as a "fall from grace, a long plunge into chaos and moral confusion."[16] It is a lucid, passionate and immensely widely informed argument, finishing with a call for urban development to balance the needs of the institutional with the needs of the individual. Mumford argued that while cities had expanded physically, "the essential social nucleus" had been treated as an afterthought. He proposed that "social facts are primary, and the physical organisation of a city, its industries and its markets, its lines of communication and traffic, must be subservient to its social needs."[17] He suggested that it was necessary to define the interrelationships between activities in order to lay down "the outlines of an integrated city",[18] which in turn would create a more humanistic city. The "industries and markets" to which he refers have come to dominate our cities through the physical mass of the buildings they occupy, reducing individual endeavour to insignificance.

The post-Second World War years were to defy Mumford's prescription. Although the war brought the physical growth of the office economy in London to a temporary halt, and post-war rationing and austerity measures delayed its resumption until the early-1950s, the period saw the ascendancy of the office economy in the national economy. However, the general approach to defining rather than explaining urban morphology continued into the post-war years. The work of Raymond Murphy and James Vance typified much of this effort.[19] They were primarily concerned with the desire to provide a

---

14 Mumford (1938) *op cit*.

15 Miller D L (1989) *Lewis Mumford: A Life* Weidenfield & Nicolson, New York p355.

16 *Ibid*.

17 Miller (1989) *op cit* p482.

18 *Ibid*.

19 Murphy R E and Vance J E (1954a) Comparative Study of Nine Central Business Districts *Econ. Geogr.* Vol 30 pp301–336; and Murphy R E and Vance J E (1954b) Delimiting the CBD *Econ. Geogr.* Vol 30 pp189–222.

uniform method for aerial definition that could replace the fixing of boundaries by haphazard and local procedures. They postulated, for example, that the CBD, as a spatial unit, could be defined through a series of measures that reflected its essential characteristics. In this way, the physical attributes of the CBD were to be measured independently of a citywide analysis of urban structure. Their measurements included the definition of uses considered to be quintessentially CBD activities. Echoes of this approach were to be found in the development of planning policy in central London many years later, where those activities not considered to have an essential requirement for a central location were to be encouraged to relocate (see chapter 6). The physical parameters used by Murphy and Vance included the volume of space dedicated at any one time to various uses, and building height and intensity indices, which could be used to define more clearly the boundaries of the CBD. They provided no insight into the emerging influence of the office economy and, like other work from the time, there was no analysis of the internal dynamics of the patterns that they mapped.

Against the flow of studies seeking spatial definition there were some that sought a more explanatory approach with a less static, less definitional interpretation of urban morphology. One of these was Ralph Turvey's work,[20] in which he argued that cities are economic systems working towards, but never reaching, equilibrium:

> It is impossible to present a comparative static analysis which will explain the layout of towns and the pattern of buildings: the determining background conditions are insufficiently stationary in relation to the durability of buildings.[21]

Turvey was suggesting that a simplistic economic model, for example a rent-bid model, had major shortcomings and that analysis had to be more behavioural:

> In other words, each town must be examined separately and historically. The features of London, for example, can be fully understood only by investigating its past: it is as it is because it was what it was.[22]

---

20 Turvey R (1957) *The Economics of Real Property* Allen & Unwin, London.

21 Turvey (1957) *op cit* p47.

22 *Ibid.*

Turvey's work was paralleled by another writer who seems to have anticipated later studies by at least 10 years. This was Donald Foley, who, in 1956, published a paper in which he traced changes in the spatial distribution of administrative offices in San Francisco.[23] But the most significant work to emerge during the 1950s was largely ignored for 20 years: John Rannells' study of central Philadelphia.[24] Rannells' study is important because of its emphasis on the role of activities, or uses, in shaping the morphology of the city. In this respect, he helped to fill the large gap in the general understanding of the city outlined above.

In a reference to earlier work, and particularly the work of the urban land economists, Rannells highlighted the difficulties and problems inherent in distinguishing between land use factors associated with location, and those unrelated to location. Thus: "location is only one factor in the operation of any given activity."[25] More importantly, he made the critical distinction between broad land use changes associated, in classical terms, with utility maximisation as a factor of access, and the influence of operational decisions on the level and structure of final demand for space:

> It is necessary to take in somewhat more than relates directly to land use, since changes in demand for space or location may come about as secondary results of business decisions or consumer preferences which, in themselves, have no concern with questions of land use.[26]

The emphasis was thus abruptly shifted away from concepts of rational decision-making, based on the assumption of "complete knowledge", into an area in which decisions that ultimately result in a land use manifestation are made for other, unrelated reasons. The decisions reached are, instead, related to the operational requirements of the companies themselves, and their linkages to one another. Rannells was less concerned with defining any preconceived area than with identifying the interlinked systems of activity that were located

---

23 Foley D L (1956) Factors in the Location of Administrative Offices Papers and Proceedings, *Regional Science Association* Vol 2 pp318–326.

24 Rannells J (1956) *The Core of the City: A Pilot Study of Changing Land Uses in Central Business Districts* Columbia University Press, New York.

25 Rannells (1956) *op cit* p5.

26 Rannells (1956) *op cit* pp55–56.

in the central area.[27] His work was not locational in the sense of spatial definition; rather he used locationally specific data to work out patterns of relationships. Rannells himself justified his approach thus:

the physical city exists because of the patterned activities of its population as they accumulate and are accommodated at definite locations, in establishments.[28]

These "definite locations" are chosen for a variety of reasons. Rannells recognised the availability of suitable accommodation, services and facilities, "as well as the associated activities of closely linked establishments or 'the market' which their operations require".[29] However, wherever these requirements are to be met, access to other establishments is crucial because:

members of every group benefit by nearness to establishments with which they have linkages and by the availability of services of all kinds which they require.[30]

Clearly, Rannells' work differed markedly from that which it followed. His was the first critical examination of the role of economic linkages in shaping urban structure. As he argued, the locational characteristics of activities are: "visible manifestations of the many systems of activity into which the city's life is organised."[31] However, he took the analysis much further by examining the impact of the activities undertaken within buildings and the nature of the urban fabric. Thus:

Activities carried on within an establishment determine, in general, the quantities and qualities of space used by itself for work, for display, for processing, for storage or for circulation.[32]

The most important contribution of Rannells' work was to shift the focus of study away from the spatial delimitation of activities, to an

---

27 Carter H (1976) *The Study of Urban Geography* (2nd Edition) The Pitman Press, Bath p240.
28 Rannells (1956) *op cit* pp16–17.
29 Rannells (1956) *op cit* p55.
30 *Ibid*.
31 Rannells (1956) *op cit* p35.
32 Rannells (1956) *op cit* p34.

examination of the characteristics of the activities that comprise the urban area, and the interactions between them that explain the process of change over time.

Despite the work of Turvey, Foley and Rannells, as the 1950s closed and the 1960s began most work on urban morphology remained doggedly focused on spatial definition, and there was no separate investigation into the evolution of the office economy. An early modification to Murphy and Vance's work was offered by Edgar Horwood and Ronald Boyce,[33] who separated the core of the CBD (the area where quintessentially CBD land uses were at their most intense) from the frame in which it was located. Even with this elaboration, the study of the structure of cities had not really progressed very far from pre-war approaches: it was still essentially about spatial description *à la* Chicago school. As late as 1964, William Alonso's influential *Location and Land Use: Toward a General Theory of Land Rent* was based on the central tenet that cities could be modelled on a featureless plain principle, ignoring the effects of "hills, low land, beautiful views, social cachet, or pleasant breezes", which while important "no way has been found to incorporate them ..."[34]

Turvey's point about historical contingency was taken up in a number of studies between the mid-1960s and early-1970s. This work took a more explanatory approach, although its emphasis was spatial rather than structural, and all placed the modern structure into the context of historic development. Hywel Davies undertook a major study of Cape Town.[35] He recognised that the core was itself heterogeneous with its own internal dynamics and changing structure and, like Horwood and Boyce, he defined a hard-core and surrounding frame. However, Davies himself conceded that: "currently there may well be diminishing returns in any delimitation studies per se."[36] Two of the primary drivers of urbanisation — access to goods and services, and contact — are ignored in spatial delineation. To describe urbanisation, as was common until very recently, simply in terms of being an expression of the competition for sites through the land pricing mechanism (eg through bid-rent curves) ignores the character and motivation of those activities locating

---

33 Horwood E M and Boyce R R (1959) *Studies of the Central Business District and Urban Freeway Development* University of Washington Press, Seattle.

34 Alonso (1964) *op cit* p17.

35 Davies D H (1965) *Land Use in Central Cape Town: A Study of Urban Geography* Longmans, Cape Town.

36 Davies (1965) *op cit* p87.

there. Of equal interest here is the fact that office activity was not seen as a distinctive activity within the fabric of the city.

In 1966 Harold Carter and Gwyn Rowley's study focused on Cardiff.[37] Their approach was to explain the modern structure of the city in terms of a process of development, dating to the medieval period, through the rapid expansion in the 19th century, taking into account physical features constraining the city's growth. The authors demonstrated the dynamic qualities of the CBD as a patchwork of specialised areas, a patchwork that had "emerged due to the needs created by the industrial hinterland."[38] David Ward took a similar approach in his study of Boston[39] by recognising distinctive areas of specialised business activity, and tracing the development of the CBD from a nucleus in the 19th century. It was not his purpose to define areas and, indeed, "At no point ... is the CBD as such defined nor is there any attempt at objective definition."[40] However, the study shed little new evidence on the influence of occupier characteristics on the development of sub-districts. Despite the fact that some studies had given an explicit office focus,[41] there was still no real explanation of the internal dynamics of the urban economy, nor of the complex relationships existing between the activities tightly clustered therein.

The quantitative revolution swept through urban geography and social sciences generally from the mid-1960s to the mid-1970s, with the force of a tornado. Suddenly, "scientific method" became *de rigeur*, and model building and multivariate analysis were used to explain urban form. The revolution had its critics, none more so than the pre-eminent David Harvey, who commented caustically:

> There is a clear disparity between the sophisticated theoretical and methodological framework which we are using and our ability to say anything really meaningful about events as they unfold around us.[42]

---

37 Carter and Rowley (1966) The Morphology of the Central Business District of Cardiff *Trans. Inst. Br. Geogr.* Vol 38 pp119–134.

38 Carter (1976) *op cit* p225.

39 Ward D (1966) The Industrial Revolution and the Emergence of Boston's Central Business District *Econ. Geog.* Vol 42 pp152–171.

40 Carter (1976) *op cit* p226.

41 See for example: Bannon M J (1972) The Changing Centre of Gravity of Office Establishments within Central Dublin, 1940 and 1970 *Irish Geogr* Vol 6 pp480–484 and Davey J (1972) *The Office Industry in Wellington: A Study of Contact Patterns, Location and Employment* Ministry of Works, Wellington.

42 Harvey D (1973) *Social Justice and the City* Arnold, London pp128–129.

While Harvey was undoubtedly correct in a broad sense, and while the statistical regime ultimately yielded to more systemic approaches, some useful work was undertaken in pursuit of explaining the internal dynamics of cities generally and of the office sector in particular. Some of this work in the 1960s embellished the activity-based approach pioneered by Rannells, and of the important strands of work in this area was that which examined the clustering of economic activities at the sub-local level and that which measured the strength of information flows between and within organisations and their influence on local level clustering. Bertil Thorngren,[43] Gunnar Törnqvist[44] and Brian Goddard[45] all published work based on contact between organisations and its relevance to the geography of office activity. For the first time, the internal dynamic of the office economy as a discrete sector of the urban landscape was being examined in detail.

The work of Brian Goddard[46] is of specific interest here not only because it typified much of the work taking place at the time, but also because his empirical work was carried out in central London. Goddard's early work[47] traced the changing location of publishing and advertising agencies' offices over an extended period, using successive editions of Post Office Directories to note changes of address, new offices and office closures. He found considerable change in the distribution of activities and suggested that "the magnitude of the shifts suggest some fundamental changes in location factors."[48]

Among Goddard's more interesting findings was the growing concentration of advertising agencies in the heart of the West End — a cluster that persists and thrives to the present day. Between 1955 and

43 Thorngren B (1970) How do Contact Systems Affect Regional Development? *Environment & Planning A*, Vol 2 pp409–27.

44 Törnqvist G (1968) Flows of Information and the Location of Economic Activities *Geografiska Annaler* Vol 50 pp99–107.

45 Goddard J B (1968) Multivariate Analysis of Office Location Patterns in the City Centre: A London Example *Regional Studies* Vol 2 pp69–85; and Goddard J B (1970) Functional Regions within the City Centre: A Study by Factor Analysis of Taxi Flows in Central London *Trans. Inst. Brit. Geogr.* Vol 49 pp161–182.

46 Goddard J B (1967) Changing Office Location Patterns within Central London *Urban Studies* Vol 4 pp276–285; Goddard (1968) *op cit*; Goddard (1970) *op cit*; Goddard J B (1973) Office Linkages and Location *Progress in Planning* Vol 1 No 2 pp111–232.

47 Goddard (1967), *op cit.*

48 Goddard (1967), *op cit* p277.

1966, there was a net growth of 54 agencies in the W1 postal district. This growth contrasted with net losses of eight firms in the SW1 area; five firms in WC1 and WC2, and 12 firms in the City's EC postal areas. The study also presented interesting data on the "births" and "deaths" of companies compared to migratory change. Thus, throughout the period in question, some 161 firms "died", that is to say, disappeared from the Post Office directories. By contrast, 207 firms were "born", or appeared in the directories for the first time. Over the same period, 69 existing firms migrated into central London.[49] These dynamics bring to life the early growth of the media industry in London during the 1960s in particular.

The changes show a texture to demand that we have not seen up to this point in other work. For the first time, there was evidence of dynamics within the office economy and evidence of spatial outcomes. Goddard's analysis showed that:

> The bulk of change between the two dates was not due to migration of firms between different parts of the centre but to the establishment of new firms in one area and the extinction of others elsewhere.[50]

It can be clearly seen from Goddard's work that a business sector's centre of gravity can be changed over time with the establishment of new firms. This has important lessons when examining the contemporary office market.

In later work, Goddard analysed taxi flows in central London in order to identify functional areas.[51] While confirming the presence and importance of activity clusters, the study offered little explanation, however, his study of office linkages and location was more enlightening.[52] His empirical evidence of patterns of telephone and face-to-face meetings suggested strong evidence that the localised spatial groups of office activities were based on functional connections.

Although Goddard's work made a significant contribution to the general understanding of the distribution of sub-districts in central London and of the level of contact between individual establishments, it was limited in its description of the relevance of operational characteristics to concentration. Moreover, the techniques used (among

---

49 Goddard (1967), *op cit* p281.
50 Goddard (1967), *op cit* p280.
51 Goddard (1970), *op cit*.
52 Goddard (1973), *op cit*.

them multi-variate analysis), lent themselves to aerial definition, rather than an explanation of the processes that operate to influence urban form. With a few notable examples, no one had peeled back the layers of spatial form to reveal the internal dynamics of the office economy. As late as 1972, Brian Goodall's standard text, *The Economics of Urban Areas*,[53] gave no separate treatment to office activity. Goodall's preference was to stick closely to a narrow bid-rent interpretation of urban land use because he believed that while spatial definition failed because urban areas never attained equilibrium, "the price mechanism always operates". He went on:

> Space and location are economic commodities subject to supply and demand forces. The urban real property market requires of each site or real property its highest and best use and this is largely determined by competition between potential users for available properties.[54]

Goodall's discussion of the CBD focused on retailing, and his reference to office activity showed only the most rudimentary understanding of the office economy:

> Besides retailing, the other major sub-core comprises offices. These offices are involved in executive and policy-making decisions in commerce, industry, and government, and are not dependent on the general buying public but need a central location in order to obtain necessary supplies of labour.[55]

There appears to be no appreciation of the fact that office activity had already, by this time, become an integral part of economic change in its own right. Its physical centrality is instead associated with the classical economic argument of access to labour. Furthermore, the interdependencies that exist in the office economy are given the most fleeting of references:

> They are especially reliant upon complementarity. Although some services are internal to an office, typing for instance, many are external and require frequent face-to-face contact between members of individual offices.[56]

Much of the work between the 1960s and early-1970s was a development of earlier work rather than a radical step forward in our

---

53 Goodall B (1972) *The Economics of Urban Areas* Pergamon Press, Oxford.
54 Goodall (1972) *op cit* p92.
55 Goodall (1972) *op cit* p98.
56 *Ibid*.

understanding of urban dynamics. Whereas the former had demonstrated the spatial structure of cities, the later work added statistical coherence to the distribution of activities. For example, the work of Goddard and Törnqvist provided some understanding of the flow of information between businesses and its impact on location. However, it was limited in two critical areas. First, with notable exceptions, it did not provide a focus on offices as a distinctive aspect of urban dynamics. Second, it did not provide an interpretation of the forces accounting for the processes of succession and change in either the supply of built space or in the occupiers themselves.

And so it was that as the 1970s began, and with the exception of a small number of important texts, there remained a primitive understanding of office activity as a feature of the urban landscape in its own right. The office economy had been largely ignored even though offices had over the previous three-quarters of a century come to dominate many city centres both in terms of land use and employment. The following two quotes from eminent geographers in the mid-1970s sum up the situation well.

> ... our understanding of the office system is in its infancy compared with progress in our knowledge of the role of retail or industrial land uses, for example, in the function and structure of cities.[57]

> To a great degree our understanding of the operative processes and consequent usage patterns in the city centre is completely inadequate.[58]

The fact that the general understanding of the office economy remained relatively poor for such a long time is probably reflective of the fact that it was not until the 1970s that the uneven development of manufacturing and services came to be perceived as a policy issue. Up to this point, public policy, academic study, employment and the bulk of wealth generation were concentrated in the production of goods. However, as we saw earlier, the ascendancy of the office economy was far from sudden. As table 3.1 shows, white-collar work had been growing absolutely and relative to manufacturing since the First World War. The table shows how the number of blue-collar jobs remained remarkably stable over a 50-year period. The growth in total

---

57 Daniels (1975) *op cit* p2.
58 Carter (1976) *op cit* p245.

Table 3.1 Growth of white-collar occupations in Great Britain, 1911–61

Year	*White-collar (millions)*	*Blue-collar (millions)*	*Total (millions)*	*White-collar (%)*
1911	3.4	13.7	18.3	18.7
1921	4.1	13.9	19.3	21.2
1931	4.8	14.8	21.0	23.0
1941	–	–	–	–
1951	6.9	14.4	22.5	30.9
1961	8.8	14.0	23.6	35.5

Source: Daniels[59]

employment was almost entirely accounted for by the rise of white-collar work, which doubled in size as a proportion of the total workforce. What happened from the 1960s onwards was a more complicated process, resulting in what has come to be referred to as the "de-industrialisation" of Britain.

Of course, blue-collar and white-collar are very broad categories, and tell us little about the nature of the work itself. Here we encounter the interminable problem in historical research of the lack of consistent, long-term historic data. Instead, we have to rely on the piecemeal gathering of different but complementary data sets.

According to one estimate, the number of office workers grew steadily between the 1950s and 1960s, rising, with the number of people with an office occupation in the UK rising from 15% to 25% of the workforce between 1951 and 1971. Between 1951 and 1961 alone, while total employment in the UK rose by 7%, employment in office occupations rose by 40%.[60] In London, specifically between 1971 and 1981, office employment rose by 21%, from 5.7 million to 6.9 million workers.[61] The London Research Centre, which published its *Office Workers in London* report in 1986, provided one of the most accurate guides to office employment in London during the period concerning

59 Daniels (1975) *op cit* p31.

60 Cited in: Goddard (1975) *op cit* p4.

61 London Research Centre (1986) *Office Workers in London* Statistical Series No 55 LRC, London.

Table 3.2 Growth of office workers in London, 1961–81

Activity	*Employment*	*1961*	*1966*	*1971*	*1981*	*% change*
Manufacturing	Office workers	385	381	354	246	(36)
	Other workers	1044	925	739	402	(61)
Non-manufacturing	Office workers	1019	1154	1173	1153	13
	Other workers	1938	1967	1818	1514	(22)

Source: London Research Centre[62]

us here, the 1960s to the 1980s (table 3.2). The first point to emerge from the data is that London's office workforce declined by over 83,000 (or 5%) between 1966 and 1981. Over the same period, office workers in the rest of Great Britain had grown by one-third. Despite the modest fall in London, the total number of job losses had fallen faster, thereby increasing the office sector as a proportion of all jobs.

The increasing role of office workers in non-manufacturing industries is clear. This component rose from 52% in 1961 to 76% in 1981. Similarly, office employment in manufacturing companies rose as a percentage of other workers from almost 37% to over 61%.

The impact of this long-term shift in the composition of employment is reflected in economic output indicators (table 3.3). For example, figures for Gross Domestic Product and Gross Fixed Capital Formation show sharp contrasts in the fortunes of the banking, finance and business services sector and the manufacturing sector. The expansion of banking, finance and business services relative to manufacturing and the whole economy, on both of these indicators, provides clear evidence of their growing importance in the national economy.

These economic output figures are reflected in the growing concentration of employment in the service sectors (table 3.4). The relative strength of the services sector shown by these employment figures helps to explain the sustained demand for offices and their growing dominance of the city skyline. The contribution of service activities to the economy in terms of, for example, output, balance of

---

62 London Research Centre (1986) *op cit* p11.

Table 3.3 Gross Domestic Product and Fixed Capital Formation, 1977–84

Sector	*1977*	*1979*	*1982*	*1984*	*% change*
Gross Domestic Product					
Banking, finance and business services	15,034	21,019	32,068	40,188	167
Manufacturing	37,972	48,832	59,165	66,424	75
All	128,938	172,388	237,297	279,053	116
Fixed Capital Formation					
Banking, finance and business services	2552	4482	7151	8584	396
Manufacturing	4730	6515	5486	7382	56
All	27,036	36,925	44,824	55,025	103

Source: Central Statistical Office, Crown Copyright material is reproduced with the permission of the controller of the HMSO[63]

payments, investment and profit, provide further context to the growth in demand for office space. Measured over time and related to demand factors, such as employment, take-up, rental changes and construction activity, these indicators provide a clear historical picture of the effect of economic trends on the demand for office space.

Trends in the balance of trade and output figures from this time underline the growing importance of services to the national economy. For example, the balance of payments figures during the late-1970s and early-1980s showed a widening gap between visible and invisible earnings, or trade and services. A major component of invisible trade is financial and business services, and overseas earnings by UK financial institutions more than quadrupled between 1980 and 1987. With the exception of a hiccup in the years of Mrs Thatcher's arrival as premier, the growth was relentless.

It is clear from the figures presented in table 3.4 that while the 1970s and 1980s witnessed the final decimation of British manufacturing jobs, the structural shift towards an office economy had been under

63 Central Statistical Office (1988) *United Kingdom National Accounts Blue Book* pp20–21 and p94 HMSO, London.

Table 3.4 Employment change by Service Industry Division, 1971–84

Service sector	*Employment change*					
	1971–76		*1976–81*		*1981–84*	
	000s	*%*	*000s*	*%*	*000s*	*%*
Distribution, hotels, etc	286.0	7.9	205.4	5.3	188.0	4.7
Transport and communications	(93.1)	(6.1)	(34.6)	(2.4)	(65.0)	(4.7)
Banking, finance, business, etc	154.6	11.7	257.9	17.5	283.5	16.6
Other services	895.5	18.2	64.4	1.1	182.9	3.1

Source: Howells & Green[64]

way for some considerable time. But while the relative decline of manufacturing is a well-documented process of decay, the rise of the office economy is less so. The mass redundancies in manufacturing during the 1970s and 1980s have been described as a process of "de-industrialisation",[65] caused by competitive weakness and resulting in a failure to maintain a positive balance of exports over imports.

As the 1970s progressed, there remained a large gap in our understanding of a key element of urban morphology. What was needed was a systematic approach that sought to explain the relationships between the activities, an approach that sought to relate these evolving relationships to changes in the physical expression of urban form. Only with a more specific and activity-related approach would it be possible to explain the internal dynamics of the office economy. What was needed was an activity-based approach that untangled the web of relationships that existed between the businesses in the office economy in order to explain its internal dynamics. What was the glue that held it together so tightly? What was the driving force of ever-increasing densities?

---

64 Howells J and Green A (1988) *Technological Innovation, Structural Change and Location in UK Services* Gower Publishing Company Limited, Aldershot p12.

65 Blackaby F (1978) *De-industrialisation* Heinemann, London.

The office economy comes of age

These questions had been partially answered in Peter Daniels' milestone book of 1975, *Office Location*.[66] This was the first major work that examined not only the locational characteristics of the office economy, but also its internal dynamics. It attempted to explain the forces acting upon and within office activities that give rise to their locational characteristics and their evolving functionality. The book was the first detailed, activity-based approach to untangle the web of relationships that existed within the office economy in order to explain its physical expression. It helped describe the glue that held offices tightly together, and it examined the nature of change that led to new demands being placed on buildings. In just one example, Daniels examined trends in office mechanisation (what we now call IT) in North America in order to help explain trends in the UK, demonstrating its impact on the development of office activity and, in particular, on the evolution of large office buildings first in the US and, later, in the UK.

In work such as that of Daniels, the emphasis in urban analysis during the 1960s and 1970s on spatial definition was gradually yielding to one where cities were seen to comprise a much richer and more complex set of relationships and activities than had previously been recognised. Cities came to be seen as mosaics of activities in which change was not only prevalent but inevitable. This transformation from a two-dimensional style of aerial analysis to approaches that were more process or activity-based has been described thus:

> Inevitably one is led towards a more realistic evaluation of the central area not being made up of a CBD ... but of a number of closely associated areas or sub-cores, constantly subject to pressures and with ... changing boundaries.[67]

The chief mystery is why it had taken so long to happen, when the evidence of change had been so plentiful. As the 1980s began, and with it the latest phase in the evolution of the modern office economy, change was continuing apace as economic activity changed. For example, in London between the 1981 and 1993, over 90,000 non-financial jobs were lost from the City, including 26,500 in printing and publishing as Fleet Street moved eastwards; 19,300 in utilities as British Telecom and the Post Office relocated; 17,500 in transport as

---

66 Daniels (1975) *op cit*.
67 Carter (1976) *op cit* p218.

port facilities moved farther east; 10,900 government jobs and 8500 in wholesale distribution.[68] Some jobs were lost altogether as the economy changed; others were simply moved, or relocated to lower-cost areas. In either case, they were the physical manifestation of a necessary and continuous process of renewal and reinvention. This process of renewal and reinvention has allowed the City as a whole to evolve and respond to new opportunities. Indeed, London's ability over the years to reinvent itself has been its saviour in economic terms. Peter Drucker[69] has illustrated how this reinvention has occurred opportunistically and structurally.

Both the Eurodollar and Eurobond markets — mainstays of the City economy for decades now — came about through the City's ability to react swiftly to unpredictable changing world events. During the Cuban missile crisis, the Russian State Bank feared having its American accounts frozen, and shifted its foreign reserves to London. However, they wanted to keep their money in dollars. Thus the Eurodollar was born — a transnational currency denominated in dollars but domiciled in London.[70] Shortly afterwards, the American administration put a punitive tax on payments of interest to foreigners "thus destroying in one fell swoop the flourishing New York foreign-bond market. It fled, giving birth to the Eurobond — again denominated mostly in dollars but domiciled and controlled in London."[71] Both markets were to be central to the City's fortunes for decades to come.

It is within events such as these that we find the rich, highly granular nature of change that helps to explain urban morphology generally and the rise of the office economy specifically. As Daniels argued:

> It may therefore be unwise to rely on conventional ideas about locational tendencies which largely reflect the influence of, for example accessibility or land rents. It is necessary to take closer account of organisational and structural change as well as the effects of technology on the future of established concentrations of service activity.[72]

---

68 Lombard Street Research (1988) *Growth Prospects of City Industries* Corporation of London.

69 Drucker P (1999) Innovate or Die *The Economist* 25 September pp25–26 and pp29–30.

70 Drucker (1999) *op cit* p25.

71 *Ibid*.

72 Daniels P W (1985) Service Industries: Some New Directions In: Pacione M, *Progress in Industrial Geography* Croom Helm, London p132.

The final phase in our journey through the rise of the office economy, from the 1980s through to the present time, has been, above all else, the "information age", during which the impact of ICT has had such a profound effect on every aspect of life. From the launch of the PC in 1981, through mobile phones, laptops, hand-held devices and the internet, this has been the age in which everyone's personal and business lives have been changed through the ability to collect, receive, transform, analyse and communicate information instantly.

During this time, there were two distinctive approaches to explaining urban form generally, and the office economy in particular, and we shall finish this chapter by reviewing both. The first approach took an institutional route. Rather than examining the behaviour of those companies whose collective locational decisions gave expression to urban form, researchers turned their attention towards those businesses involved in the creation of the physical environment. There was thus a shift in focus from the demand side of the property equation to the supply side. The importance of this shift lies in the fact that it was, not surprisingly, adopted in its entirety by the property-supply industry, further entrenching the supply-led culture that dominated the supply industry throughout the post-war period (this aspect is examined in more detail in chapters 4 and 5). One of the clearest expositions of this supply-led approach was Michael Bateman's *Office Development: A Geographical Analysis*.[73] He sought to explain the spatial characteristics of the office economy in terms of the office development process. The following quote is typical of the approach taken:

> The influence of development companies on the location of office space is inextricably linked with the sources of finance upon which most speculative office development depends.[74]

He developed the argument into one firmly stating that the primary forces behind the locational characteristics of modern office development are broader than traditionally accepted, a reference to accessibility and centrality:

> office location patterns are not simply a product of easily accessible

---

[73] Bateman M (1985) *Office Development: A Geographical Analysis* Croom Helm, London.

[74] Bateman (1985) *op cit* p5.

opportunities for information gathering and exchange (communications) but are also determined by complex financial and other vested interests.[75]

Bateman suggested that it would be simplistic to offer an explanation for office development in classical bid-rent terms "since utility maximisation by an occupier may be a secondary consideration for development to profit maximisation for the financial institution."[76] This emphasis on the explanation of locational characteristics from the perspective of the supplier is key to much of the work on property market dynamics during the 1980s. In contrast to the earlier work on demand, the occupier was no longer seen to be the key determinant of spatial patterns — this was now the role of the supplier of space, indeed:

> the notion of speculative property development by definition suggests a system where building activity is determined primarily by the supplier of property rather than by the eventual end user.[77]

Yet, if the earlier work was valid, the economic and, indeed, social linkages within the office economy suggests a self-organising market within a relatively spatially defined area. The building industry "speculates" on how much demand exists within that area, and builds to its best estimate. However, in an elaboration of his theory, Bateman went on to argue that the demand market was in fact a bit-part player in the evolving urban form: "There are a growing number of demands which bring about the process of development which are not directly linked to the needs and wants of the final user."[78]

This observation is important for it helped to provide the theoretical underpinning for much of the more specialised, supply-side analysis that was to follow during the 1980s, particularly in the arena of property industry research. Bateman argued that change in an urban area takes place not as a spontaneous response to market demand derived from abstract notions or urban land economics, but as:

> the result of a complex series of deliberate investment decisions on the part of a range of people, many of whom have little concern with classical notions of location and accessibility.[79]

---

75 Bateman (1985) *op cit* p15.
76 Bateman (1985) *op cit* p3.
77 *Ibid*.
78 Bateman (1985) *op cit* p4.
79 Bateman (1985) *op cit* p12.

While it is true that investment decisions now have little to do with classical notions of land economics, it is not clear that they ever did. By linking market demand with land economics, Bateman was setting aside some of the work undertaken during the 1950s and 1960s that sought to provide a more sophisticated analysis of demand. Once again, demand became a homogeneous entity, without internal dynamics, and with the supplier of space being the primary determinant of the changing urban form. From such analysis it is but a short step to considering property market dynamics in terms of development cycles. Richard Barras used land economic theory together with a notion of demand analysis to suggest how replacement of stock takes place in successive waves:

> At the top of the market, the most profitable activities, or those best able to pay the highest rents, compete to occupy the latest office developments offering the most suitable combination of location and facilities.[80]

This process leads to a filtering down, "inducing chains of moves", leaving successive layers of vacant stock, eventually providing a pool that "provides the redevelopment sites on which to build the next vintage of prime floorspace."[81] David Cadman and Alejandrina Catalano offered a similar explanation, proposing that alternating "phases of over- and under-supply are characteristic of the UK property market", and that the resulting cyclical pattern "is due to the time lag between the start and the occupation of the development."[82] The limitations to this proposition are examined in more detail in chapter 4.

Despite this focus on supply-side economics during the early- and mid-1980s, there was developing in parallel a renewed interest in demand explanations of urban structure and the office economy. The reason for the renewed impetus to understanding urban structure in the early-1980s was the escalating significance of developments in ICT. In particular, there was the potential threat to the future of large urban concentrations of economic activity as the result of the anticipated liberating effects of technology taking hold on the locational imperatives of business. Among the earliest exponents of the influence

---

80 Barras R (1984) The Office Development Cycle in London *Land Development Studies* Vol 1 p38.

81 Barras (1984) *op cit* p39.

82 Cadman D and Catalano A (1983) *Property Development in the UK: Evolution and Change* (2nd Edition) College of Estate Management, University of Reading p1.

of technology as a driver of structural change in urban morphology were Daniel Bell[83] and Brian Berry,[84] both in 1973. Berry's thesis spelt out the concept of technology as a decentralising agent, suggesting that the new communications technologies would "concoct a solvent" to dissolve "the core-oriented city in both time and space, creating what some refer to as urban civilisation without cities."[85] There emerged a whole series of studies that had as their focus the impact of ICT on economic change and urban morphology.[86]

The launch of the personal computer in 1981 and the spread of private data networks, however, acted as a further impetus to studies during the 1980s. Jean Gottman's *The Coming of the Transactional City*,[87] Thomas Noyelle and Thierry Stanback's *The Economic Transformation of American Cities*[88] and Mark Hepworth's *The Information City*[89] are just a small selection of the many texts along similar themes. With the benefit of at least a decade's more experience, these later studies presented a more positive view than Bell and Berry of the impact of technology on urban structures. They were suggesting that the competitive positions of already densely developed urban areas would intensify, and that innovation and demand would encourage reinvention, with Gottmann going as far as to suggest that "the centrality of the city is constantly being re-born."[90]

John Marshall suggested that the growing importance of activities involved in the production, analysis and exchange of information led to "the development of an integrated office-based sector of employment", in which "the office block has replaced the factory as a symbol of

---

83 Bell D (1973) *The Coming of Post-industrial Society* Basic Books, New York.

84 Berry B J L (1973) *The Human Consequences of Urbanisation* St Martins, New York.

85 Berry (1973) *op cit* p54.

86 See for example: Goddard J B and Pye R (1977) Telecommunications and Office Location *Regional Studies* Vol 11 pp19–30; Thorngren B (1977) Silent Actors: Communication Networks for Development In Pool IdeS (ed) *Social Impact of the Telephone* MIT Press, Boston; Pye R (1979) Office Location: the Role of Communications and Technology In Daniels P W (ed) *Spatial Patterns of Office Growth and Location* Wiley, London.

87 Gottmann J (1983) *The Coming of the Transactional City* University of Maryland Institute for Urban Studies Monograph Series No 2 College Park.

88 Noyelle T M and Stanback T J (1984) *The Economic Transformation of American Cities* Allanheld Osmun, Totowa, New Jersey.

89 Hepworth M (1987) The Information City *Cities* Vol 4 pp253–262.

90 Gottmann (1983) *op cit* p15.

modern urban development."[91] Daniels had earlier suggested that office space provided accommodation for at least 30–35% of the labour force in advanced economies, and that producer services that occupied some 20–22% of the UK labour force were prominent occupiers.[92]

This reference to producer services requires explanation before proceeding. In academic terms, the office economy is not a clearly defined entity. The actual focus of much academic research has been on the service sector generally, rather than on that element referred to in this book as the office economy, but a critical sub-sector of academic study was the producer services sector. This is broadly defined as comprising those services that are produced by one company predominantly for consumption by other organisations. For example, legal, accounting, banking and finance, insurance, management consulting, advertising and marketing are obvious examples. Others would include services in property, design and engineering, computing, R&D, personnel and procurement. In this way, producer services are distinguished from consumer services such as retailing, leisure and personal services.

Banking, finance and insurance employment is often used as a surrogate measure to describe the producer services sector. Figure 3.1 shows the rapid growth of employment in banking, finance and insurance since Mrs Thatcher's first term began in 1979. Apart from a brief pause during the white-collar recession of the early-1990s, this area of the economy has experienced relentless growth, more than doubling in size over a 25-year period.

Mark Hepworth[93] examined the office economy in terms of the interrelated roles of information and the new information technology in the process of economic development. He pointed to large, multi-locational corporations as the dominant users of advanced tele-communications infrastructure, suggesting that their increasing use of private networks would have profound implications for the future of cities and urban systems in terms of uneven development. Not least, he foresaw the issue of what was later to become known as "off-shoring":

---

91 Marshall J N (1988) *Services and Uneven Development* Oxford University Press, Oxford p32.

92 Daniels P W (1985) Service Industries: Some New Directions In: Pacione M, *Progress in Industrial Geography* Croom Helm, London p116.

93 Hepworth M (1990) Planning for the Information City: The Challenge and Response *Urban Studies* Vol 27 No 4 pp537–558.

Figure 3.1 Banking, finance and insurance employment, 1979–2004

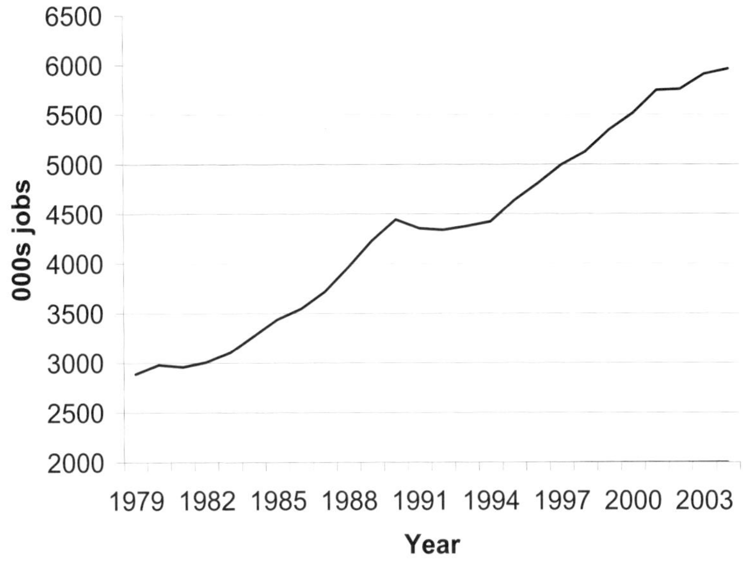

Source: National Statistics Website: www.statistics.gov.uk. Crown copyright material is reproduced with the permission of the controller of the HMSO

Arising from the distance-shrinking effects and capabilities of computer network technologies is an intensification of inter-urban competition for new markets and resources, particularly jobs.[94]

The interest in information and the role of information technology in shaping urban and economic development led to a sharp focus on those businesses where the take-up of information technology was particularly acute — the office economy. At last researchers were beginning to explain urban and economic development not simply in terms of its spatial outcomes, but in terms of the internal dynamics of the businesses that were the engine of change. William Coffey argued forcefully in an echo from earlier times that up to this time, the study of services generally, and the office economy in particular, was

---

94 Hepworth (1990) *op cit* p555.

plagued by its "non-productive" label, and that "research on services was conceptually stagnant for several decades, being largely confined to the limited framework of central place studies."[95] Coffey suggested that it was only in the later 1980s and into the 1990s that producer services (the office economy) "were finally recognised as important economic phenomena in their own right."[96]

The new activity-based approach to the office economy was exemplified by a series of papers in the late-1980s by various combinations of Peter Daniels, Andrew Leyshon and Nigel Thrift. The papers examined in great detail the structural dynamics of sub-sectors of the producer services sector, such as financial services, accountancy firms and surveying firms. For example, in their work on the City of London,[97] they explained key changes in the demand for commercial office space in the specific context of the restructuring of financial markets. Their work on the operational adaptation and spatial development of accountancy firms[98] yielded immense detail on the internal dynamics of an important segment of the office economy. We learn, for example, that the number of accountants in Great Britain grew from around 13,000 in 1945, to 81,000 four decades later, and that the number of firms grew by nearly a fifth over a similar period. The fee income of the top 20 firms quadrupled from around £260m in 1978 to £1100m in 1986, during which time they opened 83 new regional offices. Much empirical evidence was presented to illustrate the processes of business concentration, intensification, diversification and automation. And we learn how the growth of small firms, public sector work and the chase for market share all influence office expansion decisions. Such detail provides a rich insight into the nature of the activity that then drives the demand for space. For the first time, the economic and spatial characteristics of urban areas were being examined from the

---

95 Coffey W J (2000) The Geographies of Producer Services *Urban Studies* Vol 21 No 2 p170.

96 Coffey (2000) *op cit* p171.

97 Leyshon A, Thrift N J and Daniels P W (1987) *The Urban and Regional Consequences of the Restructuring of World Financial Markets: The Case of the City of London* Working Papers on Producer Services Series No 4 University of Bristol and University of Liverpool.

98 Leyshon A, Daniels P W and Thrift N J (1987) *Large Accountancy Firms in the UK: Operational Adaptation and Spatial Development* Working Papers on Producer Services Series No 2 Saint David's University College, Lampeter and University of Liverpool.

perspective of the internal dynamics of the economic activities at its heart — the office economy. The work of Daniels and colleagues directly responded to John Rannells' call over three decades earlier for a more activity-based approach to understanding urban processes.

Increasing numbers of studies drew attention to the concentration of producer services in large metropolitan areas, and empirically verified the "glue" that held the companies so tightly together in terms of the location of markets (clients and suppliers), highly skilled labour markets and the agglomeration benefits associated with minimising transaction costs.[99] Other studies showed how producer-service companies created competitive advantage in urban areas, including quality, creativity and innovation, spatial proximity, flexibility, timeliness of delivery, scope of services offered and adaptability to client needs — all a long way from the simpler explanations based on classical economics of earlier times.[100] The role of producer services in suburbanisation came under scrutiny. For example, Sven Illeris[101] traced the suburbanisation of services in Copenhagen. Similarly, studies were undertaken in Atlanta[102] and Los Angeles[103] to show how services were concentrating in clusters away from the downtown area but within the metropolitan area. Both studies offered an interesting twist on the multiple-nuclei theory of urban morphology discussed earlier.

What all these studies showed was the evolution of the office economy and its changing spatial expression. They provided evidence of the "glue" that held producer services together in tight proximity; they explained the internal dynamics of the businesses that ultimately gave rise to urban morphology, and they helped explain how change occurs. In William Coffey's terms, the decades of conceptually stagnant research on the office economy had been ended. At last there was a credible framework within which to understand the office economy.

---

99 Coffey (2000) *op cit* p172.

100 Lindahl D P and Beyers W B (1999) The Creation of Competitive Advantage by Producer Services Establishments *Economic Geography* Vol 75 pp1–20.

101 Illeris S (1997) The Changing Location of Service Activities in the Copenhagen Region *Geografisk Tidsskrift* Vol 97 pp120–131.

102 Fujii T and Hartshorn T A (1995) The Changing Metropolitan Structure of Atlanta, GA: Locations of Functions and Regional Structure in a Multinucleated Urban Area *Urban Geography* Vol 16 pp680–707.

103 Forstall R L and Greene R P (1997) Defining Job Concentrations: the Los Angeles Case *Urban Geography* Vol 18 pp705–739.

Development Booms: the Making of an Urban Myth

4

Echoes through time

Chapter 2 described the emergence of the office economy in London during the Victorian period. Even from this brief synopsis, it was clear that the scale of growth and change in the latter years of the 19th century was vast: a city being remade. Such was the scale of growth that by the end of the century London was a world city at the heart of a vast and productive Empire: "the public spaces, the railway termini, the hotels, the great docks, the new thoroughfares, the rebuilt markets, all were the visible expression of a city of unrivalled strength and immensity."[1] Nearly half of the world's shipping was controlled from London; it had become "the centre of international finance and the engine of Imperial power; it teemed with life and expectancy."[2] The City had become "the progenitor of commerce, and the vehicle of credit, throughout the world; the City maintained England, just as the riches of the Empire rejuvenated the City."[3] Amid all of this growth and expansion, it is easy to forget that, for many, London remained a city of poverty and degradation.

Old women squatted in the streets selling herbs, apples, matches and sandwiches. There was a floating population of ragged barefoot children who

---

1 Ackroyd P (2000) *London: The Biography* Vintage, London p717.
2 *Ibid.*
3 Ackroyd (2000) *op cit* p717.

slept in alleys or beneath bridges. There were costermongers with their carts selling anything from coals to flowers, fish to muffins, tea to crockery. There were also epidemics of surprising speed and savagery ...[4]

This was, after all, Dickensian London. Indeed, it was while residing in the Cubitt-built Tavistock House, between 1851 and 1860, that the great playwright penned *Bleak House*, *Little Dorrit*, *Hard Times* and *A Tale of Two Cities*. The cheek-by-jowl existence of extreme wealth and poverty has remained a powerful feature of London: today the inflated salaries of the Bond dealers working in Canary Wharf contrast sharply with the widespread poverty in the surrounding areas of Tower Hamlets.

The period of change in the latter three decades of the 19th century exemplifies the many phases of expansion and intensification that have characterised the growth of London and other European cities over the past four millennia and more. Periods of economic, social or political upheaval bring with them the need to reshape the physical fabric of the city and often very intense periods of urban change occur. In this sense, it would be wrong to perceive the overall pattern of urban expansion as a gradual, creeping process, spreading imperceptibly outwards like a tree adding its distinctive rings over successive seasons. Rather, the process of change is characterised by relatively brief, intense phases of reshaping. And these phases are not orderly, successive waves, but complex, interlocking and overlapping, often with locationally specific characteristics. Some phases of growth were driven directly by economic expansion and internationalisation (for example, the interdependent expansion of the docks and the City in the east). Some were driven by the need to house, feed and entertain the growing numbers of people required to support the expanding economy (for example, the development of the residential and retail areas in the west). Others were spurred by the arrival of new technologies (for example, in the early part of the 20th century the spread of the motor car led to rapid suburbanisation).

Many such phases of development left a trail of ruined developers and builders and half completed projects. This was as true in the 18th and 19th centuries as it was for the latter half of the 20th for developers of such famous landmarks as Canary Wharf. But the post-Second World War period was different. While the same underlying causes of economic expansion and restructuring remained, this period

---

4 Ackroyd (2000) *op cit* p719.

was different because the structure of the property-supply industry changed radically; the scale of enterprise made a step-change and development became concentrated on the purpose-built, speculative office block. Up to this point, especially in the 19th century, many major development booms had had a broader mix of uses, many comprising housing, retailing and leisure activities. But this began to change in the 20th century as the office economy became firmly established, and as "new office blocks became a familiar presence; new banks, company headquarters, insurance offices were built upon a massive scale, with intense and dramatic architectural effects."[5]

In some senses, particularly in the context of a longer historical perspective, the period between the 1950s and 1990s could be viewed as a single period of expansion, rather like the latter decades of the 19th century, in which the office economy matured. In this perspective, the development industry has simply suffered a number of major dysfunctions. In another sense, perhaps with a focus on just the period in question, and with a property industry perspective, identifiable phases of development activity are discernable that appear on the record as cycles of activity. This chapter examines the phenomenon of development booms, and particularly how they have shaped thinking about the nature of the property-supply process.

The 1970s: property in the political economy

Following the boom years of the 1960s, a period of general economic malaise settled over the UK. Full employment in 1967 gave way to a steady increase in the jobless; output began to slow, and imports of manufactured goods began their inexorable rise and eventual decimation of so much of the country's productive base. It was into these economic doldrums, in June 1970, that Edward Heath's Conservative government was elected to office for the first time. The government's response to the economic climate would prove to be pivotal to the fortunes of the property market. Through a chain of interconnected events, the decisions of Heath's government led to one of the most dramatic crashes of the post-war property market, and certainly the one with the greatest knock-on effect for the UK economy.

---

5 Ackroyd (2000) *op cit* p717.

During 1971, unemployment, inflation and public spending were all on the rise. Historically, Conservative governments would have responded with a series of liberal economic policies (principally, non-interventionism). But this time it was to be different. Instead of returning to the liberal economic tradition, Prime Minister Heath's government sought to manage the economy in a more fundamental way perhaps than any Conservative government had tried in history. Along with his Chancellor, Anthony Barber, Heath believed that he could reverse the recession in trade and industry through increasing the money supply. In a further move to boost investment in the manufacturing sector, interest rates were reduced to around 5%. Perhaps the most far-reaching of the moves was the decision to remove all lending restrictions from banks that had previously worked within upper limits to their lending. These moves to invigorate the economy were a classic dash for growth: but they also created the ideal conditions out of which an unsustainable property boom would spiral.

Unfortunately, the economic planning framework failed to have the desired effect. For example, the expected boost in investment by manufacturers failed to materialise because "it was clear to them ... that world trade was going into recession."[6] But cheap money was being borrowed: only in the wrong places, most notably the property sector. Indeed, in the summer of 1972, "the Bank of England noted from other banking reports that the expected rise in borrowing from industrialists was only 3% while lending to property interests rose by 50%."[7] This combination of a switch away from manufacturing investment, and the lifting of restrictions on lending, provided the necessary finance for a largely uncontrolled growth in property lending among secondary banks. This, in turn, led to a massive wave of speculative development.

In a move that simply reinforced the drift towards a property boom, the government also relaxed Office Development Permits (which had controlled speculative development) and repealed the Betterment Levy (a tax on development profit). The results of these attempts to manipulate the economy were disastrous for the property industry. The full horror of the economic dynamic behind the development boom can be revealed in a summary of relevant statistics:

---

6 Rose J (1985) *The Dynamics of Urban Property Development* E&FN Spon, London p164.

7 Rose (1985) *op cit* p23.

> the retail price index ... reveals a 7.9% increase in 1971, 9% in 1972, a further 7.7% in 1973 and by 1974 20%. Bank lending to industry went down by 28% in 1970 and a further 19% in 1973, whereas loans to property companies and financial institutions ... doubled between 1970 and 1973 ... The money supply went from 11% in 1971 to 27% in 1973. The growth in bank lending generally went up by 19% in 1970, 29% in 1971, 31% in 1972 and 41% in 1973.[8]

As the banks, and especially the secondary banks, piled into property, the government and the Bank of England were slow to respond, perhaps underestimating the scale of the escalating crisis. Although aware of the growing problems, the Bank of England took no action until the late spring of 1972, when it issued a letter to all banks advising them to restrict further lending on property. In April 1973, the Counter-Inflation (Business Rents) Order 1973 was introduced, which imposed a freeze on rents and which lasted until the Counter-Inflation (Business Rents) Decontrol Order No. 21, which came into effect on 1 February 1975. Although introduced as part of a broader counter-inflationary strategy, such measures could do little to halt the development boom. During 1973, in the City of London alone, work had begun on around 1.7 million sq m (18 million sq ft) of offices.[9] The dynamics were not sustainable and a slump was just around the corner.

When the end came, it was sudden and dramatic: "The end of the financial boom occurred within weeks of 9 November 1973 when the *Financial Times'* activities property share index reported an all-time high for property share prices. By 13 November, the minimum lending rate rose to 13% and on the last day of that month the Stock Exchange suspended the shares of the secondary bank, London and County Securities."[10] In December, the mini-Budget introduced further measures to dampen the economy, including the tightening of credit controls. As part of this broader strategy, the property industry was hit. The budget contained proposals for a Development Gains Tax (DGT) and a First Letting Tax. Although Labour replaced the Tories in February 1974, the proposals were carried over, and were contained within Part 3 of the Finance Act 1974.

The DGT provision was contained within Section 38 of the 1974 Act. It provided that a development gain should be regarded as income and as such constituted profits that were chargeable to tax under Case

---

8 Rose (1985) *op cit* p165.

9 Herring Baker Harris (1992a) *The Capital's Property* HBH, London p32.

10 Rose (1985) *op cit* pp165–166.

VI of Schedule D. The First Letting Tax proposed that the first letting of a property after development should be regarded as a disposal of the property at its then market value for the purposes both of CGT and DGT. In short, the measure entailed a tax on a profit that had yet to be made.

As these policies took effect, the UK economy tipped into recession once more. Interest rates and inflation both rose steeply and development projects that "had been viable with interest rates at 5% looked distinctly unhealthy with interest rates at 13%, and falling rents."[11] As banks began calling in property loans, demand for floor space plummeted and property values fell by as much as 40%.[12] In March 1974, the name OPEC was brought firmly to the fore of the national conscience following a quadrupling in the price of crude oil, (leading to what has since come to be known as the *oil crisis*). The *Financial Times'* activities all share index showed a fall of 21% during the crisis of 1973 and 1974, finally falling by almost 60%; while by December 1974, the equity market was just 27% of its peak in the summer of 1972.[13]

The wreckage of the property crash was around for all to see with the familiar proliferation of To Let and For Sale signs, together with a crop of bankrupt property and development companies. But what were the lessons to be drawn from the boom and subsequent crash? What or who was to blame? Could it have been avoided? The headlines were clear enough. A phalanx of centralised planning, including increased money supply, lower interest rates and removal of lending restrictions, was clumsily introduced by a Conservative administration. This, in turn, led to boom conditions encouraged by plentiful, cheap money. The incentive to build was further encouraged by the removal of planning and fiscal constraints. Combined with a dose of inflation, the recipe was complete. But is this adequate as an explanation?

In 1978, The Royal Institution of Chartered Surveyors (RICS) published its own *post-mortem* on the causes and effects of the property boom and the subsequent crash. The report began by identifying three factors responsible for the boom conditions in the late-1960s that preceded the crash, namely: user demand; investor requirements; and the development and construction industry. The report offered no

---

11 Herring Baker Harris (1992a) *op cit* p32.

12 *Ibid*.

13 Rose (1985) *op cit* p166.

evidence on the increase in user demand, but noted anecdotally that a "high level of user demand had built up during the 1960s", caused by "an expansion in the number of office jobs", which, in turn, had been caused by "the growth of the public service and by the trend in the private sector from manual to white-collar employment."[14] However, figures show a small fall in the office workforce in London during the latter half of the 1960s (see chapter 3).

The Institution's second presumed cause of the boom in the 1960s and early 1970s is also suspect, as shown by the data in their own report. The report showed that institutional interest in property between 1969 and 1972 actually *declined*. The great increase occurred only in 1973, when the boom was about to crash. As for the banks, the report again shows that, by the time the money gushed into the system, the boom was almost over. The report cites Bank of England data to demonstrate that bank advances on property were quite stable between 1968 and 1971, doubling in 1972, and doubling again in 1973. Institutional and bank lending, therefore, were not primary causes of the boom conditions, although they were very much features of the subsequent crash.

The final particular cause of the boom cited by the RICS was the collective behaviour of the development and construction industry. The report argued that "*Because* of the high level of demand" (author's italics), developers were willing to enter into loan arrangements that "depended on expected future increases in rents to service their loans."[15] In other words, they backed a hunch. Following a few years of economic malaise, the property industry backed an upturn: nothing unusual there. What was remarkable was the conclusion that the RICS drew from this: "it is extremely risky to borrow to the limit of available collateral."[16] This seems to be a naive and self-evident statement, and one that avoids perhaps examining the structural weaknesses of a supply process that were really at fault. As for construction, the report merely points to activity in housing and public sector construction as having provided an incentive for building firms to expand, and to borrow for the purpose.

---

14 Royal Institution of Chartered Surveyors, The (1978) *The Property Boom 1968–73 and its Collapse* A Supplementary Memorandum of Evidence to the Committee to Review the Functioning of Financial Institutions RICS, London p5.

15 RICS (1978) *op cit* p8.

16 RICS (1978) *op cit* p14.

The report then turned its attention to the causes of the crash. The report argued that "apart from the economic factors", falling demand; construction costs, the rent freeze, interest charges, DGT and the White Paper *Land* (which introduced Development Land Tax) were the specific causes of the collapse. It must be recognised, however, that falling demand and construction costs were not primary causes of this, or any other, crash. The inability of the supply process to recognise and respond in a timely manner to falling demand is a cause; the inability to reflect rising construction costs in enhanced values within a deflationary context is a cause. But falling demand and rising costs are not of themselves *causes*. The fiscal measures referred to, such as rent freezes and taxation, are direct causes because they bring about swift and severe changes in sentiment, thus: "The rent freeze shook the confidence of investors, who for many years had believed that commercial rents would go on rising indefinitely, thus providing an income broadly in line with inflation."[17]

In seeking to draw lessons from the fiasco of the collapse, the RICS argued that a highly unusual combination of international and domestic events (including inflation, a credit squeeze, economic recession, the oil crisis, and a series of legislative measures) were all to blame. Of these latter, the RICS report was particularly critical: "it is highly dangerous for any government to attempt to regulate the property market by seeking to limit the supply of property ... in response to demand."[18]

What is missing from the Institution's account of the boom and crash is any analysis of how the property-supply industry itself could have behaved differently. In its rush to blame extraneous factors (viz: "lenders too often abandoned normal standards of commercial prudence."[19]), the Institution failed to take a close look at the structure of the supply process. In fact, there was no criticism of the property industry itself, and its lemming-like desire to gorge on cheap money. The institutional market is barely mentioned, with only a reference to their ability to take the long view and "ride out short-term fluctuations in the value of their property assets."[20] There was no mention of the need for more, indeed any, market research and information. There

17 RICS (1978) *op cit* p9.
18 RICS (1978) *op cit* p13.
19 RICS (1978) *op cit* p14.
20 RICS (1978) *op cit* p15.

was no attempt to understand the dynamics of demand. The two main lessons to be drawn were:

- governments should avoid short-term intervention in the property market
- banks, and other lending institutions, should be more prudent.

Without a more trenchant analysis of the structural weaknesses in the supply industry, it was almost inevitable that another boom-bust cycle should get under way. The fact that it did, with an entirely different set of contextual circumstances, served only to underline the fragility of the official explanation for the 1970s crash. Within 10 years of the RICS report, the new boom was getting into full swing.

The 1980s: property in the global economy

In the summer of 1987, the property market was enjoying very benign conditions. The economy was expanding at more than 3% and demand for space was rising. In central London, the amount of empty space had shrunk from nearly 836,000 sq m (9 million sq ft) at the end of 1984, to just 186,000 sq m (2 million sq ft). As a result, rents were rising steeply and investment yields were falling sharply. The recession of the early-1980s was receding in the minds of lenders and prospects for a prolonged period of growth looked good. The City market was basking in the afterglow of Big Bang a year earlier, perhaps the largest spur to redevelopment since the war. Suddenly, it seemed that the whole financial services industry needed re-housing in purpose-built buildings, with dealing floors the size of football pitches. The property industry responded with an orgy of development. Not only were many old buildings demolished and replaced, but whole swathes of land were developed. Perhaps the best known of these was Broadgate at Liverpool Street Station (of which more later), where railway land, air rights and new construction technologies were all exploited to permit the creation of a whole new district in record times. Other rail stations followed suit, with major developments at Ludgate; Cannon Street and Charing Cross. And, of course, there was Canary Wharf, a largely disused dock in east London.

As the City set about transforming many of its well-known vistas, other sectors of the property industry were undergoing their own booms and benefiting, in particular, from changes to the Use Classes

Order (UCO). It was this otherwise arcane piece of planning legislation that unleashed the business park market and was responsible for the sudden spread of edge-of-town retail parks (see chapter 6 for a fuller discussion of the implications of this change in planning law). The old Use Classes Order of 1972 contained 18 classes of use that had been in existence since 1948. The new UCO reduced this to 12 in order to allow uses with broadly similar planning implications to be grouped together, reducing the need to obtain planning consent. Perhaps the most profound for its impact on the landscape was the combining together of the old Class Two (broadly, offices) with Class Three (light industry) into a new "B1" class. This meant that land and buildings previously designated for light industrial use — often sited around the outskirts of towns and cities — could be converted with ease into much more valuable office use. The business park was born.

In short, 1987 saw confidence within the property industry running high; and analysts were in general agreement about the short-term future: "the prospects for the City office market are good and we do not anticipate an oversupply of office accommodation ... within the foreseeable future."[21] Similarly: "We believe that latent demand is still underestimated ... and occupiers will continue to take up the rapidly expanding supply of new developments through to the early-1990s."[22] Even the effects of the infamous stock market crash on "Black Monday" on 19 October, appeared to have been softened by the underlying strength of demand for space. This was surprising. On the fateful day, the FT-SE fell 250 points (10%); on 22 October a further 110 points were wiped off, taking the market down to 1833; and prices fell again on Monday 26 October by another 150 points. In just one week, the FT-SE had fallen 28% from its 1987 high.

Despite one particularly dire warning that "the events of the last two weeks will bring about a property crisis comparable with that of 1974",[23] the market as a whole brushed aside the crash. One year on, while recognising that the real estate market had not been immune from events in the financial markets, property advisor Jones Lang Wootton (now Jones Lang LaSalle) stuck to the business as usual line: "an imminent collapse in tenant demand and consequent fall in rents,

---

21 County NatWest and Baker Harris Saunders (1987) *The City Office Market: An Examination of Supply, Demand and Debt* CNW/BHS, London p4.

22 Savills (1987) *City of London Office Demand Survey* Savills, London p24.

23 Winter and Company (1987) *The New Property Crisis: 1987/1988?* Winter & Co, London p3.

which was forecast in some quarters at the beginning of the year did not materialise."[24] While JLW were one of the most respected firms in the property market, with one of the most forward-thinking research teams, this view was backward-looking and failed to address closely what was looming over the horizon. There were some analysts, however, prepared to cast doubt over the strength of the market. Indeed, the first warnings of the impending disaster began to emerge as early as the spring of 1988. Geoff Marsh, then head of Applied Property Research, gave one of the earliest public warnings. His central London office market report identified 45 construction starts in 1988 — *simply on schemes of over 9290 sq m (100,000 sq ft)* — totalling nearly 1.5 million sq m (16 million sq ft). Marsh concluded:

> the central London office market is heading for oversupply ... Construction activity has actually increased significantly to levels which imply that demand has to double again from the already very high levels of 1987 and 1988.[25]

The development tap was turned to maximum flow, but who was listening? Construction completions in the City had been steady at around 232,000 sq m (2.5 million sq ft) between 1986 and 1988. Then, as property companies continued to gorge themselves on a seemingly endless supply of cheap money, in 1989 and 1990 completions leapt to 405,000 sq m (4.36 million sq ft) and 403,000 sq m (4.34 million sq ft), respectively; and in 1991 jumped to a massive 643,000 sq m (6.92 million sq ft).[26] Table 4.1 shows data highlighting the extent of lending, comparing lending with property companies in the 1970s and 1980s.

Three months after Marsh's forecasts, the *Sunday Times* asked: "Is [the] City Lost In Space?"[27] The article went on: "Are the first cracks beginning to appear in London's office construction boom?" Drawing attention to the volume of new space that was due to come onto the market in the next two years, the article noted that this was happening at a time when City firms were believed to have laid off more than 12,000 staff in the previous 10 months, and when the volume of

---

24 Jones Lang Wootton (1988) *The City Office Review 1984–1988* JLW, London Introduction.

25 Marsh G (1988) *Central London Office Market Forecasts* Applied Property Research, London p8.

26 Herring Baker Harris (1992b) *Behind the Façade* HBH, London p17.

27 Bevan J (1988) Is City Lost in Space? *Sunday Times* 21 August p3 of section D.

Table 4.1 Bank lending to property companies, comparing the 1970s and 1980s

Year end	*Total bank lending (£m)*	*Bank lending to property companies (£m)*	*Property lending as % of total*
1970s boom			
Nov 1968	9267	336	3.63
Nov 1969	10,651	327	3.07
Nov 1970	13,570	341	2.51
Nov 1971	16,792	501	2.98
Nov 1972	23,872	1155	4.84
Nov 1973	36,413	2330	6.40
Nov 1974	45,877	2802	6.11
1980s boom			
Nov 1984	150,793	5420	3.59
Nov 1985	168,440	7111	4.22
Nov 1986	202,893	9335	4.60
Nov 1987	244,749	13,333	5.45
Nov 1988	304,634	21,287	6.99
Aug 1989	395,579	29,608	7.48

Source: Phillips and Drew[28]

business had roughly halved over the same period. In the same month, August, broker Morgan Grenfell Securities warned of a "risk of oversupply" as "a risk remains that developers will still proceed with their proposed speculative schemes."[29] To round the year off, property advisor Winter & Co gave a stark warning:

> We anticipate growing problems for the market in 1989. Occupiers will shelve expansion plans in the face of expensive borrowing, an unstable Stock Market and a decline in consumer spending. Demand will begin to fall dramatically and supply of both new and second-hand space will continue to grow.[30]

28 Phillips and Drew (1989) Cited in: *Estates Times* 27 October p56.
29 Morgan Grenfell Securities (1988) *City Office Review* MGS, London p2.
30 Winter & Company (1988) *The New Property Crisis: 1989* Winter & Co, London p5.

So how big was "the risk" of oversupply? Asked another way, should it have been obvious that the market was *certainly* heading for oversupply? A simple calculation puts the quantum of supply in 1988 and 1989 into stark focus. This calculation involves a rule of thumb to calculate the number of office workers that would be required to fill all of the space being developed. Assuming a conservative occupation density of 23 sq m (250 sq ft) gross per person, the construction starts for 1988 alone represented 64,000 office workers. Even allowing for the crudeness of the calculation, against a total City working population of around 250,000 workers, and the 12,000 jobs that had already been lost, it should have been clear that the scale of development was unsustainable. And what was happening in the City was being replicated elsewhere. One observer did put the development boom into a wider geographical context, although not until late in 1989. Using slightly different calculations to those used above, but coming to the same overall conclusion, journalist David Brierley argued: "In the south east, where 95 million sq ft will be built, about 800,000 new office workers will be needed to ensure that no buildings are vacant — an impossibility."[31]

In a prescient article in the *Financial Times* at around the same time, Michael Brett compared the raging boom with the 1970s. Citing recent warnings by the Governor of the Bank of England over the level of bank lending to property companies (around £30bn in October 1989), Brett noted that one undeniable similarity between the early-1970s and late-1980s was that "on both occasions the Governor of the day sounded public warnings on property lending and the banking system roundly ignored them."[32] Brett went on to note:

> In the 1970s cycle, the warning was sounded in 1972. Bank lending to property companies grew by 131% in 1972 and by 101% in 1973 to £2.3bn. In 1974 the commercial property market collapsed.

The boom of the early-1970s was fuelled by a belief that money would continue to be freely available and that office rents would continue to rise. Then, struggling with the oil crisis and the miners' strike, the Bank of England increased the minimum lending rate on 13 November to an unprecedented 13%. Two weeks later, a little known secondary

---

31 Brierley D (1989) Tremors Shake Property *Sunday Times* 22 October p3 of section D.

32 Brett M (1989) Learning the Lessons of the Past *Financial Times* 30 October p38.

bank called London and County Securities collapsed, sparking the secondary banking crisis. Within six months, over half of the value of property companies had been wiped out. Brett concluded his article with a direct comparison to 1973:

> we have just experienced a period of rapid growth in property values, bank lending to property is at a peak, interest rates have risen sharply ... and the authorities are attempting to damp down the economy. And now, as then, we have considerable instability in the securities markets.
>
> It is not a re-run of 1973. But neither is it a background that gives much comfort to the banking and property industries.[33]

The Governor's warning in 1989 followed a 43% rise in property lending in 1987; a 60% rise in 1988; and a 39% rise in the first half of 1989; interest rates were again at an all-time high and securities were again in turmoil.

In 1990, the bloodletting began in earnest. By the end of April, shares in Sheraton Securities, Rush & Tompkins and Wiggins were all suspended, and both Finlan and Priest Marians had revealed problems with borrowings. In May, the receivers were called in to South Quay Plaza, a £50m development in Docklands. It took another two years for the full horror of the debt situation to become fully clear through collapses of well-known development companies. As Vanessa Houlder observed:

> It is more than three years since the UK commercial property sector went into decline, but 1992 was undoubtedly the year when the cracks became chasms.[34]

Noting that nearly 3 million sq m (32 million sq ft) of offices in central London lay vacant, and that bank debts to property companies stood at £35bn, Houlder referred to research by accountants Touche Ross suggesting that, since April 1990, property businesses had been going bankrupt at the rate of one every 36 hours. And it was not just small, anonymous companies that were disappearing. The roll call of well-known company collapses in 1992 was staggering. In March, Olympia & York (O&Y), one of the largest property companies in the world, and Heron International proposed restructuring of their debts. In the same

---

33 Brett (1989) *op cit* p38.

34 Houlder V (1992) Cracks Became Chasms *Financial Times* 18 December p9.

month, Randsworth, a West End company bought by US investors at the top of the market in 1989, went into receivership with debts of more than £350m. In April, Speyhawk revealed that it was technically bankrupt, disclosing that its liabilities exceeded its assets by £70m. Heron International finally collapsed weeks later. In May, with debts of about £500m, Mountleigh (a company that had been built out of an old textile mill by Tony Clegg) called in the receivers. Its shares were among the top 10 performers of the 1980s, and Clegg had sold a 22.5% stake to Nelson Peltz and Peter May, two Americans with property interests in America, for £70.4m in November 1989. They paid 200p per share, a 40% premium to the market, and Mountleigh collapsed with debts of £400m. Also in May, Rosehaugh collapsed with debts of £350m; and O&Y filed for insolvency protection in Canada and the US. Within days, Canary Wharf was put into administration.

What went wrong? What led the market to stumble from apparently benign conditions in 1988 to total chaos in 1990? The 1980s property boom was one of the greatest ever. Much of the activity was concentrated in the capital where more space was created in a shorter period than ever before. The boom even exceeded, proportionately, that of the rebuilding after the Great Fire, principally because a large proportion of the building was on land not previously used for commercial space, such as railway goods yards, disused docks and derelict land. The scale of the boom is illustrated by the fact that the City's stock of offices grew by a third between 1984 and 1991. The legacy of the 1980s development boom was breathtaking. When the crash came, 3.7 million sq m (40 million sq ft) of space, equivalent to nearly 1000 football pitches, was empty in central London alone, and there was a development pipeline of around 9.3 million sq m (100 million sq ft), representing a 50% increase in stock.[35] Vacancy rates topped 20% in the City. As well as the physical legacy, there was also the financial hangover. The boom was funded on a seemingly inexhaustible supply of money, and total lending to the property sector peaked at around £40bn. To put this figure in context, annual lending had historically run at between £1bn and £2bn.

The boom was, undoubtedly fed by a huge wall of money. And, for the first time, much of the cash came from overseas. This was an international boom, not a UK boom. During the early stages of the

---

[35] Marsh G (1991) *End of the Recession in the London Office Market?* Applied Property Research, London p2.

Broadgate project, for example, the apparent risks of the venture (off-pitch location, scale, new building types and so on) were too much for traditional UK investors, and the bulk of finance came from the Far East. Germany, Japan, Sweden, the Middle East and others piled in. According to one estimate, overseas investment in UK property stayed below £0.5bn between 1980 and 1987. Then, in 1988, it leapt to nearly £2.0bn; and in both 1989 and 1990 reached the dizzy heights of around £3.0bn.[36] But this influx of cash was a response to something, not a primary cause. Perhaps the greatest single cause was the actual and anticipated growth in office work as both the financial services industries and the technology industries expanded extremely rapidly. The planning and design communities responded with new building types, and the rush was on to supply large, highly specified buildings in city centres for financial and business services firms, and large, simpler but internally flexible buildings on business parks for technology, and a host of other office-based sectors.

The overwhelming development hubris that followed was unsustainable. Moreover, it was largely uncontrolled. Unlike the earlier boom, centralist planning was very much out of flavour and, in some senses, the burden was on the planning authority to justify a "why not" position when determining applications rather than on the applicant to justify "why". The new "B1" UCO for offices (see chapter 6) unleashed a powerful incentive to knock down and redevelop, and created the opportunity to build large office parks where once only industrial type premises would have been developed.

Development booms: inevitable or avoidable?

Edward Heath's dash for growth to combat recessionary pressures in the early-1970s involved increased money supply, low interest rates and the abolition of lending restrictions. One side-effect of these measures was to create the ideal fiscal environment for a development boom: soft money and anticipated growth. The causes of the 1980s boom were different. Although readily available money was a contributory factor, at least four other interrelated factors played crucially important roles, including:

---

[36] Debenham Tewson and Chinnocks (1992) *Money into Property* DTC, London p24.

- the expectation of exceptional levels of demand following deregulation of the financial services industry
- changes to the UCO, which led directly to new building types, especially the out-of-town business park and retail parks
- rapid developments in ICT, contributing to building obsolescence
- the availability of air rights over railway lands (for example, Broadgate and Ludgate) and regeneration land (for example, Canary Wharf).

As the histories of the 1970s and 1980s booms showed, the "profile" of each — causes, duration, amplitude and impact — were different. The only common feature of the two booms was the relative availability of finance to the property sector. However, the availability of finance by itself would not have been sufficient to count as the common, single cause of the booms. The profile of each boom was the outcome of the interaction of a unique and complex web of events and circumstances that coincided in time, and then dissipated.

The problem with this interpretation is that the two booms described were part of a sequence of four booms in the post-war period alone. The first boom, during the late-1950s and early-1960s, coincided with a period of economic growth. It began with the removal of building licences in November 1954, and ended with the Brown Ban of 4 November 1964. This first boom was then followed by a period of slow economic growth, which caused new development to decline sharply. The second boom, described earlier, saw development activity peak in 1973–74 as the national economy fell into decline and as the oil crisis took hold. Following a small economic recovery, the third boom in supply peaked in 1980–81, following the "winter of discontent" and just as the economy fell into another recession. Finally, in the late-1980s, the development industry supplied an unprecedented volume of space just as the national economy moved into the recession of the early-1990s. This frequency has led to the widespread belief that development booms are inevitable. Indeed, they are commonly referred to as property cycles, directly implying some spurious sense of periodicity and regularity.

These successive development cycles, or booms, provided a wheel of fortune on which the property industry casino swung successively from boom to bust and back again over a 50-year period. But are they really cycles? Set against the historical context described elsewhere in this book, they are but minor hiccups in another period of expansion and intensification of the urban environment. So, how are we to regard them? Are they inevitable? Or are they avoidable? The second part of this chapter looks at our understanding of modern development booms and the efforts to explain them.

Weiss observed that writers from the Duke de la Rochefoucauld had noted the boom-bust behaviour of the real estate market as early as the 18th century, but that it was only during the depression in the 1930s that "scholars began to systematically examine the historical pattern of real estate cycles."[37] It was then that the search began "for historical explanations and research methods that could help predict the timing and impact of future fluctuations."[38] It was this perceived link between analysis and prediction that was to so profoundly influence thinking about development booms for decades to come: *if only we can measure, then surely we'll be able to predict.*

American economists, such as Charles Wardwell, Simon Kuznets and Arthur Burns, were among the first cycle disciples. Working in the 1920s and 1930s, they all claimed to find results that indicated cyclical characteristics in construction and business capital investment.[39] They shared a belief that the investment and building cycles were related to, but distinct from, shorter-term, more irregular business cycles and longer-term Kondratieff swings in prices.

There were, however, detractors from this generally held belief that cycles could be identified and predicted. Joseph Schumpeter, the Austrian-born economist, who led the "depression generation" of economists at Harvard during the 1930s and 1940s, provided a robust critique in the context of business cycles:

> the question of causation is the Fundamental Question .... there is no single cause or prime mover which accounts for them. Nor is there ever any set of causes which account for all of them equally well. For each one is a historic individual and never like any other, either in the way it comes about or the picture it presents. To get at the causation of each we must analyze the facts of each and its individual background. Any answer in terms of a single cause is sure to be wrong.[40]

---

37 Weiss M A (1991) The Politics of Real Estate Cycles *Business and Economic History* Second Series Vol 20 p127.

38 *Ibid.*

39 Black J T and Hauser W E (1993) Moderating Cyclical Overbuilding in Commercial Real Estate In: *Land Use in Transition* Urban Land Institute, Washington DC p44.

40 Schumpeter J (1939) *Business Cycles: a Theoretical, Historical and Statistical Analysis of the Capitalist Process* McGraw-Hill, New York pp11–12.

Equally forcefully, Homer Hoyt, in his classic *One Hundred Years of Land Values in Chicago* argued:

> Before we go any further, we should dispose of the notion that there is anything rhythmical about business cycles ... Unfortunately for the forecaster, each business cycle seems to be unique, and its length and amplitude are determined by a combination of forces never duplicated before and probably never to be duplicated in the future.[41]

Despite these more cautionary voices, the cycle disciples cast a long shadow indeed, and during the post-war years development booms generated enormous interest among academics and researchers, all seeking some explanatory or causal mechanism from which a predictive model could be built. But how exactly do periodic phases of overdevelopment with their unique causes and events, as described earlier, fit with the concept of cycles? The distinction between "phases" and "cycles" of overdevelopment is more than a semantic one. The former describes an economic inefficiency that is periodically, and often traumatically, corrected, but that might be thought of as avoidable. The latter describes a form of regularity, with beginnings and ends, passing through an identifiable series of events during the process, and that might be thought of as predictable.

Accepted wisdom suggests that so-called development cycles are intrinsic to the market. Many commentators, notably Ian Alexander,[42] Richard Barras,[43] Michael Bateman[44] and Tony Key *et al*[45] have discussed at length the inherent cyclicality of the property market. For example, in their conclusion to the *Understanding the Property Cycle*, Key *et al* rooted their analysis firmly in the relationship between broader economic trends and the property market:

---

41 Hoyt H (1933) *One Hundred Years of Land Values in Chicago* University of Chicago Press, Chicago.

42 Alexander I (1979) *Office Location and Public Policy* Longman, Harlow.

43 Barras R (1984) The Office Development Cycle in London *Land Development Studies* Vol 1 pp35–50; Barras R (1981) *The Office Boom in London* Proceedings of the First CES Conference, London; Barras R (1979) *The Development Cycle in the City of London* Centre for Environmental Studies, Research Series 36, London.

44 Bateman M (1985) *Office Development: A Geographical Analysis* Croom Helm, London.

45 Key T, Zarkesh F, MacGregor B and Nanthakumaran N (1994) *Understanding the Property Cycle* RICS, London.

The property cycle is the compounded result of cyclical influences from the wider economy, which are coupled with cyclical tendencies that are inherent to property markets.[46]

In the forward to this work, the then President of the RICS, Clive Lewis, made clear that the research team's brief was "to make clear the enduring forces, both external and internal to commercial property that have produced this sequence of cycles — to explain cycles as a recurring phenomenon, not as the product of chance conjunctions of circumstances". In this sense, the researchers fulfilled the brief.

Barras found evidence for cyclical tendencies in the production process itself:

The supply of new developments exhibits an inherent cyclical trend, created by the delay of three to four years between the start and completion of a development scheme.[47]

These theoretical standpoints have been reflected in the more practical world of commercial property research. In a commentary following the crash of 1990, Marsh felt comfortable in stating that many commentators on the London office market:

still put their analyses firmly in the context of historic supply and demand cycles. Thus, a return to normality is simply a matter of time, before the merry-go-round of rental growth and a construction boom starts again.[48]

Clearly the property industry itself is imbued with the notion that it is a prisoner within an inherently cyclical process that leads the market to oscillate between wild optimism and frenetic activity, and periods of falling prices, negligible activity and oversupply.

There is a general acceptance within the industry itself that "the market" is cyclical. And in as much as practitioners absorb the output of academics, their "gut feeling" is supported by apparently credible research. The key issue here is that behaviour — development, funding, advice — are all profoundly influenced by an argument that is circular and that, in turn, is based on evidence that is not at all clear.

---

46 Key *et al* (1994) *op cit* p81.

47 Barras (1981) *op cit* p17.

48 Marsh G (1991) *End of the Recession in the London Office Market?* Applied Property Research, London December 1991 p21.

The first problem with the cyclical interpretation of the property market is the belief that the market is *inherently* cyclical. At the macro level, periodic influences on the property market from the wider economy are not questioned here. As economic fortunes wax and wane in the short term, there are bound to be reciprocal variations in the level of demand for accommodation, resulting in growing and shrinking supply. But are cyclical tendencies *inherent to property markets*? There was nothing cyclical about the deregulation of financial services or the introduction of the new Use Classes Order during the 1980s boom. The fact that the development industry responded over-optimistically to these events does not reflect an inherent cyclical tendency, but rather a herd instinct in a free market context. More specifically, there was no reliable feedback mechanism to act as a safety valve on the growing development pipeline.

The second problem with development cycles is that the evidence for them is based on a relatively short period of time, and on the office market in central London alone. Very rarely is data of a more general basis than this presented in the case for cycles. Consequently, the property industry continues to be profoundly influenced by a circuitous argument that has as its foundation little more than a short-term historical experience, ie four successive waves of overdevelopment between the early-1960s and late-1980s. This temporal restriction is troublesome to even some of the more ardent cycle disciples. For example, Key *et al* admit that the "behaviour of the UK property market can be traced back over no more than thirty years"[49] and that the number of recorded cycles is "too few to construct a definitive classification of cyclical patterns."[50] Of the data on which the notion of development cycles is based, the authors concede that "statistical analysis supports, but cannot confirm, the existence of property cycles."[51]

A third problem area is the dependence of the theory upon development lags, ie the time that it takes for construction to catch up with expanding demand, only to find that the business cycle has taken a turn for the worse. Yet this argument is flawed. Yes there is a lag. But fundamentally, as the 1980s boom showed, the industry simply builds too much space. Even if the economy had continued to grow at a very

---

49 Key *et al* (1994) *op cit* pii.

50 Key *et al* (1994) *op cit* p82.

51 Key *et al* (1994) *op cit* p82.

pleasant 3% per annum into the 1990s, there is no way that sufficient jobs would have been created to absorb the space being built. The situation illustrated, once again, the difference between underlying demand and the sheer greed of the development industry, as it gorges on cheap money and ill-informed buyers.

A fourth problem area for the cycle theory is that it is based on evidence of symptoms, not causes, and is therefore an abstraction. Many measures of the cycle are property indicators themselves. Key *et al* demonstrate this bias in analysis:

> Property cycles are recurrent but irregular fluctuations on the rate of all-property total return, which are also apparent in many other indicators of property activity, but with varying leads and lags against the all-property cycle.[52]

The all-property total return is an indicator of market sentiment not inherent cyclicality. It is therefore inadequate as a descriptor of cyclical behaviour. Yet the property industry continues its circuitous belief that by measuring cycles with its own self-defining measures it will achieve the goal of predictability.

The final problem with the cycle theory is the sheer improbability of it all. The property industry responds to signals from the broader economy and seeks to do what it is set up to do when conditions are perceived to be most favourable. And all this takes place within a "business as usual" context. As Key *et al* concede: it is "plausible that there is a property demand cycle directly linked to the business cycle .... longer cycles ... linked to supply-side production lags ... and still longer 'swings' ... generated by obsolescence and replacement cycles;"[53] and that:

> Theoretically, since property is subject to influences from all these factors, the final pattern in property performance would be the net result of several underlying cycles, sometimes overlapping and reinforcing each other, at other points cancelling out.[54]

The same authors also commit the "related to but distinct from" sin. In their own words: "property cycles are driven not by economic cycles,

---

52 Key *et al* (1994) *op cit* p9.

53 Key T, Zarkesh F and Haq N (1999) *The UK Property Cycle — A History from 1921 to 1997* RICS, London p26.

54 Key *et al* (1999) *op cit* p26.

but through mechanisms which give the property cycle its own dynamics and characteristics."[55] And "It is [the] lagging effect which underlies property's tendency to occasional major cycles interspersed with minor ones, to some extent independent of the accompanying economic cycles."[56]

Besides all this, why is it that offices are more "cyclical" than any other form of property development? Perhaps the risk and reward structure is such that the amplitude has little to do with inherent cyclicality and more to do with the structure of the supply industry. Geoff Keogh, Tony McGough and Sotiris Tsolacos[57] note the greater volatility of the office market compared with the industrial market. They attribute this to differences in the building, planning and construction periods in the two sectors that are longer in the office sector, thereby delaying the supply response. Again, this is a circuitous argument. The fundamental point is the sheer scale of development, not its timing.

The role of structural weaknesses

It does not necessarily follow that a market that is unstable, and therefore prone to periodic phases of boom and bust, is cyclical. Certainly phases of overbuilding occur but, as we have seen, the term *cycle* implies a regularity of periodicity and indeed common causation. Yet each of the post-war booms was varied in its length, amplitude and causes. Key and colleagues conceded that "it is essential to ... accept that cycles in economic activity are not as regular or repetitive as the everyday use of the term might imply", and that the property market "consists of recurrent groupings of upswings and downswings which vary in length, scale and composition."[58] It is surely not mere semantics to suggest that such variation in length, scale and composition undermines the very notion of a regular and potentially predictable cycle of activity.

Perhaps, therefore, we should look elsewhere for our explanation of development booms. The explanatory research that we have examined

---

55 Key *et al* (1999) *op cit* p29.

56 *Ibid*.

57 Keogh G, McGough T and Tsolacoss S (1995) *A Model of the Office Development Cycle in the UK* Paper presented to the American Real Estate Annual Meeting Hilton Head Island, SC March 1995.

58 Key *et al* (1994) *op cit* p81.

so far has been searching for its Holy Grail in the so-called *inherent* instability of the market. It has done this by linking longer-term development cycles to shorter-term business cycles, and, as we have seen, this has proved difficult. Production lags, for example, do not account for why the volume of development gets a head of steam in the first place, only why it peaks when the business cycle has moved on. Similarly, symptoms of overdevelopment, such as total property returns, do little to explain causality, let alone provide evidence of cyclical behaviour.

The real question is not whether the property *market* is cyclical, but rather whether the property *industry* is chronically inefficient in the delivery of its product. The property industry emerged from the war very differently from its pre-war guise. Aided by the need to redevelop large tracts of war-ravaged land and buildings, the era of the modern speculator arrived (see chapter 5). Developers whose sole *raison d'être* was speculative offices emerged. They were shortly to be joined by funding institutions looking for secure, long-term investment opportunities. And the already mature agency community, whose reward in the process was based on transactional activity, served both parties. As this triumvirate of interests coalesced, the involvement of the large building firms changed subtly to a subservient, contracting role.

It was this emergent industry structure, rather than any inherent market characteristics, that made the pattern of post-war speculative development booms not only possible but almost inevitable. In other words, the nature of post-war development booms is largely the outcome of the structure of the industry. This claim clearly shifts the emphasis away from exogenous factors towards an explanation based more squarely on the industry itself. Importantly, though, it does not shift the focus entirely. Property development activity has to be contextualised in the economy within which it operates: the economic context provides the ultimate demand for built space. In this sense, the development booms of the post-war period have to be seen in the context of the growth of the office economy.

As we saw in chapter 3, after a "slow burn" growth in the hundred years up to the Second World War, the second half of the 20th century witnessed a phenomenal growth in the office economy: an almost relentless growth of white-collar work, reflecting fundamental shifts in the national (and international) economy, in which white-collar office work came to dominate. This growth in the office economy (and the service sector generally) represented a fundamental shift in the national economy, and one that required a novel solution to its accommodation needs: it needed the new accommodation quickly, efficiently and in significant bulk. The property industry responded with large-scale speculative office development. It is possible that the pre-war property and construction industry would have been structurally ill-equipped to deliver what was needed. Despite discontinuities during recessions, the overall pattern of growth of the office economy was one of relentless expansion, and this economic restructuring actually needed a speculative development process to keep pace with the demand for purpose-built office space to replace old and obsolete stock. The property industry responded: on occasions it oversupplied, prior to a supply-side correction; on others there was drought. Overall the broad trend was for the office property sector to expand in response to the need to accommodate a growing army of office workers.

Seen thus, the post-war development booms were a part of a longer-term process of economic restructuring. As part of this process of change, the property industry expanded and provided the accommodation necessary to house the growing office economy. But the key question remains: do the post-war property booms reflect an inevitable, "cyclical" process of supply, or have supply-side weaknesses played a central role in market instability? As noted earlier, and seen in the context of the Tudor boom, or that of the 19th century boom in which Thomas Cubitt played such a central role, the post-war development booms and their associated crashes might be seen as supply-side weaknesses within a single period of economic expansion and restructuring. We have therefore to look to the industry itself for at least a significant part of the explanation. Before examining supply-side weaknesses, it is worth briefly reminding ourselves of the classic interpretation of a boom cycle. Barras[59] provides a classic conceptual model of building cycle dynamics, and we will examine supply side weaknesses in the context of this model. Barras outlines the main phases as follows.

1. Strong upturn in the business cycle coinciding with a relative shortage in the available supply of property, following a period of low development activity during the previous business cycle.
2. Strengthening demand and restricted supply cause rents and values to rise, improving the profitability of development and triggering the first wave of building starts.

[59] Barras R (1994) Property and the Economic Cycle: Building Cycles Revisited *Journal of Property Research* Vol 11 pp185–186.

3. If credit expansion accompanies the business cycle upturn, then it can lead to a full-blown economic boom, while at the same time banks fund a second wave of more speculative activity.
4. A major building boom is under way, but lags inherent in the development process mean that little new space is completed, and rents and values continue to rise.
5. As the bulk of new buildings reach completion, the business cycle has moved into its downswing, money supply is tightening and interest rates begin to rise.
6. As the economic boom subsides, demand for property weakens, just as the new supply reaches its peak. Rents and values begin to fall and vacancy rises.
7. As recession looms, the fall in rents and values accelerates; the credit squeeze hits property companies with un-let buildings.
8. The outcome is a property slump with depressed values, high levels of vacancy and widespread bankruptcies in the property sector.

The reasoning of this explanation is clear, but it ignores the role of contingent factors that determine the timing and scale of change in economic activity that feed through to heightened confidence in the development sector. Let us now examine the supply-side weaknesses in more detail.

The first weakness to be highlighted here, perhaps the most obvious, is the supply-led nature of the development process. The notion of speculative property development, by definition, suggests a system where building activity is determined primarily by the supplier of property rather than by the eventual user.[60] Although not necessarily inevitable, the speculative development process is a production process that is distanced from the demand process. It is an activity in which confidence plays a crucial role, where the provider takes a view on the market and makes a judgement on the timing and pricing of a particular project. As shortages of space lead to rising rents and higher capital values "developers initiate schemes without full appreciation of the total volume of development being started" and, by the time the new wave of buildings is being completed, "a potential oversupply has been created."[61] The evidence of this chapter shows that the enthusiasm with which the development industry

---

60 Bateman (1985) *op cit* p3.

61 Barras (1981) *op cit* p17.

responds to an upturn in demand has often been over-optimistic. Rising rents and values caused by low availability, followed by softer money supply, provide successive boosts to the confidence of the speculator. In this latter context, the proclivity to build is often encouraged by the fact that the developer will see its customer not as the end user of the building, but the financial institution that is prepared to forward fund or buy upon completion the newly created asset.

The weakness here is the herd-like instinct of developers: what kind of developer would make the altruistic gesture of delaying a project simply because he believed that others were in the process of supplying sufficient space to meet anticipated demand? It is this herd-like behaviour that leads to the delivery of large volumes of real estate in a concentrated period of time. This is a supply-side weakness rather than an inherent cyclical characteristic.

The next weakness of the supply side is the role of the funding institutions particularly, and the availability of finance generally. Development booms are not caused solely by the behaviour of developers: "It is now apparent that market disequilibria is further heightened because there may be not one source, but rather two sources of demand for new buildings, ie user demand and investor demand".[62] This suggestion is reinforced by Helga Leitner, who gives an American perspective on the supply-side factors that strongly influence profitability and office building dynamics. She argues:

> The importance of the supply of investment capital is consistently downplayed in neoclassical research, yet booms in commercial building are increasingly attributed to the increased supply of capital for property investment by financial institutions.[63]
>
> The increasing tendency towards equity investment since the late-1970s brought with it a progressive transfer of ownership of commercial property from developers to their financiers, disarticulating building development from ownership. One consequence of this is that developers became less concerned about the risk that the revenue generated by the building would not adequately compensate for the cost of development.[64]

---

62 Barras R (1987) Technical Change and the Urban Development Cycle *Urban Studies* Vol 24 No 1 p14.

63 Leitner H (1994) Capital Markets, the Development Industry, and Urban Office Market Dynamics: Rethinking Building Cycles *Environment and Planning A* Vol 26 pp784–785.

64 Leitner (1994) *op cit* p795.

Key *et al* also point to the behaviour of the funding community:

> Part of this inherent instability is because property is traded in an investment market, and any investment market is the subject of swings in sentiment and expectations that are wilder than those in the real economy.[65]

It is notable that Key *et al* refer here to instability rather than cyclicality. The difference between market equilibrium (ie new supply and the level of demand being broadly similar) and major disequilibrium can be simply the appetite of the investment market. A small movement in investment allocations in favour of, say, offices, can have a dramatic impact on the perceived risk of a building project. If institutional demand is seen to be running high, then developers will feel more confident in their ability to find a customer for their product. This case is illustrated well by the events surrounding the dot.com boom between 1999 and 2001. While technology, media and telecoms (TMT) shares were reaching undreamt-of heights, the property industry was looking forward to boom times. And, in the short term, boom times arrived. To provide a flavour of the market at the time, in 2000 MCI Worldcom pre-leased 30,000 sq m (330,000 sq ft) at Reading International Business Park, by junction 11 on the M4, and in an even bigger set of deals Cisco Systems completed Scotland's largest ever pre-let, with 28,000 sq m (300,000 sq ft) in Glasgow and a massive 56,000 sq m (600,000 sq ft) at Green Park, near Reading. Everything looked set to go. But not only did these two companies fail to occupy the space they had leased, the whole sector collapsed — or did it? Employment in the technology sector barely changed; while many of the new upstarts collapsed, it seems their employees quickly found alternative sources of employment. In other words, the demand side of the equation actually changed very little. What did change, and changed massively, was the property sector's expectations. The development tap had been turned to full on, and space flooded onto the market on a scale wholly unjustified by the underlying economic principles. The market lived with the consequences at least for the next five years.

The third structural weakness is the lack of feedback from demand to the supply sector. This refers to the notion that intelligence from the demand market should be fed back, interpreted and acted upon by the supply process. This activity is examined in more detail in chapter 7,

---

65 Key *et al* (1994) *op cit* p84.

but it is relevant to highlight here the fact that user research was virtually absent during the four booms of the post-war era. There was no recognisable research industry during the first two; some semblance of information gathering had begun by the third; and full-blown research departments were only just getting under way as the 1980s boom unfolded. Thus, in terms of market research, the industry was operating almost blind for almost the whole period: there was no composite view on the scale of development, and there was no structured demand analysis. This weakness within the development industry was a contributory factor in the phases of over-building. Thomas Black and William Hauser have highlighted the problem of imperfect information:

> the failure to take into consideration the response of others appears to be a long-standing factor in speculative excesses near the end of a boom period and also in panic withdrawals once the bubble has burst.[66]

Of course, earlier booms had no market-wide research either. But the difference in the post-war period was the scale of output of speculative office blocks. Space built specifically and only for white-collar workers was being churned out in increasingly large volumes and in ever-increasing densities. Just as agriculturalists become more vulnerable when they rely on a narrow range of products, so the property market became more unstable as it became dominated by one product — speculative offices. The supply industry made little effort to understand supply and demand dynamics because its dominant market position encouraged a culture of confidence that, given reasonable location, space of any quality would eventually be taken up by occupiers whose choice was limited. It is legitimate, therefore, to highlight the fact that the development industry operated, by and large, without market-wide data on the development process for most of the post-war period. The same is true of those whose role it was to manage the supply of new offices.

Despite clumsy interventions by policy makers (for example Office Development Permits), the planning process did not take a market-wide view of development levels in order to inform decisions on applications. Yet the planning process is a key actor on the supply side

---

66 Black and Hauser (1993) *op cit* p47.

through its role in consenting development. Despite this pivotal role, the planning process was, by and large, almost completely uninformed about the level of demand for property for most of the post-war period. Arguably, it lacks the tools to this day with which to make informed decisions about the volume of demand for new space.

The development process is one in which the "replacement of older offices by new buildings forms part of a continuous process of redevelopment which is going on within the office stock."[67] This brings us to the fourth structural weakness. Because of the length of time taken to deliver a building, the supply process has normally lagged rises in demand. This lag has contributed to rapid rises in vacancy levels as demand falls away. However, a feature of recent times, particularly since the 1980s, has been the ability of the development and construction industry to speed up its delivery process. This had the rather adverse effect of worsening over-building because more space could be delivered in a shorter time. For example, construction techniques and building costs have made significant advances in recent years:

> greater offsite prefabrication of building components and progress in site-management techniques and construction times ... greatly improved construction productivity and noticeably shortened building times.[68]

Michael Ball goes on to argue that improved construction techniques may have "intensified the amplitude of the property cycle" as lower costs reduced risk and as more developers sought to "beat the bust."[69] Furthermore, while there has historically been a lag between demand and construction, this is not a *de facto* cause of periodic oversupply. Rather, it is the apparent inability of the industry to stop building that is the greater problem. This latter fact is inextricably linked to a poor understanding of the level and profile of demand.

The property-supply industry is a highly fragmented one, which is a source of further weakness in its ability to address the tendency to overbuild. In the aftermath of the property market collapse in 1990, management consultants Ernst & Young argued that the industry was

---

67 Barras (1984) *op cit* p38.

68 Ball M (1994) The 1980s Property Boom *Environment and Planning A* Vol 26 p680.

69 *Ibid*.

"poorly managed because it is both flawed and fragmented."[70] They went on to explain that it was flawed because of the lack of a "common willingness to understand or accept the implications of transactions, which tend to be large, elaborate, expensive and slow ..." and fragmented because "occupiers, developers and investors have different and non-complementary agendas, objectives, market leverage, and decision-making standards."[71] The consultants argued that very few players exhibited a strong business strategy that would enable them to take decisions within a strategic framework; most developers tended to focus on projects as investment opportunities rather than their attractiveness to occupiers, and that because of these first two factors, developers tended to overreact to market changes, thereby exacerbating market volatility.

Analysis of the property-supply industry, and specifically of speculative building, has largely failed to address the structure of the supply industry itself, and the role that this has played in the magnitude of development booms. Therese Byrne and David Kostin hinted at the effect of the structure of the development sector:

> London's established property cartel comprised not only the property companies and lending institutions, but also the chartered surveyors, who apparently have a vested interest in underwriting and valuing the properties in the clients' portfolios.[72]

In many other markets, both business-to-consumer and business-to-business, there is a direct feedback from market to supplier in which it is relatively straightforward to control supply to more-or-less match market demand. But this does not happen in property. There is no industry "thermostat" that controls over-heating. On the contrary, as the market heats up, opportunists pile in and, without a market-wide understanding of the actual level of demand, or any kind of central planning mechanism, the industry proceeds to over-build. John Henneberry and Steven Rowley point to the ease of entry as a weakness in the supply industry. Using the 1980s boom as an example,

---

70 Ernst & Young (1993) *The Property Cycle: The Management Issue* Ernst & Young, London p5.

71 *Ibid.*

72 Byrne T E and Kostin D J (1990) *London Office Market II: Breaking the Code* Salomon Brothers, London p5.

they cite the relaxed attitude of institutions, coupled with the use of new financial instruments that:

> made it easier for speculative risk takers new to the property market to undertake development. This group, predominantly trader developers, lack the benefit of market experience, have little understanding of the requirements of property users and have no long-term commitment to the buildings they produce.[73]

The final weakness to be addressed here, and the one that is covered least of all in the literature, is the human vulnerability to risk. Property development is an exciting process: its very essence is risk. Finding a site, piecing together a development opportunity, securing financial backing, the construction process — all are highly charged activities that keep the adrenaline high. In cycle theory, developers are characterised as responding mechanistically to market signals provided by prices and price changes; but in fact they are far more complex. Adarkwah Antwi and John Henneberry recognised the "inadequate treatment of developers' behaviour in econometric analyses of the development cycle," and how these more complex issues can, in aggregate, reflect and reinforce asymmetry in the development cycle."[74] Similarly, while recognising the usual issues of business cycles, long production times and easy money, Black and Hauser also highlighted behavioural causes, such as psychological responses to growth periods, the industry's risk and reward structure and unrealistic financial appraisals as accounting for excessive activity.[75] Ball went even further to illustrate how the development hubris of the individuals involved can contribute to the severity of a development boom: "Media curiosity with their business and personal lives then creates the impression that the individuals have discovered some new formulae for business success."[76] Whether it can be defined as hubris or not is a moot point, but developers certainly have an infectious desire to create. Whatever the precise nature of their motivation they are, generally, enormously

---

73 Henneberry J and Rowley S (2002) Developers' Decisions and Property Market Behaviour In: Guy S and Henneberry J *Development and Developers* Macmillan, London p98.

74 Antwi A and Henneberry J (1995) Developers, Non-linearity and Asymmetry in the Development Cycle *Journal of Property Research* Vol 12 p221.

75 Black and Hauser (1993) *op cit* pp 46–47.

76 Ball (1994) *op cit* p682.

positive and creative people prepared to spend a long time pulling together a complex project and then have the satisfaction of seeing it become reality. This huge, positive drive is in fact a weakness for the industry in the absence of thermostats elsewhere in the system.

In this chapter we have seen how during the half century since the Second World War the emergent office economy was accommodated in an ever-expanding stock of office space. We have also seen how, during this period, the supply process was interrupted by occasional collapses as the weight of activity became unsustainable in a wider context. However, the notion that the property development process *per se* is cyclical has been questioned here and structural supply-side weaknesses have been highlighted as major factors contributing to the periodic phases of oversupply. The post-war structure of property development was one built on speculative finance for speculative product. It was highly concentrated in a single product — offices — and was structurally weak in terms of its internal fragmentation. The contingent factors of the 1970s and 1980s booms, as examples, were highly specific and cannot be generalised through all time and across all space.

In summary, the structure of the post-war property-supply industry was different from that which it succeeded. It evolved very quickly to meet a fundamental need within the economy to accommodate a rapidly growing office economy. It was based around speculative finance and it suffered major dysfunctions as its structural limitations allowed it to over-extend itself several times. Of course, the question that emerges is whether this model is an appropriate one for the current time and the future. Given the longer-term evolution of the office economy outlined in previous chapters, it should not be assumed the model of the previous five to six decades is one that has any permanency. Quite plausible economic, environmental and urban planning issues, not to mention issues rooted within the changing nature of the office economy itself (see chapter 9), could be marshalled to suggest that a new model is overdue.

5 Investors and Developers: A Triumph of Hope Over Experience

The property riddle

A riddle wrapped in a mystery inside an enigma. This was how Winston Churchill described Russian foreign policy at the outbreak of the Second World War. Famous for his rhetoric, Churchill found a way of both simplifying a very complex set of relationships while at the same time conveying his own sense of perplexity. There can be no better way to introduce a chapter that focuses on the supply side of the post-war commercial property market — at least from an occupier's perspective. The structure of the market was entirely supply-driven and it created buildings that, with notable exceptions, bore little relation to the changing needs of the businesses that rented them. Among the mysteries was the commercial lease — the central, contractual agreement between the owner and occupier of a building. The Landlord and Tenant Act 1954 introduced the standard lease (also known as the institutional lease), which remained virtually unchanged for over four decades. Throughout this time, it offered security of tenure to occupiers in return for long-term, onerous commitments, while appearing to create immense value for investors and owners. Above all this, the central riddle of the market is why its prime customer was, for so long, the investor and not the occupier. Imagine renting your home. You cannot find a decent property on offer unless you commit to a lease of 25 years. During that time, you are responsible for the cost of all repairs and insurance of the building and you must keep it in its original condition. Should you decide to move before the 25 years are up, you must continue to pay the rent or find a replacement tenant. And that is not all, if the replacement tenant should at any time fail to pay his or her rent, the landlord could come back to you as the original signatory to the lease and demand payment.

This is how it was for businesses who signed a commercial lease from the 1950s until the late-1990s. It is, of course, only possible where the landlord is in total control of the market. Such control was secured through the establishment of a central contract, namely the Landlord and Tenant Act 1954. This was an update of the Landlord and Tenant Act 1927, which was concerned mainly with shop premises. The legislation, complete with its feudal terminology, survived massive changes in the world around it, only to be challenged when it was clear that new ways of delivering property would be required if the current actors in the process were not to lose their relevance.

Businesses who typically planned no further than three, possibly five, years ahead were asked to commit their businesses to a property for 25 years. Not only that but, every five years, the rent would be adjusted and could only increase. To cap that, there was privity of contract. This particularly invidious clause described the relationship between the original parties to the lease. It meant that once a tenant signed a lease they remained responsible for the rent throughout its full 25-year term — even if, and here is the twist, they assigned it to another business and moved to new premises. As if that were not enough, there was the full repairing and insuring component. This onerous clause effectively divested the landlord of all management responsibility and placed it squarely on the tenant's shoulders.

By locking occupiers into long leases with severe disincentives to moving, the institutional lease provided a secure income to owners. In short, it became a predictable cash flow, which was enormously attractive to long-term investors. In this sense, it helped create the highly liquid market in commercial property that provided an alternative to gilts and equities, and that proved a magnet to foreign capital. The problem with predictability is that it can lead to complacency. In this case, apart from the problems that it created for occupiers by, in effect, engaging them as actors in the property process through their responsibilities, by locking them into such long lease arrangements, a prevailing supply-led culture evolved in which the development supply industry treated its most important customer as the owner, or investor, rather than the occupier. So buildings were developed with a view to selling to an institution and we grew accustomed to "institutional specification" and the "institutional lease"; neither of which recognised the needs of the occupier. What the institutions needed was product uniformity to underpin valuation and tradability: it was a short step to the "rent slab".

There were two generic actors who dominated the property-supply process in the early post-war years: the institutions and the property companies. The institutions comprise the pension funds and insurance companies (and to a lesser degree Property Unit Trusts), who invested vast sums of money in UK property during the second half of the 20th century on the premise that it would generate secure returns. Their primary motive for investing in property is risk management. They seek to create portfolios of property spreading, typically, offices, industrials and shops, with geographical diversity, and which will be part of a broader portfolio, including gilts and equities. They are the companies in whom we entrust our savings to build a secure future. Names such as Legal & General, Prudential Corporation, Scottish Widows and Standard Life exemplify this group.

Institutional investors began to put their money (that is to say, our money) into the commercial property market during the late-1950s. Their priorities as owners of the buildings and landlords to most of British business were to balance their portfolios by offsetting the risks of investing in gilts and equities, with security and long-term growth, achieved through the strictures of the standard commercial lease. Property became synonymous with the phrase "hedge against inflation". It was in part this hedge that led so many of us to believe that the value of our pension savings would continue to rise. The institutions gave the property market a kind of credibility that the property companies had failed to create, and it was the mutual interest of both that perpetuated a unique system of provider-occupier relationship for nearly 50 years.

Property companies, or developers, come in a wide variety of guises. They range from the small to medium-sized company led by an entrepreneurial and often flamboyant individual, to larger companies with a more sober, or corporate outlook. They also split between trader-developers, who buy and develop sites in order to sell on the developed asset (often to institutions), and investor-developers, who develop sites with a view to holding them for their asset value. While their history pre-dates the Second World War, they first came to the general public's attention in the post-war building boom. The names of Harry Hyams, Charles Clore, Jack Cotton and Joe Levy came to symbolise development at this time. Smaller, more entrepreneurial companies, almost by definition, come and go, but more enduring examples include Bride Hall, Chelsfield, Greycoat, Helical Bar and

MEPC. The larger companies are typified by the likes of British Land, Grosvenor, Hammerson, Land Securities and Slough Estates.

It is the changing roles and interactions between the institutions and property developers that resulted in the property riddle, and so fundamentally shaped the dynamics of the post-war commercial property market, not least through its enduring impact on the office economy. How did this iron grip of the supply industry come about? Why did it last for so long? And what is its future? For the answers to these questions, we have to go to the immediate post-war period.

The era of speculation

In the aftermath of the Second World War, a huge rebuilding programme was required to help repair the ravages of the Blitz. Central London lost around 880,000 sq m (9.5 million sq ft) of offices and in the City, around one-third of the stock "was completely flattened."[1] However, as Hedley Smyth argued, an overriding brake on development at this time was "the insufficient accumulation of capital to justify expenditure on new offices and retail outlets."[2] In other words, there were many greater priorities than commercial property, for example, economic and social reconstruction. Consequently, the development market remained relatively subdued for around eight years after the war. Many of the workers displaced by the Blitz stayed away, only returning once the economy of the city began its slow recovery. Between 1951 and 1961, floorspace in the City grew by about a third, and its working population increased from around 337,000 to 390,000.

Two further constraints suppressed development during this period of austerity and nationalisation. First, building resources were rationed through building licences, introduced during the war. Second, there was the Town and Country Planning Act 1947. This was introduced by the Labour government to constrain developers by introducing 100% development tax and a new system of development planning.

Some developers found ways around the system and got new projects under way but, overall, new development was sparse. Perhaps

---

1 Jenkins S (1975) *Landlords to London: The Story of a Capital and its Growth* Book Club Associates, London p209.

2 Smyth H (1985) *Property Companies and the Construction Industry in Britain* Cambridge University Press, Cambridge pp131–132.

the most significant additions to office stock during this time were those built specifically for government departments. These were developed under "lessor schemes" in which the government granted a license to a developer with a suitable site. The other way for developers to avoid licence control was by pre-letting new developments to companies involved in export industries.

It was not until 1953 that commercial property development was to get its first big post-war break. The new Conservative Minister for Housing and Local Government, Harold Macmillan, introduced the Town and Country Planning Bill to repeal the financial provisions of the 1947 Act and abandon 100% development tax. As Oliver Marriott relates the story, he believed "that laws which the public found hard to understand were bad laws."[3] Further, that while "the development charge is alright in theory ... it will not work in practice", and that "if there is something wrong in practice it is just possible there is something wrong with the theory."[4] In a remarkable comment, Macmillan argued that "the people whom the Government must help are those who do things: the developers, the people who create wealth whether they are humble or exalted."[5] Of course, this comment must be taken in context: it demonstrated the government's desire to kick-start reconstruction without dipping into its own reserves. However, it sowed the seeds for a wave of activity that Harold Macmillan probably never envisaged.

Together with the repeal of building licences in November 1954, these measures opened "the floodgates for commercial property development."[6] There is no doubt that the pressure to develop was already being compounded by an expanding economy and growing pent-up demand. Consequently, the conditions were evolving for a new era in property development: that of mass commercial property speculation. The growth in property companies and floorspace consents illustrate this point.

The number of property companies grew rapidly in number from 25 quoted companies in 1939 to over 150 by 1965.[7] Reflecting this growth in interest from property companies, the scale of development began

---

3 Marriott O (1967) *The Property Boom* Pan Books Ltd, London p15.

4 *Ibid.*

5 *Ibid.*

6 Marriott (1967) *op cit* p11.

7 Bateman M (1985) *Office Development: A Geographical Analysis* Croom Helm, London p16.

to increase dramatically. Central London office consents grew from around 158,000 sq m (1.7m sq ft) in 1951 to 279,000 sq m (3,002,100 sq ft) in 1953, and as high as 545,000 sq m (5,858,300 sq ft) in 1955.[8]

It is perhaps ironic that just as the development boom was getting under way, pressure from business occupiers for greater protection led to the introduction of the Landlord and Tenant Act 1954. Concern over the shortage of office space following the war led to calls for greater protection, and the Act was passed to give tenants security of tenure, the right to apply for a new tenancy and a right to compensation should continued tenancy be refused. The result was enhanced value for the property industry generally and a boom time for property companies in particular. The dynamics of the time is demonstrated by the growth in the total value of quoted property companies. This grew from £103m in 1958 to £800m in 1962.[9]

The image of this time has something of a frontier feel about it and the mood was encapsulated well by Jack Rose, citing personal experiences:

> An estate agent instructed to sell a site would telephone a prospective purchaser who, with no further details than the address, price required and the approximate size, would take a taxi to verify the location. Satisfied on this he would telephone his architect ...[10]

The architect would then seek clarification from the local authority on plot ratio and permitted uses, and the developer would calculate construction costs, fees and interest charges. A deduction of 20% from the gross building area would provide the net area available for calculating rental income.

> A profitable deal would emerge if this income, capitalised at 10%, equalled or exceeded the addition of the development costs and site cost. Within hours of the first telephone call a deal could be struck.[11]

It really was as crude as this. Speculators rushing around to grab pieces of land that they could "turn", and create, sometimes, personal fortunes. Social historian Anthony Sampson described the period in vivid terms.

---

8 Marriott (1967) *op cit* p312.

9 Marriott (1967) *op cit* p311.

10 Rose J (1985) *The Dynamics of Urban Property Development* E&FN Spon, London p151.

11 *Ibid*.

In five years several of Britain's biggest cities have been face-lifted: they have changed from horizontal to vertical skylines. Steel and glass cliffs have pushed up between old churches; rows of Victorian shops have given way to big white office buildings; skyscrapers have grown up around St Paul's.[12]

Sampson referred to the patience involved in assessing and visualising the potential of sites, bargaining and buying up clusters of old buildings and negotiating with local councils in order build new office blocks that crammed in the maximum office space. He went on to suggest that:

it is the property developers — subject to the wayward controls of local councils — who are taking over the role of master town planners, which was once the prerogative of dukes, earls or the monarch himself.[13]

One of the more powerful figures from this time, but perhaps typical of the genre, was Jack Cotton, an "exuberant character"[14] who worked out of a permanent suite at the Dorchester Hotel, where he was "surrounded by Renoirs, vivacious secretaries, brisk surveyors, maps of London, press cuttings, and a stream of visitors. He sits talking, drinking and laughing at the long table in his drawing room, sometimes till two in the morning ..."[15] By contrast, his weekends were spent at his house by the Thames at Marlow listening to the Crazy Gang and collecting miniature bottles.[16] Cotton's single mindedness led to a string of extraordinary deals. The son of a Birmingham Jewish export agent, Cotton set up an estate agency business at the age of 21 and was soon developing sites.

He acquired a public company in 1946, to develop London and Birmingham properties with insurance companies — which grew enormously in the following 10 years. He formed a host of subsidiary companies with insurance businesses (notably Pearl Insurance and Legal & General) and various corporate businesses (including ICI, Shell-Mex, BP and Barclays Bank) to undertake development projects.[17]

---

12 Sampson A (1962) *Anatomy of Britain* Hodder & Stoughton p415.
13 Sampson (1962) *op cit* p416.
14 Erdman E (1982) *People and Property* Batsford, London p114.
15 Sampson (1962) *op cit* pp416–417.
16 Sampson (1962) *op cit* p417.
17 Sampson (1962) *op cit* p418.

In 1960, Cotton merged his company with that of his friend Charles Clore to create the biggest property development group in the world, with assets of £67m, and with Cotton at the helm."[18]

While the Klondyke nature of the mid-1950s disappeared, and the process became more sophisticated, the basic role of the property developer has not changed much since then. He spots a site with potential for development and will risk capital to buy the land, or at least an interest in the land; obtain planning consent and design and manage construction in the hope that he will reap the rewards of a greatly enhanced value at the end. Actually there are a few points along the way when the developer may decide to take his profit and move on. For example, he might choose to sell the site as soon as he gains a planning consent and make a capital gain without having to manage the risk of actual development.

As the 1950s gave way to the sixties, the fruits of the first post-war development boom began to emerge. And the weaknesses of the speculative process became apparent. Much of the criticism for the sixties architecture was laid firmly at the doors of the men who orchestrated the process. Marriott highlighted the image of the developer as someone for whom the development process was no more than an opportunity to create profit:

> (the) developer is like an impresario. He is the catalyst, the man in the middle who creates nothing himself, maybe has a vague vision, and causes others to create things.[19]

The prospect of building something of real aesthetic or architectural merit did not seem to be high on the agenda. This led to the widespread criticism that developers were responsible for creating rent slabs (in property market terminology) or urban wastelands (in populist terminology). Marriott was blunt in his assessment:

> Only a minority of developers were particularly concerned with the aesthetic design of their buildings. Since the developers were often men of little formal education, and since they were promoting their buildings for entirely commercial reasons, this is hardly surprising.[20]

---

18 Sampson (1962) *op cit* p418.
19 Marriott (1967) *op cit* p36.
20 Marriott (1967) *op cit* p40.

Commercially, developers did not need to worry about quality. In the booming 1960s, there was so much demand for property that quality just did not matter: in short, it was a sellers' market. Rents were growing faster than development costs and developers could make serious money from mediocre buildings. An architect would produce plans, a specification and an artists' impression; a quantity surveyor would calculate a construction cost, and the developer would select the construction contractor that submitted the lowest bid. As Rose observed, the developers favoured those architects who maximised rentable area, compromising in the process specification and external aesthetics. "Hardly a single building incorporated air-conditioning. Central heating boilers were oil-fired rather than gas fuelled and there were generally insufficient electric power outlets."[21] No one was concerned that cutting corners might come back to haunt the property market in future decades, but when the long leases granted at this time began to come to an end in the 1980s, the alternatives were demolition or refurbishments costing more than the capital value of the buildings.

It is little wonder that, in the public psyche, property development became a byword for greed and avarice, and that developers came to be widely held solely responsible for some of the most despised buildings in the country. No other single phase of development has done more to reinforce this unfavourable image of the developer than that of the 1960s and 1970s. Members of the general public would probably not distinguish between institutions and developers; nor would they typically be cognisant with funding requirements on property development or the internecine aspects of planning law, such as plot ratios. Instead, the general public blame the "property developer" for putting profit before community benefit.

The buildings from this period have come to represent in the public mind everything that is bad about property development and the people whose business it is. The buildings are drab, uninspiring, cheap and dysfunctional. And the people responsible for them are caricatured as uncaring, money-grabbing speculators. The period left a legacy of despised town centres, in which the shopping centres and office blocks owed more of their architectural heritage to Victorian prisons than centres of commerce and community. The term "speculative development" (where buildings are built without an

---

21 Rose (1985) *op cit* p153.

occupier already signed to ownership or leasehold) has become synonymous with gambling. And there was always too much of it, with development booms leaving a glut of empty space that served only to reinforce the image of the developer as the drunken gambler making one last visit to the roulette wheel.

The emergence of the institutions

In the early post-war years, financial institutions played a passive role in the development process by providing fixed-interest mortgages, often secured against leased assets. But as the 1950s progressed, the institutions increased their influence. Insurance companies were first in, followed by pension funds. They became progressively more directly involved in the development process, until they arrived at the pivotal and powerful position that they would occupy for the rest of the century. One of their most influential roles was to define an "institutional specification" for buildings that prescribed key aspects of design, paying little reference to the needs of the market and militating against innovation. Churchill's riddle was a very apposite description. How could a market come to be dominated by a relatively small number of large, faceless financial institutions, whose relationship to the customer was so tenuous?

There was no single architect or grand design to account for the way in which the post-war property market evolved in the UK, but rather a complex web of interconnecting and related economic, political and social factors. Angus McIntosh and Stephen Sykes (1985) named a few:

> Inflation, national economic policy, entrepreneurial skill, the poor performance of gilts and equities, town planning and taxation have all contributed in different ways to the growth of the institutional investment market.[22]

The lifting of building licences in 1954 also played its part. It happened at the same time as the government decided to re-introduce lending restrictions in an attempt to counteract rising inflation and a deteriorating balance of payments, which had the effect of pushing up interest rates. Meanwhile, the Capital Issues Committee clamped

---

22 McIntosh A P J and Sykes S G (1985) *A Guide to Institutional Property Investment* Macmillan, Basingstoke p19.

down on company applications to raise finance through rights issues. All of which meant that the number of opportunities to develop multiplied just as the sources of finance diminished; it was inevitable that property companies would look elsewhere for money. And so it was that they turned to the insurance companies for loans on low, fixed-interest rates. As their indirect involvement grew, however, the opportunities offered by direct involvement became irresistible to the institutions. They wanted a slice of the action, and they were in a hurry. By 1960, the *Investors Chronicle* was able to remark that:

> The granting of straightforward mortgages are a thing of the past. Equity shares and fixed returns have been demanded by insurance companies as they have wanted to benefit from the "anti-inflationary principle" too.[23]

Insurance companies would commonly take an equity stake in a property company by obtaining shares or an option to convert loans into shareholdings. The maturing relationship between property companies and institutions was further encouraged as a side-effect of government measures to curb speculative building activity. Chancellor Selwyn Lloyd's credit squeeze combined with the rise in bank rates from 4% to 7% between 1959 and 1961 served only to reinforce the increasingly complex relationship.[24] The commitment of financial institutions to the property sector had thus matured from one of indirect investment during the 1950s to a direct role by the 1960s.

With greater commitment from the institutions came power and influence. In fact, they fundamentally altered the workings of the property market. The institutional lease and institutional specification became dominant. And as their grip tightened, they determined where, how and what got built. In the process, the direct link between the producer (developer) and consumer (tenant or occupier) was broken.

The growth of direct involvement by financial institutions in property and property companies was rapid. By May 1962, "the insurance companies held ordinary shares in nearly 50 property companies and, by 1965, the figure had risen to over 100."[25] Before long, the institutions found a way to share in the development profit by

---

23 Associations with Insurance Companies *Investors Chronicle* 29 April 1959. Cited in: Smyth (1985) *op cit* p147.

24 Smyth (1985) *op cit* p155.

25 Lean W and Goodall B (1966) *Aspects of Land Economics* The Estates Gazette Ltd, London p94.

forming joint ventures with developers, or by providing fixed-interest finance in return for subscription rights to some of the companies' share capital.

The 1965 Finance Act, however, introduced double taxation of company profits, making it highly unattractive for institutions to receive their share of rental income in the form of dividends from a property company. The response of the institutions was quite predictable. They began to seek greater involvement in the development process itself and:

> to buy property directly, often by entering sale and leaseback agreements whereby the institution had an equity interest in the property rather than in the company.[26]

At first, institutional developers were willing to grant long occupational leases of 25 or 35 years without rent review. Until that is, inflation caused building values to rise rapidly and landlords introduced rent reviews to keep pace with inflation during the course of the lease. From there, the standard institutional lease emerged with its five-yearly, upwards-only rent reviews. Institutions also granted mortgages on variable rates of interest to developers, adjusting the interest payable periodically, becoming "related to the rental value of the property."[27] However, the institutions realised that if they actually purchased the investment themselves and then leased it back to the developer they would have far more control over their investment. Thus, in the early-1960s, the sale-and-leaseback became common practice. And as money poured into institutions from the investing public, their demand for property could not be satisfied by "let investments" and so they became involved in the pre-funding, construction finance and eventually direct development.

As the 1960s drew to a close, there were the early signals of an economic downturn. Falling investment, growing government debt and falling employment. However, by this time the property companies were returning to the banks for short-term borrowing, and between 1971 and 1974 bank lending to property companies increased sixfold.[28] Furthermore, the bulk of the lending for this speculation

---

26 Herring Baker Harris (1992) *The Capital's Property* HBH, London p31.

27 McIntosh and Sykes (1985) *op cit* p20.

28 Barras R (1984) The Office Development Cycle in London *Land Development Studies* Vol 1 p44.

came from the secondary banking system and, when interest rates were increased from 5% to 13% between 1972 and 1973, just as rental values were beginning to fall, the market crashed. It crashed in a most spectacular fashion, leaving a litter of ruined property developers and secondary banks. The property industry made one of its rare appearances in the public arena when Prime Minister Edward Heath (in sharp contrast to Macmillan's post-war remarks) referred to property development as the unacceptable face of capitalism.

The institutions circled the market like a flock of vultures over a bloated corpse. And they gorged heavily. Table 5.1 shows how an annual average investment of around £350m between 1968 and 1972 suddenly leapt to over £600m in 1973, reaching £1bn for the first time in 1976. Table 5.1 shows how institutional involvement grew in the period following the crash. As they bought up land and buildings, the institutions tightened their grip on supply and increased their power in the industry. So much so, that one perception was that the role of the developer, whether property company or individual, had been relegated to that of project manager or dealer.[29] Between 1975 and 1981, the total property assets of the institutions grew from £7.2bn to £27bn; or from 16.4% to nearly 20% of their total assets.

Table 5.1 Investments by financial institutions, 1968–79 (£m)

Year	*Insurance companies*	*Pension funds*	*Property unit trusts*	*Total*
1968	119.4	93.0	40.2	252.6
1969	185.9	112.0	43.3	341.2
1970	197.5	97.0	24.8	319.3
1971	198.1	91.0	22.7	311.8
1972	131.1	121.0	38.9	291.0
1973	306.8	248.0	56.9	611.7
1974	405.1	305.0	14.5	724.6
1975	406.3	339.0	33.8	779.1
1976	449.7	520.0	71.2	1040.9
1977	410.1	535.0	66.2	1011.3
1978	549.1	590.0	109.4	1248.5
1979	631.0	510.0	91.0	1232.0

Source: Central Statistical Office[30]

29 Rose (1985) *op cit* p167.

30 Cited in: Smyth (1985) *op cit* p211.

When the third post-war boom erupted in the late-1970s, the institutions had established their dominance in the development process and many developers were unable or unwilling to risk too much exposure to a downturn. In the new model, institutions guaranteed forward funding for the construction process and to buy the let investment on completion, while the developer used his skills to manage and facilitate the project. In return, they laid down "industry standards" concerning location, design and construction.

The industry understood what was meant by an "institutional lease" an "institutional specification" or an "institutional investment".

The fortunes of the owning sector in recent decades has scaled dizzying heights and plumbed extraordinary depths. What has been consistent — particularly for property companies — is the dismal performance of the companies themselves. A report from Commerzbank noted that:

> During each of the past 5, 10, and 15 years the sector's total returns have lagged those shown by Datastream's Total Market Index by circa 9% pa, while over the past 20 years they have lagged by an average of 5.5% pa.[31]

And the same is true of returns on the property itself. In 1994, Matthew Oakeshott observed that office investment had been "a triumph of hope over experience". He argued that: office property sector had consistently:

> underperformed other property sectors as well as other investment media. He showed that between 1980 and 1993 all property performance produced a total return of 9.8% pa. During this time, offices achieved just 8.4% pa.[32]

In the same year, Simon London of the *Financial Times* used Investment Property Databank figures to point out that, over the period 1970–93, the average annual return from property amounted to 12.4%. This is available to a passive investor owning properties directly. Likewise, over the same period, quoted property companies had also shown an average total return of 12.4%.[33] They had, in other words, added nothing in terms of management expertise or gearing.

---

31 Atkins J, Jones R and Gough C (1998) *Property Perspectives* Number 16, 19 February Commerzbank, London p12.

32 Oakeshott M (1994) One for the Gamblers *Financial Times* 22 July p18.

33 London S (1994) Quote, Unquote *Financial Times* 25 November p15.

The underperformance of the office sector in financial terms (and property generally) was reflected in the fact that institutional investment in property peaked during the 1980s, when international investment in the London office market reached record levels. In 1987, *Business* magazine commented that:

> The traditional investors in property have already pulled out. The financial institutions, like pension funds, which put up the money in the late-1970s and early-1980s are now investing a mere £1 billion of new money into the property market each year, and little of that into City office blocks.[34]

The position of the institutions was progressively occupied by overseas banks and funds (principally US, Japanese and German). By the end of the decade, overseas investment was at record levels. Foreign investment in the UK property market increased from £1.9bn in 1988 to £3.1bn a year later.[35] A follow-up report in 1994 showed that, while 1990 exceeded 1989 with well over £3bn, new investment quickly fell away in the early-1990s as the global recession took hold. The report showed that, for 1991 and 1992, overseas investment in UK property had fallen to just over £1.5bn and around £1.3bn, respectively.[36]

Overseas interest in UK property has been underpinned by the nature of the institutional lease. Nowhere else could investors find real estate with a guaranteed income stream for up to 25 years. Perhaps one of the most spectacular examples of this interest was the arrival in London of Olympia and York in the mid-1980s. Not only is this a tale *par excellence* of the changing fortunes of property companies, but also it demonstrates clearly the role of developers in a wider economic context, the interplay with public policy and the scope for innovation in the property process. The story begins with the brilliant vision of one man and a government-inspired regeneration project, before passing through widespread ridicule from a sceptical property industry and local and Greater London Council politicians. Initial success was promptly followed with the developer falling into financial administration, with the inevitable *schadenfreude* of its detractors. But, despite everything, the project eventually became a spectacular success.

---

34 Jardine C (1987) Japanese Funds to Fuel Boom *Business* July pp66–68.

35 Debenham Tewson and Chinnocks (1990) *Overseas Investment in the UK Commercial Property Market* DTC, London.

36 Debenham Tewson and Chinnocks (1993) *Overseas Investment in UK Commercial Property* DTC, London.

The emergence of Canary Wharf as a new urban quarter in London had its roots in the long-term decline of the London docks. As we saw earlier in this chapter, the fortunes of London's modern docks were relatively short-lived, from modest beginnings in the early 19th century to a peak in the latter part of the 19th century. By the 1980s, they had been in terminal decline for decades as a result of international competition; obsolescence; the growth of containerisation at larger ports with direct access to the sea; high labour costs and an appalling record of labour relations. The East India dock closed in 1967, and the whole area fell into a vicious spiral of economic and social decay. The last operating docks, the Royal Docks, closed in 1981. Of course, Docklands' parlous state was not unique. It was just one example among many of the impact of the restructuring of the UK economy. Up and down the country, docks and shipyards, factories, car plants, mines and so on were falling victim to the same forces afflicting Docklands.

Facing crippling unemployment and economic shrinkage, together with inner-city decay, the Thatcher administration, recently elected in 1979, set about implementing measures to combat the decline. The Local Government Planning Act of 1980 was used to establish the London Docklands Development Corporation (LDDC) that came into operation in July 1981. The LDDC was charged with the regeneration of Docklands, an area of some eight square miles — the largest regeneration project in Europe. However, for Canary Wharf, it was the more specific designation of the Isle of Dogs as an Enterprise Zone that was to have the greater long-term impact.

The genesis of Enterprise Zones is widely attributed to town planning guru professor Sir Peter Hall. Concerned at the level of decay and deprivation that was ravaging many of Britain's inner cities at the time, Hall addressed the Royal Town Planning Institute's annual conference in June 1977. His proposals to reverse urban decline included selecting small areas of inner cities that would be thrown open many kinds of initiative, with minimal control, thereby recreating the entrepreneurial characteristics of Hong Kong in the 1950s and 1960s in the hearts of UK cities such as Liverpool and Glasgow.

Hall's ideas appealed to the Conservative opposition party and, in particular, to Sir Geoffrey Howe, then opposition economics spokesman. The ideas offered a largely free market solution, with government acting merely as catalyst. A few small areas of unfettered entrepreneurial activity, so the thinking went, would act as engines of growth, pulling their surrounding areas in the direction of growth. Howe advocated a variation of Hall's ideas to encourage investment back into inner cities. When the Conservatives were elected to government in May 1979, he became Chancellor of the Exchequer and set about establishing Enterprise Zones. Eleven were designated, with the first opening formally in 1981. Michael Heseltine, Secretary of State for the Environment, was charged with their management. The Isle of Dogs Enterprise Zone opened in summer 1982. The zones offered businesses a range of benefits, including:

- exemption from Development Land Tax
- exemption from rates
- corporation and income tax allowances for capital expenditure on buildings
- relaxation of planning restrictions and speedy decisions.

The Isle of Dogs presented a huge challenge in urban regeneration terms. Three miles east of the City, in abandoned docks and with negligible public transport and hopelessly inadequate road links, the area was a wasteland. It was difficult to imagine at the time what could possibly be achieved, but slowly new buildings were created, and new businesses began to appear. But is was a fateful visit by an American banker, on a tour of the area in search of a site for a food processing plant in 1984, whose single-minded vision and boldness was set to change the fortunes of the area forever.

The late Michael von Clemm, then chairman and chief executive of Credit Suisse First Boston (CSFB), was making his visit at a time when he had also been struggling with City planners to resolve CSFB's urgent need for large, open trading floors to cope with the firms' activity in the Eurodollar market. In Docklands, he was shown an abandoned banana warehouse that, because it had received bananas from the Canary Islands, was known as Canary Wharf. The building he was shown comprised two 3700 sq m (40,000 sq ft) open floors and his idea was to fill them with financial traders. Immediately, he contacted Morgan Stanley's chief executive, Archie Cox, to invite him to view the site and to join his plans to move there. It was at about this time that the then Governor of the Bank of England, Robin Leigh Pemberton, relaxed the controls over where banks could locate, removing the requirement to be close to the Bank of England's back door. Von Clemm then called developer G Ware Travelstead.

> In December 1984, Michael Von Clemm ... called me from London and said: 'Can you come over? There's an old banana warehouse on Canary Wharf; could we use this as a solution to our trading situation?'

I said 'It won't work, Michael, there's no transport and there's no critical mass. We can't sit there in isolation.'[37]

However, Travelstead took up the challenge and joined the project. Under his guidance, the project was transformed into a plan for a 1 million sq m (10 million sq ft), 29ha (72 acre) development, including twin towers. He launched a major PR campaign, the like of which had rarely been seen in London, and the press reacted with predictable incaution, with many articles following the "Manhattan-on-Thames" theme. The one thing Travelstead did not have was committed financial backing from his anchor tenants — only intent. As the months dragged by, he faced increasing pressure to "come up with the goods". Negotiations dragged on and on, and discussions were held with many other financial institutions and developers, including Canadian developers Olympia & York (O&Y). Then, in mid-1987, CSFB and Morgan Stanley withdrew as financial backers to the project.

As the project floundered, O&Y swooped. Within a month of Travelstead's consortium falling apart, the project had new owners. The Toronto-based O&Y was run by three brothers, Paul, Ralph and Albert Reichmann, and had immense financial stature. At the time of its takeover of Canary Wharf, it owned huge tracts of Manhattan and was said to have around $12bn of assets. The deal gave O&Y virtual ownership: First Boston International retained a residual stake in the project and CSFB and Morgan Stanley were committed as anchor tenants. Within three months, O&Y unveiled its revised plans for the project and the development programme was gearing up for major activity. The project was set fair, and the first phase was expected to come on line in 1989.

But, of course, no matter how fast O&Y could build, and no matter how hard it sought to attract tenants, it was not immune from the travails of the wider London office market. As we saw earlier, tremors began to shake the London office market in 1989, and a year later it imploded. Just as new supply reached maximum flow, and tenants disappeared, Canary Wharf phase one reached completion. The efforts to attract tenants were redoubled and rumours were abounding of huge incentives to attract occupiers to the project, including two-year, rent-free periods, a long fixed rent, generous fit-out allowances and the

---

37 Gardner J (1987) Calling the Canary's Tune *Chartered Surveyor Weekly* Vol 18 1/8 January pp10–11.

assumption of responsibility by O&Y for premises left behind with obligations. Suddenly, the audacity of one the world's strongest developers began to many to look like outright foolishness. Inevitably, market talk was of how long Canary could last.

Then, like an earthquake following tremors, O&Y filed for insolvency protection in Canada and the US. It was May 1992. Debts were estimated at $3bn (£1.6bn). The sense of shock within the property market was palpable. The developers fought a rearguard action, and were reported as saying that Canary Wharf would be unaffected by the move and would continue on schedule.[38] But the glue was undoing. Two weeks later, the project itself was placed in administration, with debts of £576m. Under the headline "Banks abandon Canary Wharf" the *Financial Times* reported "on Wednesday the 11 banks [the leading creditors] told O&Y that an insolvency filing was the only option."[39] The shock was palpable. O&Y had seemed invincible, and the stakes at Canary Wharf too great to fail. A torrid time followed, with endless speculation over the future of the project and its chief sponsor. Various international personalities were linked to the project, including Sheik Maktoum al Maktoum of Dubai and Li Ka-shing of Hong Kong, reflecting the increasingly international nature of the UK office market.

Eventually, the 11 banks that had financed the O&Y project brought Canary Wharf out of administration in the following year, 1993. After a slow start, the project saw visible signs of activity. Major lettings were achieved with the Personal Investment Authority and the European Medical Agency. Morgan Stanley increased its commitment to the project with a further 46,500 sq m (500,000 sq ft) letting in 1994, and in spring 1995, BZW, the investment-banking subsidiary of Barclays Bank, committed to a similar-sized letting. In April, confidence in the project was sufficiently high to allow construction to restart.

In fact, such was the renewed success of the project that the Corporation of London once more began agitating about companies moving away from the City. BZW's decision to relocate was too much for some in the Corporation to bear. Referring to a "furious row" between the Corporation and Canary Wharf, the *Independent on Sunday* reported that Michael Cassidy (chairman of the Corporation's

---

38 Preston R and Stephens P (1992) Banks Face $3bn Losses on Their O&Y Loans *Financial Times* 16 May p1.

39 Preston R (1992) Banks Abandon Canary Wharf *Financial Times* 29 May p1.

influential Policy and Resources Committee) had accused Canary Wharf of breaching "a gentlemen's agreement not to poach financial institutions."[40] He had "accepted" BZW's decision on the basis that Canary Wharf would not seek further defections.

The Wharf's remarkable rise from the ashes was given further impetus in August 1995 when Prince al-Waleed bin Talal bin Abdulaziz of Saudi Arabia joined forces with Paul Reichmann to make a bid for the project that only a year earlier had been valued at £500m. The prince owned 24% of Euro Disney, and was the largest single shareholder in Citicorp (a major creditor and, later, occupier of the project). The bid was accepted in October, with the bidders paying nearly £800m, and Reichmann retaining a 5% stake.

In October 1998, it was announced that Canary Wharf was preparing for flotation, and these plans were realised the following spring. By October 2000, Canary Wharf overtook Land Securities as the UK's largest property company, with a market capitalisation of £3.94bn, compared with Land Securities' £3.91bn. The *coup de grâce* came in October 2000, when Canary Wharf entered the FTSE100 index. By 2003, Canary Wharf was up for sale again, and a protracted battle for control of the project began.

Thus, it was that Canary Wharf came full circle. Its 20-year history was a complete microcosm of the 1980s boom and 1990s collapse, followed by a measured recovery. It was reminiscent of the earlier *grands projects* that were perfected by Thomas Cubitt. Today, Canary Wharf is a new urban quarter in its own right. It is a large, 35ha (86 acre) estate of 18 dramatic, mainly steel and glass, tall buildings, totalling some 8m sq ft (with a further 4m sq ft yet to be constructed). Its cavernous interiors and lower levels accommodate all the frontages of a typical high street: shops, travel agents, banks, numerous cafes, coffee shops and restaurants; fitness clubs. All of this is set within a manicured landscape of gardens, sculptures and water features. And through and around it all each day bustle some 55,000 workers. When it is complete, it will house 90,000 workers, equivalent to around one-third of the City employment market.

While the project was criticised early on for diluting the strength of the City of London, it has quite possibly saved London as one of the three key financial centres in the world, alongside New York and

---

40 Rodgers P (1995) City Outrage at Being Sold Down the River *Independent on Sunday* 9 April p1.

Tokyo. It is home today to many of the leading investment banks, several of which occupy in excess of one million square feet (see table 5.2). And it has successfully diversified its occupier base with a range of other companies relocating there since 1991, including: Clifford Chance (law); BP and Texaco (oil); Ogilvy & Mather (advertising); Financial Services Authority and European Medicines Evaluation Agency (government); Reuters (media), and Independent on Sunday, McGraw Hill Group, Readers Digest and the Telegraph Group (publishing). And there are numerous other smaller occupiers in the multi-let 1 Canada Square — the iconoclastic tower — and elsewhere on the estate.

Table 5.2 The Canary Wharf "million square foot club"

Barclays Bank
Clifford Chance
Citigroup
Credit Suisse First Boston
HSBC
Lehman Brothers
Morgan Stanley Dean Witter

Canary Wharf has become a spectacular success in terms of responding to the changing needs of the office economy with real estate that met a need in terms of building specification. It was also perhaps the zenith of speculative development in the UK. What it did not do was to address the underlying concerns of occupiers in terms of offering different terms. It replicated what was available throughout the market and, as the 1990s recession took hold, the nature of the standard lease once more came to the fore.

First glimmerings of reform

The last decade of the 20th century began with a deep recession. But more than this, it marked the beginning of a new era. Following the long consumer and investment boom of the 1980s, the slump had a particularly shocking effect; a sure case of hubris to nemesis in one very sharp, precipitous fall. Between 1983 and 1990, 3.5 million new jobs were created in the UK, taking the total employed to 27.2 million.

Two years later, two million of those jobs had disappeared. While manufacturing growth effectively stopped in 1990, house prices slumped, and many homeowners discovered negative equity. The service sector continued its inexorable climb, capturing three out of four jobs by the mid-1990s. By the mid-1990s, more people worked in Indian take-away shops — over 60,000 — than in ships, steel and coal combined. The recession hit the commercial property sector particularly hard (see chapter 4). The market crashed when lending was at an all-time high; vacancy rates rocketed and property companies were going bust at unprecedented rates. Amid all this chaos, the seeds of structural reform were sown.

As the effects of the 1990s recession percolated through, businesses struggling to minimise fixed costs, such as rents, began to put pressure on the supply industry to introduce flexibility into commercial leases. At the same time, the supply industry itself began to contemplate the impact of a period of prolonged low inflation in which rental and capital growth would suffer. Traditionally, property companies relied upon inflation to bail them out. They began to consider the rather daunting prospect of having to create value themselves, rather than relying on a frothy market to do it for them. Thus, the recession of the early-1990s saw the beginnings of real reform, leading ultimately to major changes in the leasing market.

During the recession, occupiers began to organise themselves in a way that had not happened before. They started to voice their concerns through representative bodies, such as IDRC and NACORE. Later to merge into CoreNet, both organisations were imported from the US and, along with the growth of the British Council for Offices, the Urban Land Institute and the British Property Federation, they were symptomatic of the growing professionalism of the property market generally (see chapter 8). As they became more vocal, they demanded more from their landlords than rent collection: they wanted flexibility in lease terms and they wanted better service. Most of all, they wanted a real estate supply chain that was responsive to the increasingly complex, uncertain and competitive environment in which they operated. The arrival in the UK (again from the US) of serviced offices provided a partial answer, but more fundamental change was needed from the large landlord community.

As occupiers lobbied for lease reform, the owning community became increasingly concerned at soaring vacancy rates, and landlords found themselves presiding over growing amounts of non-income-earning property. So great was the overhang of space in the aftermath of the crash in 1990; so apparently few the number of occupiers looking for space, and so prolonged was the recession expected to be, that landlords, for the first time in the modern era, began to contemplate the unimaginable — service provision. Thus it was in the aftermath of the recession, in the mid-1990s, that the first signs of a new approach emerged. Almost inevitably the precedents came from the US. Whether through necessity or choice, a number of US property companies began to push their businesses towards providing real estate services. For example, a profile of Trammell Crow in *Business Week* described how the company was seeking to establish itself as a one-stop shop for property management, leasing, construction management and information services. The transformation was not without its cultural difficulties, as many partners "couldn't or wouldn't make the transition from development to management"; a process rather colourfully described as "taking a bunch of fighter pilots and telling them that now they have to maintain the aircraft carrier."[41]

Walter Steucklin, head of corporate real estate at Asea Brown Boveri in Europe, endorsed this new process. He argued that developers would have to build to meet end users' requirements, leading to a wholesale restructuring of the corporate real estate industry in which the "real estate developer [would] become a member of the service industry."[42] Significantly, the message was also endorsed by the financial community, which had borne the brunt of the property collapse. In a briefing note to highlight BAA's "Fair Deal" initiative that sought to improve customer service, BZW argued that:

> Landlords are increasingly having to recognise that they operate in a service industry providing accommodation to customers. The confrontational approach to landlord and tenant negotiations is not appropriate in a market characterised by oversupply and limited demand, and where tenants are generally well aware of the strength of their bargaining positions.[43]

However, the UK property industry had to be dragged through several years of attritional debate over the structure of commercial leases before it could properly contemplate adding value to the process through the provision of services.

---

41 Zellner W (1992) Guess What Trammell Crow is Eating? *Business Week* 2 March pp36–37.

42 Steucklin W (1993) Look Who's in the Driving Seat Now? *Site Selection Europe* September pp22–25.

43 BZW (1995) Flying Lessons *Property Briefing* 23 January.

As company failures grew during the recession of the early-1990s, the standard lease came under intense pressure for reform from occupiers, who were increasingly regarding themselves as customers rather than merely tenants. Growing numbers of businesses found themselves facing demands for rent from landlords in whose buildings assignees were defaulting on rent. The occupational market challenged owners to meet the needs of an increasingly dynamic and competitive business environment. They found support from the Bank of England, which declared that the upwards-only lease pattern was predicated on upwards-only property values and that the thrust of its anti-inflationary policy would be to make it obsolete.

Initially, the attack focused on the principle that rents should only go upwards at review. Other issues to come under attack were privity of contract and lease length (highlighting the absurdity of signing 25-year leases when most companies have business plans stretching no more than five years). The retail community led the charge, urging government to promote flexibility in the market. As a result, the Property Market Reform Group was set up. A period of government consultation took place through 1993 and 1994, leading in 1995 to the publication of a code of practice for commercial leases. The first success came in 1995, when the Landlord and Tenant (Covenants) Act 1995 repealed privity of contract.

In April 2000, the DETR reported on the operation of the Code of Practice. Significantly, it found that the limited number of changes favouring occupiers had been driven by market forces (ie recession) rather than as a result of the Code. This is best illustrated in trends in lease lengths. It was reported in 1997 that of 4713 leases granted in 1996 and reported in the Investment Property Databank, some 55% were granted for five years or less. Moreover, in central London where the property recession had been most severe, the average new lease length in 1996 was eight years, compared with 20 years in 1989.[44] During the summer, the government put further pressure on the industry to reform itself. In September, planning minister Nick Raynsford stepped up the campaign for lease reform with an attack on upward-only rent reviews. He said:

The present situation is not sustainable. The present situation is not

---

44 Cohen N (1997) Power to the Tenant *Financial Times* 17 October p17.

satisfactory. I hope the industry will recognise it must adjust, hopefully on a voluntary basis.[45]

There was a clear hint in this statement that if voluntary reform were not forthcoming, then some form of legislation would be considered. In the same month, the DETR called a meeting of key players in the industry, and the Commercial Leases Joint Working Group (CLJWG) was formed, comprising various interests including owners, occupiers and intermediaries. The debate over lease reform grew increasingly bitter over the next couple of years.

Government continued to push for more flexibility and choice in commercial leases. Raynsford told the Property Industry Forum in January 2001 that he wanted concrete proposals for alternative leases by the end of March. A DETR spokesman was reported as saying that if the deadline was not met, legislation banning upward-only rent reviews would be drafted.[46] The University of Reading's Department of Land Management produced a research report in February 2001 called *Lease structures, terms and lengths: does the UK lease meet current business requirements?* The report found that up to 40% of corporate occupiers believed the UK leasing system to be unsatisfactory.[47]

In April 2001, the CLJWG admitted that it had failed to secure agreement on a way forward. It had discussed alternative lease terms, but these were defeated by vested interests. The first of these was a standard default lease, which had a 10-year term, security of tenure and up and down rent reviews, including an occupier's break without compensatory payment. Landlord representatives on the CLJWG rejected this option. Three alternatives were proposed. Option one proposed a short-term (five-year) lease, with no security of tenure, a fixed rent and assignment subject to reasonableness. Option two proposed a longer-term (10-year) lease, with a conditional occupier break and security of tenure. It offered a review in the fifth year to market rent, but at a minimum of the initial rent. The occupier had rights to terminate at review with six months' notice if the rent was to rise. Alternatively, the owner could agree to continue the passing rent.

---

45 Cited in: Smith K Raynsford Raises Stakes on Leases *Property Week* 1 September p1.

46 Marriott R (2001) March Deadline to Scrap Upward-only Rent System *Property Week* 26 January p128.

47 Cited in: Barrie G (2001) Lease Terms Threatening UK plc's Competitive Position *Property Week* 23 February p3.

If the break was exercised, the occupier should pay six months' rent compensation to the owner. Option three was also a 10-year term with an unconditional occupier break and no security of tenure. The fifth-year review was the same as option two. These options were rejected by occupier representatives on the CLJWG.

The reluctance of occupiers to embrace the proposals appears to have revolved around giving up security of tenure in return for shorter leases and unconditional break options. Landlords, on the other hand, were concerned that greater flexibility would affect values. At the General Election in June 2001, Nick Raynsford was replaced by Lord Falconer. Anyone expecting that the change would result in lease reform slipping down the agenda was to be disappointed. In November, the CLJWG announced that it had found a compromise between landlord and occupier interests. A new code of practice, in which landlords would offer priced alternatives to upward-only reviews, was agreed. Occupiers agreed that downward reviews would be settled no lower than the initial rent.

In April 2002, the industry inched towards reform with the unveiling of a revised code of conduct. Among the terms of the new code, the following were pivotal:

- rent to be priced according to the terms offered
- choice of term length to be offered
- alternative rent reviews
- repairing obligations appropriate to the lease length and condition of property
- landlord's consent to assignment not to be unreasonably withheld
- no requirement for tenant to remove permitted alterations unless reasonably required.

Despite this progress, the fact that government ministers had to warn that failure to reach agreement would result in regulation of commercial leases demonstrated the level of reluctance to move to a more flexible system. In 2005, Government and the industry reached a compromise. While the Government backed down from its plan to ban upward-only rent reviews, the industry began to accept a loosening of restrictings on sub-leasing and assignment.

As the debate over lease reform raged through the late-1990s and into the new millennium, property companies and institutions themselves failed to provide a lead. Clearly, their vested interest in retaining the status quo would prevent them from proposing radical reform. But they were also largely mute over how the continued underperformance of the sector could be addressed under any scenario. While, to some extent, the large institutions sat back and ignored what was going on, the continued lacklustre performance of the sector encouraged some traditional property companies to redefine their role. They began to accept that the rent collection role was not providing their shareholders sufficient value, and that if they were to succeed in an environment where growing returns from property investment were no longer guaranteed, then a different approach would be required. It was argued that the traditional lease was unsuited to a more dynamic business environment, and that the answer lay in "a more customer-focused approach ... based on flexible leasing and enhanced service provision."[48] But, as with lease reform, it was with some discomfort and pain that the sector approached change.

In 1990, the UK-quoted property sector comprised around 100 companies and accounted for nearly 4% of the stock market. Ten years later, and after significant underperformance, it accounted for just 1.4%.[49] Furthermore, property's role as a hedge against inflation was diminished as the economy flattened, and while property shares were looking cheap

> this is no longer sufficient reason to buy into the sector. The big threat is looming deflation. This concern has punctured hopes of rental and capital growth and companies will now have to work hard to create value; inflation will no longer help them out.[50]

Property shares remained in the doldrums through the late-1990s, and into the new millennium. Indeed, their very *raison d'être* actually came into question. Trading at discounts to net asset values in the region of 25%, property companies offered very little to their investors. And if they were unable to add value for shareholders, what future did they have? Consequently, they came under increasing pressure to return value (ie cash) to their shareholders. In February 1999, Chesterfield announced plans to liquidate itself and hand back the proceeds to its investors. It was a radical step but one that signified how poorly rated

---

48 Taylor P (1999) A New Dawn for Tenants: the Landlord that Likes to Say Yes *Property Week* 9 July p18.

49 Waples J (1999) Property Firms Face Pressure to Break Up *Sunday Times* 14 February p9, section 3.

50 Waples (1999) *op cit* p9, section 3.

the sector's small- to medium-sized companies had become. In other high profile deals, Bilton surrendered to Slough Estates, and Rodamco bought Scottish Metropolitan. The retreat from public gaze on the stock market gathered speed. In summer 2000, the news that had been rumoured for some time finally broke: MEPC was to be taken private by institutional investors GE Capital Europe and Hermes Pensions Management. MEPC's very public move to private ownership was followed by Allied London, Bourne End, Burford, Capital Shopping Centres, Eskmuir, Frogmore, Prestbury, and Raglan. During 2000, "nearly 20 quoted property companies, with around £2.4bn of assets, disappeared from the public sector".[51] In 2001, Pillar bought Wates City of London, a specialist City development company; and Warnford Investments and Regalian also went private.[52]

The threat of long-term deflation and poor rental and capital growth were real, and the very business model of the traditional property company was being called into question. Although property companies had traditionally traded at an average discount to net asset value of around 25% (even trading at significant discounts when the underlying market fundamentals were strong), it seemed that a certain point had been reached when the patience of investors had begun to run out. Significantly, performance was not the only feature of criticism of the sector. For example, when MEPC announced its exit from the stock market, Norma Cohen of the *Financial Times* commented:

> Institutional shareholders have expressed growing impatience with the traditional management style of property companies, in which estates are viewed as assets rather than coherent businesses.[53]

The same article quoted Alistair Ross Goobey, chief executive of Hermes, as saying that "the model being abandoned is one in which you buy property and demand more rent every five years". Goobey's position was very clear:

> We can see no merit in investing in what is effectively a rent collection organisation ... We can see no merit in investing in the Rolls Royce lifestyles of so many property company managements.[54]

---

51 Watson S (2001) Privates on Parade *Property Week* 12 January p36.

52 Waples J (2000) Pillar Property Eyes Wates City of London *Sunday Times* 12 November p2, business section.

53 Cohen N (2000) MEPC to go private for £3bn *Financial Times* 2 June p1.

54 Cohen N (2000) Quoted Sector in Question *Financial Times* 2 June p34.

Others were even blunter:

Does anyone care that these companies have gone .... They are the squalid remains of empires .... They are small versions of British Land that have no future.[55]

Most of the quoted property companies were relatively small, run by "characters" with well-rewarded management teams. Their focus was entirely on maximising returns from "deals". They were ill-equipped to address the kind of change that was beginning to emerge and were not inclined to relinquish their traditional role easily. In an editorial, the *Financial Times* took an acerbic swipe at the property sector and its apparent inability to reinvent itself:

Few property companies show much sign of strategic planning or reacting to rapid change by turning themselves from dull leasers of bricks and mortar into imaginative accommodation service providers.[56]

Yet, it was this shift to service provision that was to provide the first glimmerings of reform, the start of a process of reinvention. Perhaps the most striking example was Land Securities. During 2000, Land Securities made radical changes to its management team and to its business strategy that would have been considered inconceivable just two or three years earlier. Suddenly it was talking less about rents, asset values and projects, and more about service provision. Joint ventures and external capital were to feature in the new Land Securities. And, perhaps most radical, the business was to move into service provision and Private Finance Initiative work in order to grow earnings-based business as a proportion of its revenues.

The second half of the 20th century saw four great property booms and four associated slumps. It also saw the nature of property development change as the smaller property companies of the immediate post-war period yielded to the domination of the anonymous institutions. Then as the institutions themselves began to lose their appetite for property, so changes in the global economy highlighted the need for a more efficient way of delivering real estate. But perhaps of greatest significance, occupiers became empowered.

---

55 Nick Leslau, Chairman Prestbury Cited in: *Property Week* 2 February 2001 p11.

56 *Financial Times* 2 June 2000 p20.

The property industry began to learn some important lessons, and to recognise the need to be structured and managed in a way that corresponded more closely with the demands and characteristics of the occupier market. This meant moving towards the provision of services as well as floorspace.

6 Public Policy: A Tale of Indifference and Ineptitude

Throughout much of the post-war period, both local and central government were pre-occupied with policies aimed at limiting the growth of office activity. This preoccupation was mostly politically inspired: it was at least in part underpinned by the romantic notion of preserving blue-collar work in one of the most expensive city centres in the world. Perhaps more significantly, it was also caused by a lack of understanding of the forces that were underpinning the inexorable rise of the office economy. Moreover, and reflecting the more specific context of the property industry, it showed an obsessive concern with supply-side dynamics. A growing concern with "the office problem" during the 1960s and 1970s, manifested in a myopic focus on growth in aggregate levels of floorspace and led to reactive planning frameworks that consistently failed to address the requirements of office occupiers. Right up to the eve of Big Bang in the City in 1986, there was an almost complete absence of policies based on the operational and occupational needs of the office economy that had by then become such an important element of the London and UK economy.

Central and metropolitan intervention

As early as 1940, the Royal Commission on the Distribution of Industrial Employment (The Barlow Commission) raised concerns over the proliferation of commercial and administrative buildings as industry moved away from the central area of London.[1] However, at this time, the planning policies of the local authorities of Greater London paid relatively little attention to office employment in central London.[2] The *County of London Plan* of 1943 set the tone for much of what was to follow. In his forward to the plan, the Right Honourable Lord Latham, Leader of the London County Council (LCC), stated that:

> Our London has much that is lovely and gracious. I do not know that any city can rival its parks and gardens, its squares and terraces. But year by year as the nineteenth and twentieth centuries grew more and more absorbed in first gaining and then holding material prosperity, these graces were over-laid, and a tide of mean, ugly, unplanned building rose in every London borough and flooded outward over the fields of Middlesex, Surrey, Essex, Kent.[3]

The plan itself, which was to form the basis of post-war planning in London, barely referred to office activities, and asserted that central London "must continue to be of many and varied uses and, in the main, redevelopment can take place without serious disturbance to the present natural zoning."[4]

An identifiably anti-office stance first appeared in the LCC's *Draft Development Plan* of 1951 (approved in 1955). The main strategic consideration of this plan was the decentralisation of industry and commerce and the expansion of residential development to address depopulation of central London, through the use of zoning and plot ratio controls. While the retention of industry was later to fall back into favour as a desirable generator of jobs, herein lay the genesis of an obsessive concern within public policy with "the office problem". It was an obsession that was to dominate the development and implementation of office policy, at local, metropolitan and central government level, for the next 35 years. It was an obsession that was to show a singular lack of focus on the evolving role of London generally, and the rise of the office economy that was so acutely expressed therein particular.

Although damage to the fabric of London during the Second World War was extensive, post-war austerity measures constrained

---

1 Town and Country Planning Association (1962) *The Paper Metropolis* TCPA, London p25.

2 TCPA (1962) *op cit* p25.

3 Forshaw J H and Abercrombie P (1943) *County of London Plan* Macmillan & Co, London piii.

4 Forshaw and Abercrombie (1943) *op cit* p22.

redevelopment activity. However, as business gradually returned to something resembling normality, pressure to redevelop bomb-damaged sites mounted and gradually the planning system yielded. Between 1948 and 1954, the LCC issued planning approvals for the construction of nearly 2 million sq m (21 million sq ft) of new office space in central London. In addition, permissions for a further 560,000 sq m (6 million sq ft) of conversions to office use were granted.[5] But this large build-up of consents was merely a prelude to the boom of the mid-1950s and, as many of the consents were sought to secure value rather than real development opportunities. The operation of building licence controls, introduced by the post-war Labour government through the 1947 Planning Act as part of its austerity programme, placed suppressed the ability of developers to build. Together with 100% development charges, they proved highly effective in discouraging development. This fact became clear as soon as they were abolished in 1954, when development applications increased markedly and a spectacular construction boom began. Between 1954 and 1958, the annual rate of construction completions increased nearly tenfold, from 65,000 sq m (700,000 sq ft) to 550,000 sq m (5.9 million sq ft) in central London.[6]

Until this boom in development, office employment had not formed any part of central government's employment policies. But, as redevelopment led to a growing concentration of office employment, and as the plan's strategic concern with the decentralisation of industry and commerce appeared to be not working, concern began to grow in central government over its impact on the capital's employment structure and on congestion.

In 1954 (while the LCC's development plan was still in preparation), the Minister of Housing and Local Government, Duncan Sandys MP, asked the LCC to undertake a survey to determine land use allocations and to provide a factual basis for an attack on congestion. The ground was laid for a determined and sustained attack on the expansion of office activity, and Ministerial comments on post-war development plans hinted at the types of measures that were to follow. For example, in approving the LCC plan in 1955, the Minister inserted a policy statement aimed at preserving residential uses in the central area. This

5 TCPA (1962) *op cit* p22.

6 Barras R (1979) *The Development Cycle in the City of London* Centre for Environmental Studies, Research Series 36, London p41.

stipulated that on the expiry of their permits for temporary use as offices, buildings would revert to their former, residential use. The attitude hardened, and the attack gained momentum. In 1956, Sandys approved the *County of Middlesex Plan*, suggesting that: "It would afford considerable relief to the congested central areas of London if more business concerns could be persuaded to establish their offices in the outer parts"[7] of Middlesex. Then, in 1957, the LCC published *A Plan to Combat Congestion in Central London*. While conceding that it was essential for London's position as the administrative and commercial capital of the country to be maintained (remarkably parochial ambitions given the city's already-established role in world commerce), the plan argued that policies needed to be amended. In particular, it sought restrictions on the areas in which large office buildings could be built.

As well as a concern over increasing congestion, "the office problem" was also related to a growing concern over the increasing polarisation of "productive activity" and the service sector. Manufacturing activity in London was declining severely during the 1950s, and policies aimed at decentralising office activity from central London were, in part, based on a fear that continued and largely uncontrolled growth in the centre would encourage further loss of manufacturing jobs. Thus, manufacturing employment was seen to be more "worthy" of protection than service jobs. In this sense, policy frameworks were addressing the historic role of the city centre rather than a more progressive stance that would have recognised the inevitable rise of services generally, and the office economy in particular.

The plan to combat congestion did little in practice to halt the rise of offices, and it did even less in central government circles, where the perception was growing that the metropolitan authorities were unable to prepare a coherent impact on the location and development of office activity. All the while, pressure was building among those property developers and speculators who had amassed their property portfolios during and immediately after the war. Development began to spiral as soon as the wartime rationing on building was relaxed by central government in 1954, with the ending of building licenses. As controls on construction effectively lapsed, the years 1953–63 were ones in which, with the support of clearing banks and insurance companies, developers "were unleashed on the London environment to enjoy a

---

7 TCPA (1962) *op cit* p27.

decade of uncriticised and virtually untaxed profiteering."[8] Despite its potentially strong grip on development through the local development control process, central government perceived that the LCC failing to control the spread of development, and eventually its frustration surfaced in the form of a full-scale review of London government:

> A multitude of motives went into Henry Brooke's decision in 1957 to set up the Herbert Commission to examine the root and branch reform of London government. But there is little doubt that the LCC's shortcomings in the planning field ... played a major part in it.[9]

The report of the Herbert Commission in 1962 led directly to the Local Government Act 1963, which replaced the LCC with the Greater London Council (GLC) in 1964 as the strategic planning authority for London. At the same time (and in direct parallel with a move 10 years earlier), the Act recommended that the GLC should carry out a survey of Greater London, so that it could submit to the Minister a *Greater London Development Plan* (GLDP). The results of the survey and a Statement were published in 1969. However, the government did not wait for the metropolitan authority to establish itself and its policy regime. Its long-held perception that London-wide planning lacked the teeth and co-ordination to step into the office market and contain the office problem led it to intervene directly, for the first time, in the office development system. This was a bold change in direction for public policy on land use control, especially given the fact that it was based on at least two questionable assumptions.

The first of the questionable assumptions concerns the actual scale of growth in office employment. It seems that there was a significant gap between perceptions and reality of office employment growth. For example, the employment estimates on which the introduction of policy measures was based were themselves incorrect. The LCC had fuelled the debate over numbers in the First Review of its Development Plan in 1960. It had argued that the number of people employed in central London had been increasing by 15,000 each year, or nearly twice the national rate of growth.[10] The Town and Country

---

8 Jenkins S (1975) *Landlords to London: The Story of a Capital and its Growth* Book Club Associates, London p215.

9 Jenkins (1975) *op cit* pp226–227.

10 Cowan P (1971) Employment and Offices In: Hillman J (1971) *Planning for London* Penguin, London p65.

Planning Association added its weight to the argument, stating: "the increase was almost entirely in office employment."[11] However, these comments were misleading. The 200,000 jobs thought by the government to have been created in central London offices between 1951 and 1964 was in fact a "very inaccurate" estimate.[12] On the basis of quite misleading statistics, government took critical decisions about employment policies in order to justify its attempts to retain blue-collar work in central London.[13]

The inaccuracy of the estimates on which the government had based its approach to office policy emerged when the results of the 1961 Census were belatedly published in 1966. These showed that the actual rise in office employment was significantly less than had been estimated. The results showed that between 1951 and 1961 the average annual growth in London's office employment had been less than 6000 jobs, or just over one-third the rate on which the previous policies, thinking and planning had been based.[14] Moreover, the figures showed that the bulk of employment growth in the South East had taken place not, as had been previously assumed, within Greater London, but in the rest of the South East region.[15]

A second questionable assumption that had an equally important impact on the office market in London was that office employment was itself responsible for worsening congestion problems in the central area. There is, however, little evidence to verify that this link exists. The specific focus on macro supply dynamics, such as employment trends, distracted attention from other related issues, such as traffic management, which are much more difficult, more expensive and sensitive to tackle. Consequently, instead of being "seen as an integral part of an overall urban growth and adjustment strategy, relating closely to transport, housing, manpower questions and other policies",[16] office activity was beginning to resemble a scapegoat for London's perceived ills. The assessment of aggregate trends in employment lacked any clear understanding of the causes and structure

---

11 TCPA (1962) *op cit* p20.

12 Alexander I (1979) *Office Location and Public Policy* Longman, Harlow p64.

13 Hall P (1969) *London 2000* 2nd Edition Faber & Faber, London p77.

14 Cowan (1971) *op cit* p66.

15 Manners G and Morris O (1986) *Office Policy in Britain: A Review* Geo Books, Norwich.

16 Manners G and Morris O (1981) Does London Need an Office Policy? In: Barras R (1981), *The Office Boom in London* Proceedings of the First CES London Conference p6.

of the increased demand for office employment. Most of the growth was taking place in industries that were tied to central London through a complex network of economic linkages, which were shaping London's role as a global centre of finance and commerce. And the introduction of restrictive office policies was unnecessary not only because estimates of office employment were exaggerated, but also because the growth was taking place in activities that were tied to the centre.[17]

The government's preoccupation with controlling office development was undaunted by questions over the validity of its policy assumptions. On the contrary, frustration at the continued, seemingly uncontrolled growth of office space, and the apparent ineffectiveness of the metropolitan authorities, led to direct intervention. In 1963, and without waiting for the outcome of the GLDP process, the government began a two-pronged attack on office development in central London. The first of these measures saw the principle of office decentralisation established as part of central government policy for the first time, and the establishment of a public agency — the Location of Offices Bureau (LOB) — to make it happen. The second prong of the attack was to ration the amount of office space that could be built through tight development controls — the Office Development Permit system.

The LOB was established in 1963, with the declared aim of encouraging the decentralisation of office employment from central London. Its remit also included the promotion of publicity and research, and the provision of information. During its tenure, there is little doubt that the scale of decentralisation from London increased markedly. Table 6.1 shows that the number of jobs that were relocated between its inception in 1964 and closure in 1979 amounted to some 105,000, involving 374 businesses.

The extent to which these moves could be wholly attributed to the activities of LOB has been hotly debated. Some argue that LOB's impact was only marginal: for some "the horse had bolted and the government locked the stable door."[18] For others, its success in decanting office jobs from central London could be attributed in large measure to the operation of market forces.[19] The annual reports published by the LOB provide some evidence to support these claims. The results presented

---

17 Evans A (1967) Myths About Employment in Central London *Journal of Transportation and Policy* Vol 1 pp214–225.

18 Marriott O (1967) *The Property Boom* Pan Books Ltd, London p23.

19 Manners and Morris (1986) *op cit* p116.

in the *1978/79 Annual Report*, for example, are typical. During the year in question, 10,428 jobs were moved out of the whole of London by 142 clients of the LOB. Only half of the jobs (5005), and one-quarter of the clients (36) moved between regions, ie beyond the South East. Furthermore, "relatively few of these moves involved complete relocation of a company's offices."[20] Indeed, 3000 jobs were relocated by five banks and insurance companies — mainly comprising administrative staff. Of the remaining 5346 jobs, only 54% originated in the central area.

Table 6.1 Number of jobs and moves from central London, 1964–79

Year	*Number of jobs moved from central London*	*Number of moves from central London*	*Mean size of move from central London*
1964	4500	16	281
1965	6650	24	277
1966	7800	26	300
1967	9200	27	340
1968	7500	21	357
1969	6000	26	230
1970	6100	23	265
1971	6400	26	246
1972	4800	27	178
1973	9200	31	296
1974	9200	33	279
1975	8400	32	263
1976	7350	26	283
1977	3500	9	389
1978	5700	11	518
1979	3180	16	199
Total	105,480	374	300

Source: Location of Offices Bureau[21]

20 Location of Offices Bureau (1979) *Annual Report 1978/79* LOB, London pp11–13.
21 Location of Offices Bureau, reprinted in Jones Lang Wootton (1987) *The Decentralisation of Offices from Central London* JLW, London pp3–4.

While there was evidently some limited decentralisation of employment, there was negligible deconcentration of economic activity. Cost cutting is a primary reason for relocation, and this can be relatively easily achieved by moving a large proportion of clerical and administrative staff, rather than the client-facing departments and decision-makers. For 1978/79 at least, the LOB's success at redistributing employment was limited and, in addition, appeared to complement the established process of relocating administrative functions to cheaper, "back-office" locations. So what of the government's other anti-office policy — restricting the amount of new space that could be built?

Encouraging companies to leave London was not, by itself, considered to be an effective strategy for slowing down the rate of growth in the central area. In order for central area congestion to be significantly reduced, it was argued, relocation policies would have to be reinforced through a rationing of new supply. So it was that in November 1964, government announced its proposals to do just that. First, it restated the problem by pointing out that outstanding planning permissions, together with existing use rights, could result in over a quarter of a million further jobs in London, half of them in central London.[22] Without clarifying the causes of this development pattern or the economic context that might have been leading to the growth in demand for space, the statement went on to announce the need to call a halt to the rapid growth. It stated in bold terms that:

> We have to call a halt to this rapid growth. First we must have a standstill on new offices in London. To this end, the Government will shortly be introducing a Bill under which, in stated areas, any new offices will require Office Development Permits ...[23]

To meet this objective, it proposed to introduce a Bill under which, and in stated areas, new offices would require Office Development Permits (ODPs). This reaction to the perceived problems associated with a further 250,000 office jobs in central London showed a startlingly simplistic view of the growth dynamic in the office economy and its implications for the city's evolution as a world city.

---

22 HMSO (1964) *Offices: A Statement by Her Majesty's Government* SO Code No. 63-9999 4 November 1964 HMSO, London.

23 HMSO (1964) *op cit.*

Thus, it was that from 4 November 1964 the "Brown Ban" came into force. Any proposals for new office developments amounting to more than 232 sq m (2500 sq ft) would require an ODP. Furthermore, the ODP was subject to "named user" restrictions and would only be granted where the developer could establish a definite need for the office space in the proposed location. The Board of Trade (which was responsible for the control of office development before it was transferred to the Ministry of Housing and Local Government in 1969) required strict criteria to be met before granting an ODP. Where an occupier was specified, three further qualifying criteria were applied:

- that the activity for which the office accommodation was being sought could not be carried on outside the area of control
- that no suitable alternative office accommodation could be found
- that the development was essential in the public interest.[24]

It is clear, also, that the "public interest" catch all clause could, potentially, be used against most schemes that passed the first two criteria. The named user clause clearly favoured the further concentration of large occupiers because it "operated with an in-built bias in favour of large national and international concerns by comparison with smaller firms, without any objective reference to real user needs."[25]

Table 6.2 shows the number of ODPs granted during the full period of their implementation. The figures are not directly comparable for the whole period because the exemption limits for ODPs were raised on three occasions. In 1970, the 232 sq m (2500 sq ft) limit was lifted to 929 sq m (10,000 sq ft); this was then raised to 1393 sq m (15,000 sq ft) in 1976; before reaching its final limit of 2787 sq m (30,000 sq ft) in 1977.

Table 6.3 shows the amount of space in the Greater London development pipeline in 1964 and between 1968 and 1975. Complete and vacant floorspace stood at over 465,000 sq m (5m sq ft) before the introduction of ODP controls, with a further 1.3 million sq m (14 million sq ft) under construction. By 1968, the impact of the controls was beginning to show. Complete and vacant space had fallen by a quarter, space under construction had fallen by nearly two-thirds, and outstanding planning permissions had fallen by 86%. The suppressing

---

24 Board of Trade (1967) *Annual Report by the Board of Trade for the Year Ended 31 March 1967* HMSO, London.

25 Manners and Morris (1986) *op cit* pp127–128.

Table 6.2 Office development permits issued in central London, 1965–78

Year	*Number of permits*	*000s sq ft*	*000s sq ft relinquished*
1965	33	1242	587
1966	69	1229	676
1967	84	2483	1052
1968	127	6601	4051
1969	154	6308	2237
1970	266	10,921	4827
1971	198	12,246	4212
1972	139	10,302	3788
1973	126	7677	2567
1974	–	–	–
1975	64	4883	448
1976	75	6545	1119
1977	57	5674	328
1978	52	7753	333

Source: HMSO. Crown copyright material is reproduced with the permission of the controller of the HMSO[26]

effect of ODPs on development allowed the GLDP *Written Statement* of 1969 to claim that the system had prevented developments that "could have caused a runaway demand for office workers."[27] This self-congratulatory remark is strange for its apparent suggestion that employment grows to fill the available space, rather than being a response to economic growth, but was symptomatic of the supply side policy framework of the time.

The complete and vacant space continued to fall over the period, reaching less than 25% of its 1964 level by 1975. However, in 1970, when the ODP exemption limit was lifted from 232 sq m (2500 sq ft) to 929 sq m (10,000 sq ft), the number of outstanding planning permissions doubled, and a year later construction levels began to rise.

26 Office Development Statistics in the Fourth Quarter and the Year 1972 *Trade and Industry* 15 March 1973 pp578–579 HMSO, London; Office Development Permits in the First Quarter *Trade and Industry* 8 June 1979 pp449–450 HMSO, London.

27 Greater London Council (1969) *Greater London Development Plan Statement* Planning Department p20.

Table 6.3 Office space in the pipeline in Greater London, 1964 and 1968 to 1975 (million sq ft)

Year	*Complete and vacant*	*Under construction*	*Outstanding planning permissions*	*Total*
1964	5.1	14.1	17.9	37.1
1968	3.8	5.4	2.5	11.7
1969	3.0	4.4	2.9	10.3
1970	1.4	4.3	6.2	11.9
1971	1.9	5.2	9.5	16.6
1972	1.6	10.9	9.0	21.5
1973	1.0	12.7	10.5	24.2
1974	1.1	14.1	12.3	27.5
1975	1.2	4.5	6.3	12.0

Source: *Estates Times*[28]

As with the LOB, the impact of ODPs has been hotly debated over the years. As long ago as 1971, the highly respected academic planner, Peter Cowan, went on record as stating that "there is no longer any doubt that the Office Development Permit system is weak and ill-considered."[29] Irrespective of its validity as a supply-side mechanism, it is clear that one of the most significant though less understood impacts of the ODP system was its effect on the businesses occupying office space in central London. Companies were being forced to occupy whatever space was available. As new space was in increasingly short supply, they were forced to occupy second-hand space that itself was of a poor design standard and increasingly obsolete for the changing operational needs of occupiers. As Gerald Manners and Diana Morris argued:

employers failed to find accommodation in places which they preferred ... working conditions for the office workforce were poorer than they might otherwise have been, with floorspace per worker remaining relatively small

28 *Estates Times*, 1 November 1973 p9 citing Annual Report by the Secretary of State for the Environment and the Secretary of State for Wales, 1974 and 1975.

29 Cowan (1971) *op cit* p68.

and the age of the occupied office stock somewhat older than might have been the case without government intervention.[30]

While central government was pursuing its anti-office policy, metropolitan government was slowly preparing its strategic plan. When the 1969 Statement mentioned above was eventually produced, it served to reinforce central government's anti-office stance. For example, on office jobs, the Statement recognised that while total employment in London was falling overall, the number of office workers was rising and would continue to rise.[31] Its rather weak response to this growth in demand for space was that "it should be met to the extent that it can, for those activities which need to be in London, within the context of a declining labour supply overall."[32] There was also a rare recognition of the changing requirements of occupiers. The additional space to meet demand was required "to relieve the cramped conditions in out-of-date buildings and to provide the more spacious conditions which modern business methods require for achieving the maximum output."[33] Despite this positive stance, there was to be no reprieve as the noose of control tightened.

The policy framework that emerged in the 1976 Statement focused on locational priorities. The need for more efficient land use in central London was emphasised in preference to extending central London activities and, consequently, growth of those activities considered appropriate to central London would be achieved through further decentralisation. For those that remained, the plan stated: "some areas of central London are more suitable for the development of offices than others."[34] It sought to direct office growth to "preferred office locations", or areas in which offices "can be located with benefit."[35] However, this was little more than lip service to the control of office development because the authority lacked "both the necessary executive powers and the financial muscle" to implement its policy.[36] The Council could not directly intervene in the office market, and in

---

30 Manners and Morris (1986) *op cit* p128.

31 GLC (1969) *op cit* p20.

32 *Ibid*.

33 GLC (1969) *op cit* p20.

34 GLC (1976) *Greater London Development Plan Written Statement* Planning Department paragraph 7.6.

35 GLC (1976) *op cit* para 4.13.

36 Manners and Morris (1986) *op cit* pp108–109.

this sense was less effective than central government. For example, Third Schedule rights limiting local authority control over the development industry, and their ability to initiate development in preferred office locations, restricted the actual effectiveness of the paper commitment to control office development.

The 1969 Statement was subject to a public inquiry, and it was a full seven years before this, the consideration of findings and a modified plan, were completed in 1976. It had taken 12 years from the setting up of the GLC to the publication of a comprehensive plan for London — twice as long as it had taken to prepare the *London Development Plan* of 1951.

The combined effect of central and metropolitan government lining up against the growth of office employment in London was to constrain occupiers geographically and in inappropriate space. The policy framework was myopic in its approach, and what was perhaps fundamental to the weakness of London-wide policies was that they operated in isolation: questions about office location policy:

> were discussed and debated in the absence of viable solutions to metropolitan (economic and physical) planning problems as a whole. Yet ... office policy must be seen as an integral part of an overall urban growth and adjustment strategy.[37]

Just as importantly, however, the policies appeared to be working in isolation to the needs and aspirations of the occupiers themselves. There was no real understanding of the nature of the office economy nor of how it was changing or in what direction future changes in office requirements would move. Certainly, none of these were made explicit in policy statements. Indeed, the scale of policy makers' ignorance of the changing needs of occupiers and, therefore, the way in which the central London economy was evolving was breathtaking. There was evidence around if they had gone looking for it, and there were a significant number of prescient forecasts in this area; the following from 1971:

> The central clustering of London's office activities will remain the most important single element in the country for the exchange of money, ideas, and information — the invisible "transactional society", which will become even more dominant between now and the year 2000.[38]

---

37 Manners and Morris (1981) *op cit* p61.

38 Cowan (1971) *op cit* p72,

However, overriding concerns with perceived congestion, with the concentration of office activity at the expense of manufacturing and other "productive" economic activity, and with preserving the "essential character" of central London, precluded any notion of an activity-based approach to policy making. As we saw in chapter 3, there was plenty of evidence around which set out the dynamics of the expanding office economy, the emergent knowledge economy, and particularly its locational characteristics. Yet UK policy makers, obsessed with supply-side economics, failed to grasp the significance of what was happening in city centres and sought instead to control "the problem".

It was inevitable that this constraining pressure would eventually be released in a new cycle of demand. And it was only three years after publication of the GLDP in 1976 that the opportunity for release occurred. The new cycle of demand was to be released by an almost total withdrawal of central government from the office market along with the change of government in 1979. The arrival of Mrs Thatcher in Downing Street signalled a more hands-off approach to many aspects of the economy, the planning process included. Just two months into the new administration the DoE announced:

> The Government has reviewed the control of office development. This was introduced as a temporary measure in 1965 against the background of an office building boom and was primarily conceived as a counter to congestion in London.[39]

Without appraising how successful the ODP system had been in relieving congestion, the Notice went on to declare that the "Government is satisfied that office development within London ... can be adequately controlled through the normal planning system.[40] Neither statement suggested a fresh understanding of the office economy, nor a more positive approach to its development; simply that supply-side policies would be repealed. Later that month, the DoE announced: "Special control of office development ends on Monday 6 August."[41] Fifteen years after directly intervening in the office market for the first time, central government was retreating. The relative indifference displayed towards office policy in the pre- and immediate post-war years by central government had come full circle by the return

---

39 DoE Press Notice 270, 5 July 1979.

40 *Ibid.*

41 DoE Press Notice 320, 30 July 1979.

of the Conservative administration in 1979. And the anti-office stance of metropolitan government was somewhat stifled by its own battles with central government that eventually led to its abolition in 1986.

Policy makers yield to the office economy

The 1980s witnessed two events that demonstrated, once again, the schizophrenic approach of public policy towards the office economy and, more specifically, the different agendas of local and central government. On the one hand, there were many local authorities that adopted a highly insular approach, ignoring the immense external pressures of change. On the other hand, there was a central government with a clearly liberalising agenda, intent on rolling back the dead hand of control. What emerged by the end of the decade was a recognition within policy frameworks that offices were a fundamental facet of urban growth.

As central government rolled back controls over offices and encouraged a generally more *laissez-faire* approach to economic management, it fell squarely on local authorities to devise their own policy approaches to the built environment. It was not long before the dreadful flaws in such an approach to the management of a world city became patently clear and nowhere was the folly and potentially damaging effects of this approach more exposed than in the experience of the Corporation of London.

As the local authorities took centre stage in the office policy process, there was a softening of approach, although many years of anti-office policies paid dear in terms of a very poor understanding of the contemporary role of offices in the economy and the changing character of occupiers and their demands on built space. By 1982, the Corporation of London was beginning to understand the link between stock and demand:

> It is becoming increasingly apparent that prospective tenants are giving greater attention to the quality of the construction and design of the building. Poor standard of development is much harder to let than good quality of work. Funding institutions are now readily investing in refurbished schemes of good quality.[42]

---

42 Corporation of London (1982) *City of London Information Report: Offices* Department of Architecture and Planning p16.

> One section of property that is causing concern is the late-1950s/early-1960s speculative blocks. These units need drastic refurbishment if they are to be fully effective in their central locations. However ... to bring them up to scratch means a very costly operation and no short-term solution readily comes to mind.[43]

But such sentiment failed to transpose into a realistic policy framework, partly because the City continued to operate within the shadow of the strategic planning authority. The position of the latter was made abundantly clear in 1984 by George Nicholson, then Chair of the GLC's Planning Committee. Nicholson reinforced the Council's position on offices with the following statement:

> There are no forecasts indicating that there is a real demand for office space much in excess of past take-up rates. Indeed, many firms are cutting back their corporate staffing and are occupying smaller suites and not the quarter or half million square foot monsters so beloved by developers.[44]

While it is not difficult to forgive the fortune-telling abilities of the GLC (after all, plenty of others have got the future wrong), it is difficult to conclude that this position was not driven by political considerations rather than a consideration of the operational needs of the evolving office economy. The fact is that the strategic planning authority for Greater London failed completely to anticipate any quantitative increase or qualitative shift in demand for office space. The sharp increases in demand and shortages of space that were recorded in 1986 and 1987 were the result of long-term change. Yet take-up rates and aggregate employment trends were thought sufficient to guide Nicholson in his decisions on the level and type of office development to be permitted in the capital.

The fact is that less than two years before Big Bang there was simply no appreciation of the recent changes in the office economy, let alone any insight into the radical shake-up that was about to happen. At the city-wide level, and as late as the mid-1980s, there remained a fundamental misunderstanding of what was around the corner, and this reflected itself in the local planning process of the City of London. The disconnection between the evolving nature of the office economy

43 Corporation of London (1982) *op cit* p17.
44 Nicholson G (1984) The GLC Answers on Offices *Building Design* 11 May pp14–15.

and the planning process took a dramatic turn when the *City of London Draft Local Plan* was published in November 1984.[45] The plan fell woefully short of any coherent understanding of the relationship between City business and City property, and attracted a level of interest and criticism rarely raised over a local plan. The central weakness of the plan was that despite its claims to represent a world financial centre — with 5.1 million sq m (55 million sq ft) of office space; 220,000 office workers and a residential population of just 4000 all concentrated into one square mile — it continued to reflect the essentially anti-office stance of the metropolitan planning authority.

In the *Draft Plan*, 70% of the City's core area was designated a Conservation Area. Demolition and replacement there were to be strictly controlled in order to preserve the special character and architectural heritage of the City. The plan sought to resist a reduction in the diversity of uses affecting employment opportunities; and to restrict large-scale office development to the fringe areas. This it sought to achieve by exercising discrimination relative to location and existing uses; restricting new buildings to existing sites; preventing land assemblage by developers, and by designating Special Policy Areas. One of these, the eastern City area, sought to restrict the loss of wholesale and industrial premises; to restrict the loss of "small" and "very small" units of business accommodation, and to discourage developments entailing the unification of several sites.

High buildings were seen in the plan as incompatible with the scale and character of the City; and demolition of certain non-listed buildings that contributed to the special character of a conservation area would be resisted. Echoing George Nicholson's comments, the *Draft Plan* went on to argue that new technology would lead to a rationalisation of space requirements, and a general fall in unit size. It also claimed that proximity to the Bank of England would remain paramount for financial activities. It seems incredible that these statements were being made just 23 months before Big Bang, when the lessons of financial services deregulation were available from New York, which had gone through a similar process of deregulation in 1975.

The Corporation invited comments on its plan. Many detailed comments were submitted, with a significant number coming from concerned City businesses. One of the most detailed (and published)

---

45 Corporation of London (1984) *Draft Local Plan* Department of Architecture and Planning.

of these was that put forward by the Centre for Policy Studies that outlined five major criticisms of the *Draft Plan*:[46]

- First, it argued that the plan demonstrated little apparent understanding of the City's economy or the economic and technological changes affecting the type of buildings required. This was clearly true and struck at the heart of the credibility of the plan.
- Second, that it was based on an uncritical acceptance of outdated policies contained within the GLDP. While true, it should be remembered the *Local Plan* worked within the framework of the strategic plan, and was therefore constrained by its policies.
- Third, that it did not indicate the Corporation's desire to promote the financial economy of the City. Again, this is true, and reflects a naive understanding that was apparent at all levels of government in terms of understanding the contemporary role of the office economy.
- Fourth, that the *Draft Plan* had not justified the restrictive policies that would frustrate development. This point was related to the second criticism.
- Fifth, that the proposals illustrated the shortcomings of a planning system that was cumbersome "when faced with a fast-changing environment."[47] This point is underlined by the long gestation periods that many local and metropolitan plans had from initial draft to final statement.

While the Corporation of London was considering the criticisms of its plan during the summer of 1985, G Ware Travelstead announced his intention to build up to 750,000 sq m (8 million sq ft) of space in London's Docklands. Travelstead was quoted as saying that the scheme represented "a massive boost of confidence in the future of London", and that "London needs offices that meet today's and tomorrow's needs if it is to continue to thrive."[48] Travelstead's move, while opportunistic, was a direct challenge to the City: if it did not want to accommodate the new financial players, then other locations could. It should also be recalled that, at the time, Paris and Frankfurt were

---

46 Centre for Policy Studies (1985) *Comments on the City of London Draft Local Plan of November 1984* CPS, London.

47 Centre for Policy Studies (1985) *op cit* p36.

48 Mallett L and Gardner J (1985) US "Star Wars" Scheme Set for Docklands *Chartered Surveyor Weekly* 13 June p776.

making overtures to challenge London's dominant position in financial services in Europe. Suddenly, the City was under threat, and it was no surprise that the Corporation radically revised many of the central tenets of its earlier statement.

In depositing the revised plan in May 1986, Michael Cassidy, then Chairman of the City Planning and Communications Committee, wrote in the forward that in formulating the plan, the Corporation had:

> sought to strike a balance between providing adequate office accommodation for the financial services industry, which predominates the City, and at the same time maintaining the unique character and quality of the townscape of the City.[49]

Indeed, the revised *Draft Plan* had absorbed some of the key criticisms of its predecessor. In an important development, the new *Draft Plan* recognised the significance of the space requirements of the City companies. Economic policy number two aimed:

> To encourage office development which meets the requirements of new office technology and which is flexible to cater for variations in office layout and use.[50]

The new attitude of the Corporation towards development was welcome. Nevertheless, two critical conclusions are inescapable. First, the Corporation had left itself open to the widespread opposition to the initial *Draft Plan* by failing to consult its key constituency. The occupiers knew what was happening to their businesses (it did not take the Centre for Policy Studies long to ask them). Discussions would have avoided many of the fundamental flaws of the *Draft Plan*. Second, if consultation with occupiers during preparation of the *Draft Plan* had occurred, then the Corporation could have anticipated the major effects of Big Bang on demand for office space. As it was, they were caught off guard and faced with a hostile development industry eager to satisfy the pent-up demand. The Corporation's only option, made all the more necessary by the revitalised Canary Wharf scheme (under its new owners Olympia & York), was to take the pressure off pent-up demand by rushing through a swathe of consents that were to trigger one of the

---

49 Corporation of London (1986) *Local Plan Written Statement and Proposals Map* Department of Architecture and Planning.

50 Corporation of London (1986) *op cit* p24.

largest development booms in the City's history. But, yet again, it had reacted to rather than anticipated the changing dynamics of demand.

At the same time as the Corporation was rewriting its local plan, central government was, once again, gearing up for a major intervention in the planning process — this time to the benefit of the office economy. Government had signalled its intent with respect to the planning system, and particularly The Town and Country Planning (Use Classes) Order 1972, in its 1985 White Paper *Lifting the Burden*. The Use Classes Order (UCO) contained 18 categories of use for buildings and land, which had remained unchanged since 1948. The UCO controlled development by requiring that consent be granted for a building's use to change from one class to another. Applications for consent were typically time consuming for applicants, and used large amounts of manpower within local planning authorities. In addition to these process issues, it was also becoming clear that the classes had not kept pace with the changing needs of occupiers, particularly in the emergent high-technology industries and the service economy.

Following industry consultation, the government published *The Town and Country Planning (Use Classes) Order 1987*. The new UCO reduced the old 18 classes to 12 but, perhaps most significantly, introduced a new Business Use Class, or B1. This combined the old classes of offices and light industrial, together with laboratories, R&D and studios. From this apparent tinkering with a piece of planning legislation sprang one of the most profound changes in the office property market of the whole post-war period. The change in legislation had a major impact in city and town centres, where it allowed the conversion of light industrial buildings that had stubbornly clung on to their expensive, central locations simply because conversion was too difficult, and often because the local authority sought to protect "productive" jobs (and buildings) against the further spread of office jobs. But perhaps the even greater impact of the new legislation was that it resulted in the proliferation of an emergent building type and the transformation of large tracts of land, often on the edges and beyond of built-up areas. The new building was the "high-tech building" and its setting the "business park".

During the early-1980s, the technology industries were growing rapidly. Such companies were looking for a new type of building that allowed them to accommodate office and clean production activities into a single, flexible and simplified building type. The traditional office was, physically, too restrictive. They wanted to put office space, laboratory space, and elements of light production, assembly and storage all in the same building. On top of this, they wanted to be able to change the configuration of the space as the needs of their businesses dictated. Many such companies were experienced in the North American market, where business parks had become commonplace. These kinds of buildings were not available in traditional office centres.

The development industry responded by providing high-tech buildings, typically simple, two-storey buildings that allowed for a mix of office and production/warehouse. The early examples were characterised by their brightly coloured cladding. However, these early buildings were little more than smartly designed light industrial units. The earliest examples, starting in around 1980, included Abingdon Business Park, Kembrey Park in Swindon and Aztec West, near Bristol. To cope with the growing demand and to overcome the restrictive nature of the UCO, certain planning authorities began to grant planning consents with special conditions and others began to reach agreements outside the UCO.

As the market matured, a more sophisticated building type emerged that looked more corporate but still provided genuinely mixed space. The early phases of Stockley Park typified this kind of building, as did Frimley Business Park, Winnersh Triangle in Reading and Capability Green at Luton. These parks were typified by higher-quality master planning and the buildings included atria and generally higher-quality materials. It is significant that Stockley Park, one of the earliest and perhaps the most successful park of its genre, was strongly influenced by research into occupier needs by design firm DEGW, particularly of founding partner John Worthington, which itself was commissioned by developer Stuart Lipton of Stanhope Properties. The research undertaken for Stockley was highly influential in convincing government of the need to revise the UCO as well as setting the standard for the new business park market. The success of this partnership between developer and advisor is all the more remarkable given that the same team was, simultaneously, having a similar impact on the City of London (see chapter 7).

Pressure continued to grow on the increasingly outdated UCO, and, in June 1987, the new Order was introduced. This formalisation of what had by now been happening by stealth for several years swept in a third phase of evolution in which the high-tech, mixed-use schemes yielded to straightforward office campuses for corporate head offices from a host of different sectors. The impact of the legislation was dramatic. Of course, change of use also meant change of value: the new legislation meant that suddenly developers could convert land and buildings that had previously been consented to accommodate light industrial uses into the new business use class. The temptation to pile in and benefit from the uplift in value led to a flood of new developments.

The new legislation underpinned one of the largest-ever speculative development booms. By 1990, there were nearly 800 developments calling themselves business parks; around 4.5 million sq m (48 million sq ft) had been built; a further 1.5 million sq m (16.5 million sq ft) was under construction, and a massive 13.7 million sq m (148 million sq ft) had been granted consent.[51] Thus, within less than 10 years, a new form of demand emerged; enabling planning legislation was enacted, and the market moved from starvation to glut. This was not a cyclical phenomenon but a structural one.

A new approach to strategic planning

Government abolished the GLC in 1986 and along with it the strategic planning authority for London. Responsibility for strategic planning was absorbed into the government's own responsibilities. However, perhaps learning from the experience of the Corporation of London's Local Plan in 1984, and recognising that a complex world city such as London needed at least some form of land use planning framework, and overcoming ideological concerns over interventionism, the government set up the London Planning Advisory Committee (LPAC) in 1986. The LPAC comprised representatives from each of London's 33 boroughs, and its remit was to provide the Secretary of State with planning advice during the preparation of strategic planning guidance for London.

The Committee published a report on the principal *Policy Issues and Choices for the 1990s* in January 1988,[52] which was then subject to consultation before publication of the *Draft Strategic Planning Advice* in June.[53] Finally, in October, the *Strategic Planning Advice for London* was published.[54] This last document summarised the advice that the LPAC

---

51 King A and Bryant S (1990) *Living with B1: UK Business Parks 1979–1999* Applied Property Research, London.

52 London Planning Advisory Committee (1988a) *Policy Issues and Choices: The Future of London in the 1990s* LPAC, Romford.

53 London Planning Advisory Committee (1988b) *Draft Strategic Planning Advice* LPAC, Romford.

54 London Planning Advisory Committee (1988c) *Strategic Planning Advice for London: Policies for the 1990s* LPAC, Romford.

wished to give on the scope and content of the Secretary's Strategic Planning Guidance; and it dealt with planning problems that the LPAC believed would probably not be included in the Guidance.

In its *Policy Issues and Choices* document, the LPAC proposed a fourfold vision for London. This vision comprised:

- London as a civilised city offering a high quality of environment for all Londoners
- London as a world centre of international trade and business
- London as a city of opportunities for all
- London as a city of stable and secure residential neighbourhoods, capable of sustained community development.

The advice argued for a more interventionist style of planning than the Secretary was anticipating, with the greater use of planning measures to achieve a balance between economic growth and social and environmental considerations.

In the section on economy and employment, the report noted that employment in London fell from 4.5 million in 1966 to 3.5 million in 1984, and that there should be no return to the decentralisation policies of the 1960s and 1970s. In order to stem the loss of jobs, the report continued, the broad goals of the 1990s should be to foster economic growth and regeneration. The advice recognised the need for flexibility in planning by suggesting that, in the face of economic uncertainty:

> Planning policies to meet the resulting accommodation requirements will have to be contingent on different possibilities, and be responsive to demands which could change quite rapidly over short time periods.[55]

The LPAC argued that strategic guidance should promote and support London's international and national roles by the accommodation of those sectors that export their services and products outside London. This could be achieved in part by encouraging the expansion of large-scale business uses in a "core zone in central London, in West Docklands, and at a limited number of key public transport interchanges".[56] This, it argued, could involve a growth of around 300,000 jobs by 2001 (broadly equivalent to the size of the City of London

---

55 LPAC (1988a) *op cit* p18.
56 LPAC (1988a) *op cit* p19.

workforce). A major failing of the report, however, was that it offered no strategic advice on the potential demand for office growth in central London: "The Committee has attempted to estimate industrial and commercial requirements in London. It has concluded that the essential information required is not available."[57]

It is curious, to say the least, that three decades after central and metropolitan government first began to contemplate and prepare policies to control office activity in London that such an admission could be possible. However, despite the absence of relevant information, the committee did argue that central London's international and national role as a centre for business, financial services, transport and communication networks "should be supported" and that "London must be able to offer high quality office sites in central London and a number of strategic centre locations."[58]

The report noted that there was a current development pipeline of around 4 million sq m (43 million sq ft), with further commitments of more than 3.7 million sq m (40 million sq ft). It argued that if the relevant sectors were unable to sustain their recent levels of growth, then the sort of retrenchment that occurred in the early-1970s and 1980s should be anticipated. It argued that, at "the highest possible growth levels", there could be demand for a further 5 million sq m (54 million sq ft) of new business floorspace "over and above the existing pipeline and other likely commitments".[59] While the benefit of hindsight has shown the forecasts to be somewhat optimistic, the message was clear: the broad thrust of the LPAC's approach was one of encouraging economic development and providing all business with the space it needed. The Secretary of State's draft response was a much shorter document (17 pages, plus one map) that stressed the need for planning to focus on land use planning "to facilitate development while protecting the local environment".[60] The Guidance argued that the primary purpose of the newly established Unitary Development Plans was to provide "a framework for development control. This guidance therefore deals with matters that are directly related to the use and development of land".[61] The clear message in

---

57 LPAC (1988a) *op cit* p19.

58 LPAC (1988a) *op cit* p21.

59 LPAC (1988a) *op cit* p22.

60 Department of the Environment (1989) Draft *Strategic Planning Guidance for London* DoE, London p2.

61 DoE (1989) *op cit* p2.

this statement was that borough councils were expected to avoid many of the broader social and economic issues that had been brought into borough plans within the framework of the GLDP and were, instead, to concentrate on the core subject of land use planning. This meant a sharper focus on the office economy that, by this stage, had become such a dominant facet of the urban scene.

The Guidance emphasised the role of the private sector in the regeneration of London, and argued that "boroughs should adopt a positive, flexible and realistic approach to business development throughout London".[62] Such a philosophy was in sharp contrast to the anti-development stance adopted by the GLC in the 1970s and early-1980s. The draft Guidance, in effect, was directed at shifting the balance in land use planning away from one in which an applicant needed to justify a scheme (within the normal framework of development control), to one in which the local authority would have to justify a refusal. Five key statements in the Guidance illustrate this shift in balance:

- development in central London should not be restricted to a tightly drawn core zone
- UDPs should reflect the changing needs of industry and current or likely future demand for such development
- boroughs should not seek to distinguish between activities within the B1 Use Class
- boroughs should not reserve land for general industrial use when there is no realistic prospect of such use materialising
- a local planning authority is not entitled to treat an applicant's need for permission as an opportunity to obtain some extraneous benefit or advantage.

Clearly, the government was taking a more positive stance towards the growth of the office economy in London than had been the case for decades. The Guidance set the tone for the 1990s, and provided a lead for strategic policy makers to follow. By the early-1990s, a far more accommodating policy framework for the development of the office economy was emerging than at any time since the war.

Slowly but surely a new understanding of the office economy was emerging within public policy. For example, a study commissioned by

---

62 DoE (1989) *op cit* p4.

the LPAC urged a new strategic urban framework for London,[63] and presented a more sophisticated understanding of the role of the office economy in the late-20th century than anything that had preceded it in planning policy terms: "Wealth creation in world cities is to be found in the agglomeration and network of interlocking and mutually supportive businesses serving world markets with products and services based on knowledge, information, technology and creative skills."[64] In the LPAC's first five-yearly review of its advice to government (Regional Planning Guidance (RPG) Note 3), a new strategic context specifically for offices was included that recognised that London's future as a world city was dependent upon the financial and business services sectors. It was not the prescriptive kind of guidance of bygone years, in which strategic policy had sought to directly steer office development, but rather was aimed at reducing uncertainty "by improving the availability of strategic information to planning authorities, and to help the market operate more efficiently by lessening the risks of developers and investors misreading it ..."[65] This was a major step forward in terms of providing the kind a information-rich environment that was a prerequisite for addressing the volatility of the development industry that was at least in part due to a lack of market-wide information.

The early- to mid-1990s were dominated by the recession and, consequently, there was little pressure to deal with increasing demand for office space in public policy. Indeed, RPG3 specifically sought a shift of emphasis from providing further office supply to managing the surplus. The next major event to influence the office market was yet another change to the strategic management of London. This time, and under the guidance of the new Labour government of Tony Blair, strategic management of the capital was to be introduced, although in a more modest way than the all-embracing GLC of earlier years. Following American and European experiences, a city mayor was to be elected, and the mayor was to head a body called the Greater London Authority (GLA), with effect from July 2000. Following a brief squat in a non-descript office in Victoria, the newly elected GLA, under the mayoralty of the all too familiar Ken Livingstone, moved

---

63 Coopers & Lybrand Deloitte (1992) *London: World City Moving into the 21st Century* HMSO, London.

64 Coopers & Lybrand Deloitte (1992) *op cit* p3.

65 Simmons M (1994) Planning for Office Development: A Strategic Approach *Property Review* December/January p213.

into a smart new headquarters on the South Bank of the Thames adjacent to Tower Bridge. The GLA's planning remit included the preparation of a Spatial Development Strategy (SDS) for London, into which all UDPs were expected to dovetail. The SDS replaced the guidance previously prepared by the LPAC, and its aim was to provide an overall land-use strategy to support the Mayor's social, economic and environmental policies.

The first stage in the preparation of the SDS was *Towards the London Plan*,[66] a consultation vision document, which was followed by debate and then, in June 2002, the *Draft London Plan*.[67] The plan committed to a review of the long-held opposition to high-rise buildings, and looked to earmark a series of sites around mainline rail termini for high-density development.[68] The *Draft Plan* was then subject to an Examination in Public during spring 2003, before being adopted in February 2004.[69] The *London Plan* represented a sea change in attitude towards the office economy compared with its predecessors — some of which it must be said were signed off by the same Mr Livingstone now installed as Mayor. The plan began by recognising that "London has changed dramatically" over the past 20 years, particularly due to "the globalisation of many economic sectors, and the dominance of the finance and business sectors, frequently interlinked with dramatic changes in technology".[70] This was a prelude to outlining a growth-based strategy for London that had four key implications for policy:

- higher densities and a more compact city were to be expected
- the scale and phasing of development should be integrated with the public transport system
- the supply side should respond by providing commercial floor-space
- spatial priorities should help redress the balance of development.[71]

The plan stated that the Green Belt would be sacrosanct and good design would become paramount. It said that London would have to

---

66 Greater London Authority (2001) *Towards the London Plan* GLA, London.

67 Greater London Authority (2002) *Draft London Plan* GLA, London.

68 GLA (2002) *op cit*.

69 Greater London Authority (2004) *The London Plan: Spatial Development Strategy for Greater London* GLA, London.

70 GLA (2004) *op cit* p1.

71 GLA (2004) *op cit* p3.

grow without expanding beyond its boundaries. And it recognised the increasingly polycentric nature of London. The scene was thus set for a concentration of development in the core area and at strategic nodes. While the positive approach to the office economy was welcome, there was little surprising in any of these policy statements. What was perhaps surprising was the underlying assumption of growth upon which the plan was based.

The plan was based on projections suggesting an overall increase of 636,000 jobs through to 2016, and that "given the dominance of the office-based business sector ... the availability of suitable office accommodation is a critical issue".[72] Table 6.4 shows the plan's forecasts for financial and business services employment, with growth of 33% in London between 2001 and 2016. The table shows particularly rapid growth for Tower Hamlets (focused on Canary Wharf) and the City.

Table 6.4 Financial and business services employment, 2001–16

Area	*2001*	*2016*	*Change*	*(%)*
Tower Hamlets	58,701	145,451	86,750	(148%)
City of London	226,970	313,089	86,118	(38%)
City of Westminster	232,489	291,620	59,130	(25%)
Greater London	1,402,333	1,865,000	462,667	(33%)

Source: Marsh *et al*[73]

The plan argued that to meet the projected growth of 463,000 office jobs, London's 27.4 million sq m (295 million sq ft) stock of offices might need to grow by 8.1 million sq m (87.2 million sq ft) — a potential 30% increase.[74] There was little evidence or justification given for the projections in the plan, but six months after publication, its direct impact on the development industry was becoming clear:

72 GLA (2004) *op cit* p26.
73 Marsh G, Chippendale D and Sadek F (2003) *London Offices Policy Review 2002* London Property Research, London p84.
74 *Ibid*.

> Despite the 60% fall in demand between 2000 and 2003, and with top rents 40% below 2000 levels, developers ... are already lining up at the starting blocks, poised to set off another development dash. One significant factor behind this optimism is the *London Plan* .... The office development industry broadly supports the philosophy and policies of the *London Plan*, and accepts its office employment forecasts as being soundly based, and not wishful thinking.[75]

The impact of the plan's broader acceptance of tall buildings was also becoming clear. During the early-2000s, a host of proposals for tall buildings emerged. Table 6.5 shows proposals for buildings in excess of 30 storeys in 2005. The table suggests a high level of confidence in the London office economy and its prospects for continued growth.

Table 6.5 Tall building proposals in central London, 2005

Project	*Location*	*Area (sq m)*	*Start*	*Completion*
Riverside South (Bldg 1)	Canary Wharf	140,000	2005	2008
Riverside South (Bldg 2)	Canary Wharf	140,000	2005	2008
London Bridge House	London Bridge Street	60,000	2006	2008
London Stock Exchange	Old Broad Street	42,000	2005	2008
Paddington Basin (Ph3)	Paddington	56,000	2005	2008
Minerva Tower	Houndsditch	93,000	2005	2008
	Eastbourne Terrace	45,000	2006	2008
	Leadenhall Street	55,000	2004	2008
Citygate Ecotower	Aldgate High Street	150,000	2004	2009
	Folgate Street	100,000	2005	2009
	Bishopsgate	62,000	2005	2009
London Bridge Tower	London Bridge Station	65,000	2005	2009
Columbus Tower	Canary Wharf	30,000	2005	2009
Heron Tower	Bishopsgate	34,000	2005	2009
Indescon Court	Millharbour	60,000	2004	2009
Canary Wharf	North Quay	221,000	2006	2009
Southwark Tower	Newington Causeway	60,000	2005	2012

Source: CityOffices.net[76]

75 Marsh G and Chippendale D (2004) *London Offices Policy Review 2004* London Property Research, London p2.

76 *www.cityoffices.net*.

History will decide whether the *London Plan*'s central projections on growth were wishful thinking. However, what is clear from a contemporary viewpoint is that the projections appear to be optimistic. A few salient statistics suggest that a more cautious approach might have been appropriate. In mid-2004, around 3 million sq m (30 million sq ft) of office real estate stood empty in central London. Nearly half of this was in the City, representing a 16% void rate. While central London availability had previously peaked at around 3.3 million sq m (35 million sq ft), in 1992, following the largest speculative development boom in history, the current level of vacancy followed several years of economic growth and effective full employment. Take up of office space in central London in 2003 was even less than in the previous trough of 1991. Out of London, along the Thames Valley that has the UK's largest concentration of technology-based companies, the picture was no less bleak. A further 1.4 million sq m (15 million sq ft) stood idle, reflecting the aftermath of the misplaced expectations of the dot.com boom and the downturn in demand from US companies.

In addition to these hard facts of market dynamics, there is an overlay of change within corporate occupiers themselves, suggesting that the nature of their occupancy is changing and that current demand trends might be structural rather than cyclical. Discussed in more detail in chapter 9, these trends include the more efficient use of space and the widespread introduction of flexible working in which desks are shared, thereby reducing the overall demand for space. These trends are being driven in large part by the desire of office occupiers to reduce their financial exposure to real estate and to drive out cost wherever possible. In addition, and echoing what had earlier decimated the manufacturing industry, high employment costs have resulted in office jobs beginning to disappear overseas in a process labelled offshoring. The high cost of being located in London was reflected in the government's review of its own cost base. The Lyons Review,[77] published in July 2004, recommended the relocation of 20,000 civil servants to the regions.

Such trends add up to the possibility of structural change in demand for office jobs. Perhaps even the first signs that the office economy generally has experienced its maximal growth phase — just at the point that London's metropolitan authorities have, for the first time,

---

77 Lyons, Sir Michael (2004) *Independent Review of Public Sector Relocation* HM Treasury, London.

put in place a welcoming policy framework to accommodate the office economy. However viewed, the fact is that growth in the office economy in recent years has not been accompanied by increased demand for space in quite the same way that it has done historically. The spectre of jobless growth in the office economy, where increased output is not reliant upon increased employment, has begun to haunt the property market, and could haunt public policy as the fruits of recent policy measures begin to appear on the London skyline.

Learning from a Victorian polymath

Sir Patrick Geddes (1854–1932) was one of the founding fathers of modern urban planning. A great influence over Lewis Mumford, who featured in chapter 3, Geddes was one of the last great Victorian polymaths. He was a biologist (having been tutored under Charles Darwin's great friend and defender Thomas Henry Huxley at the London School of Mines), a botanist (holding the Chair of Botany at University College Dundee), sociologist (co-founding the Sociological Society in 1903) and urban planner. He was well travelled, having worked in India, Palestine and the US, and was extremely well connected. His ideas and studies roamed over broad swathes of history, the arts, science and philosophy. Like Lewis Mumford, he was a humanist, and greatly concerned over the increasing enslavement of society on the alter of technological progress, and the implications for environmental degradation.

But one of the most important aspects to Geddes' broad knowledge and experience was the fact that he understood the interconnectedness of life. His fascination for the organisation of social structures and their physical arrangement in space drew extensively from natural systems and philosophical thought. He saw society as a natural organism, one that required nurturing and caring for to ensure its long-term health, and one that depended upon the well-being of those other organisms sharing the same ecosystem for its own survival. He was a pioneer of environmentalism.

What Geddes would have made of post-war planning, and specifically its approach to the office economy, can only be guessed. But it is quite probable that he would have found the ad hoc, reactive and ill-informed measures described here as quite absurd in the context of his more holistic approach. Geddes' Outlook Tower in Edinburgh, complete with its camera obscura, expressed his vision of the flow of ideas and knowledge from the community to the wider world. Somehow, profoundly, British town planning lost sight of the notion of outward-looking policies for much of the post-war period, and took an inward-looking, myopic approach to the office economy.

Just as the supply of office space in London has lurched from phases of oversupply to undersupply during the post-war years, so has planning moved in to and out of phases of strict control and more relaxed regimes. What is clear is that throughout almost the whole of this period there was a failure to understand the office economy within the machinery of planning policy. The depth of this ignorance encompassed its role within the national economy; its internal dynamics; its locational needs and its requirements for built space. The central problem was that there was no feedback mechanism, nothing to explain how changes within the office economy were driving changing demand for built stock within city centres. Policies generally, at central, metropolitan and local levels were reactive, inflexible and unresponsive to the diverse characteristics and requirements of office occupiers. Manners and Morris concluded that the results of policy "were on balance quite modest" and that:

> Undoubtedly, the central lesson of intervention in the 1960s and 1970s must be that old and unadapted policy vehicles should not be employed to secure new policy ends.[78]

They continued:

> The original rationale for intervention was rooted in certain perceptions of the Central London office "problem". Subsequent policy changes were merely tacked on to that original initiative, and on to a set of attitudes and initiatives towards manufacturing industry.[79]

Only in more recent times, with the setting up of the GLA, has a more strategic and supportive public policy context emerged. The question that arises, however, is what should the policy framework be supporting? Having so dismally failed the office economy for most of the post-war period, there is a strong chance that the sudden impetus to provide for major growth in the office economy might be too late.

---

78 Manners and Morris (1986) *op cit* p145.
79 Manners and Morris (1986) *op cit* p145.

Perhaps, just as the office economy is reaching its maximal expansion, planning policy is about to release the development tap to produce large amounts of the kind of space that has been provided over the past 20 or more years. Very little evidence exists to support the growth assumptions within this strategy, which is built instead on theoretical econometric models of the future. However, there is plenty of evidence to suggest that major changes in working patterns are on the way (see chapter 9) and that the demand for office space is likely to change accordingly.

7 A Developing Understanding

A market without intelligence

The Boeing complex at Everett, Seattle is an awesome sight. At nearly 13.3 million cubic metres and 39.8ha (around 470 million cubic feet and 16 acres), the main facility is the largest building, by volume, in the world. Its 400,000 sq m (4.3 million sq ft) footprint is the equivalent of over 100 full-size football pitches. It houses an enormous production line, where every year around 100,000 visitors observe 747s, 767s and 777s being assembled. Viewing the scene from gantries positioned high above the ground the scale of the aircraft becomes curiously lost against the vastness of the internal space. Sections of fuselage, wing, tail plane, nose cone and engine coalesce to create the iconic shapes of the Boeings, prior to the interior fitting out. Hundreds of assembly workers are dwarfed by the scale of their enterprise, scurrying like worker bees attending their queens. The fact that such a complex product emerges at the end of the production within eight weeks of beginning leaves one in awe of the process and the people behind it.

There are a number of interesting parallels between the Boeing facility and the property industry. The aircraft are produced by an aircraft company, owned by a leasing company and leased by an airline — a very similar model to the property process with developer, owner and occupier. Each has a capital intensity broadly similar to a large city centre office building. Their components are brought from around the world to a specific site for assembly. The 777 has three million components provided by 900 suppliers. This is more complex but not entirely unlike the logistics for delivering the components and materials that go to make up a modern office building. And aircraft are built in low volumes, as are office buildings.

However, there are also some significant differences between Boeings and buildings. First, buildings are fixed in space, and are not built repetitively on a production line. Second, the aircraft have to be built to extreme design safety standards, whereas the typical unit of measurement on a building site seems to remain the width of a shovel, and buildings frequently leak. Third, and more seriously, while client airlines help design and tailor a base product to suit their specific needs, this is the antithesis of speculative property development. The manufacturers of the hugely complex and capital-intensive aircraft live a symbiotic existence with their customers, in which the needs of the customer inform the decisions and strategies of the producer. Tailor-made buildings are a rarity in the property industry, and the feedback loop from user to producer is, by contrast, very weak.

Until the 1980s, there was a total disconnect between customer and supplier in the property industry: there was no feedback into the design process; there was no co-operation in the procurement chain, and the product was of a "one size fits all" nature. Indeed, before the mid-1980s there was virtually no market or product research in the property sector. There was some technical research into materials and construction technologies at the construction and engineering end of the process; and some of the surveying firms, had research departments, but their main effort went into collecting transactional statistics, such as rents and yields, take-up levels, vacancy levels and so forth: all supply-focussed. There was virtually no research examining the nature of the industry's product in terms of, for example, its ability to meet customer needs, the durability of its specification or its quality as an investment. It is no exaggeration to state that, in the early-1980s, the product tests and assessments published in The Consumer Associations' magazine *Which?* were more rigorous than those applied to commercial office buildings.

For much of the post-war period, design was driven primarily by consideration of how cheaply buildings could be constructed. There was little product differentiation, either in terms of physical attributes or tenure arrangements; and there was virtually no consideration of what infrastructure would be required within buildings to ensure that they performed to an acceptable standard through their life cycle. During the 1950s, and particularly in the 1960s, the majority of speculative office development consisted of buildings designed and built with an inflexible floor plan, low-capacity service provision and a low-quality internal specification. Small, shallow floors were standard with a structural floor to ceiling height of 2.4–3.0m (8–9 feet), and limited potential for horizontal distribution of power, data and telephony cabling was common. The buildings were designed to accommodate highly structured and unchanging organisations, with staff in small or individual offices, and little attention was paid to the environmental or ergonomic conditions on the occupied floor. Centre Point, in London's West End, is a classic of this building genre.

Floors were generally finished in woodblock or tiles, with no provision for underfloor cabling; while suspended ceilings were largely unheard of — light fittings being fixed directly to the plastered ceiling. Single glazing, coupled with large window areas gave rise to problems of heat gain in many buildings. To let accommodation, the minimum of tenant facilities was required by the developer, and toilet areas and entrance halls were generally extremely basic. Externally, a standard concrete structure with coloured glaze cladding of little architectural merit was standard. The life expectancy of the buildings built during this period (around 50 years) seems, in retrospect, to have been ill-judged. Although it might be argued that the buildings were functionally successful for the time, in so far as they responded to the immediate needs of their users; it might also be argued that in planning and investment terms they were woefully inadequate. Buildings with expected life spans that would leave them still in use in the early part of the 21st century were being demolished for redevelopment just 20 years after they were built. Clearly, the buildings lacked the flexibility in their design to respond to the changing economic, technological and political conditions.

It is not simply with the benefit of hindsight that one can draw these conclusions on the inadequacy of buildings from an earlier period. As long ago as 1966, Marian Bowley observed that:

> there has been woefully little general interest in research, in economic rationality in design, or in the problem of providing building owners with adequate opportunities of choice. Co-operation between all the people concerned with the design and production of buildings has been, and still is, inadequate and, moreover, there is an astonishing absence of stimulus to either innovation or efficiency at various stages of the building process.[1]

---

1 Bowley M (1966) *The British Building Industry: Four Studies in Response and Resistance to Change* Cambridge University Press, Cambridge p325.

The industry was simply not organised to address the needs of the companies who occupied its buildings. There was no perceived need for intelligence, or research: the industry had a standard product (designed to institutional specification), available on standard terms (the FRI lease). Property's triumvirate of investor, developer and agent, in which the investor was the customer, the agent the intermediary and the developer the supplier, prescribed a passive process in which there was no impetus for innovation, and there was no reward for added value. The FRI lease secured the income stream, and the income stream was the triumvirate's *raison d'être*. This inertia helped to underpin the notion that property was a supply-driven process. The process was rigid and unchanging, and one of the side-effects was that the industry's products, namely its buildings, were, at best, mediocre and more often than not, of poor quality.

However, during the past 20 years, there has been a paradigm shift in the way in which the property industry understands its products and how they are used by its customers. Not least, the occupier of the office is now more widely recognised as the customer, rather than the institutional owner. The use of research in the development process over the past two decades has contributed to a better understanding of the role of property and, most crucially, helped inform decision-making in both its delivery and management. Our understanding of how buildings perform in use has changed dramatically in recent times, enabling a far more sophisticated approach to their management and specification. This chapter shows how our understanding of offices has evolved during the past 20 years by examining three strands of research: product development, market research and building performance.

Product development

In 1984, Number One Finsbury Avenue in the City of London was completed. The 28,000 sq m (300,000 sq ft) building was developed by Rosehaugh Greycoat Estates and designed by Arup Associates. But this was no ordinary building; for a variety or reasons it set the development agenda for the next 10 years and more. The building was a magnificent addition to the City's office stock and remains one of the most elegant commercial buildings in London. It was the first joint project of Godfrey Bradman and Stuart Lipton, then of Rosehaugh and Greycoat, respectively. Sometimes referred to in the trade as "Phase One Broadgate", the project was indeed the test bed for the development duo's most famous project on the adjacent site — that of Liverpool Street station and the neighbouring Broad Street station — where Lipton, with his new company Stanhope, again in partnership with Rosehaugh, was to create Broadgate, the most significant development in the post-war history of the London commercial property market.

The building was pioneering, although not entirely experimental. Arup had tried the striking, modernist approach on earlier projects of a clearly similar pedigree, including the Wiggins Teape building in Basingstoke and for IBM in Portsmouth. For Lipton, the watchword was evolution rather than revolution, after experimenting with Cutlers Gardens in the City and Victoria Plaza in Victoria. But Finsbury Avenue was infinitely more refined than anything constructed during the 1960s and 1970s, the period of the London speculative office market that produced such monstrous additions to the skyline as the "famous five" tower blocks on London Wall. Something had changed; but what exactly? Essentially, the building challenged three fundamental principles of the development industry.

The first challenge to accepted wisdom was on location. Sited as it was just beyond the sharply defined City boundary, it was one of the first City buildings to be built outside the square mile, in the London Borough of Hackney. It is necessary to be familiar with London politics in the early-1980s to fully appreciate this latter point, suffice to say that, in popular terms, the "capitalist City" and the "socialist republic of Hackney" presented rather contrasting neighbours. Much has changed since. While the building now sits comfortably among a number of other City buildings, all providing for the needs of City companies, in 1982 when the project got under way, "bank walks" (that defined the acceptable walking distance that banks could physically locate from the Stock Exchange) dictated that Finsbury Avenue was well beyond the pale. The building was fully let within four months of completion. Finsbury had successfully challenged the age-old monopoly of the square mile and shook traditional thinking about location.

The second area of development thinking that Finsbury Avenue challenged was that of design. It demonstrated that speculative buildings did not have to be cheap, built to a maximum density and to a minimum quality. Instead, its architectural style represented a significant break with tradition: it showed that speculative buildings could be bold, exciting and of high quality. The building has bronze coloured facades with horizontal metal grille sun screens and exposed cross-bracing, a stepped section, planted roof terraces and, what became a Lipton trademark, a large atrium with sculpture and large-scale planting. The finishes are beautifully detailed, and components such as balustrades and light fittings are made of fine metal sections, demonstrating craftsmanship in manufacture and attention to detail in specification. It is relatively low rise (at eight floors), with large rectangular 14m (46 ft) deep floor plates, and structural floor heights of 3.5m (11.5 ft). More importantly, it was specifically designed so that the internal environment could be repeatedly redesigned without compromising or being constrained by the longer life span structural elements. It was delivered to a "category A" finish, meaning that while suspended ceilings and raised floors were provided, internal fittings, such as carpets and partitions, were not, thereby avoiding the age-old tradition of new tenants ripping out developers' finishes in order to get a finish suiting their needs.

The third key principle that Finsbury Avenue challenged was that speculative development was, by definition, an entirely supply-led process. Indeed, what really set the building apart was the effort that was invested in understanding the needs of the companies that might be expected to occupy the completed space. This was the first time that a commercial developer had commissioned a building specifically to meet the needs of targeted occupiers and therefore represented a major shift in approach. It signalled the beginnings of a new approach to development in which the product was subjected to major advances in specification and design as the result of research into occupier needs. The essence of this work is captured here in order to convey how our understanding of office buildings has changed as a result.

One of the earliest signals that Finsbury Avenue was going to be different was the fact that Greycoat was a co-sponsor of the first study on the impact of information technology on the design of office space, the *ORBIT* study. *ORBIT* is an acronym for Organisations, Buildings and Information Technology, and the project was a multi-client study, carried out in 1982 by DEGW with Building Use Studies and EOSYS.[2] There were 10 sponsoring client organisations including, significantly, Greycoat. Privately published in 1983, under the authorship of Frank Duffy of DEGW, it examined the growing impact that information technology was having on buildings. More specifically, it was the first research to link the physical characteristics of buildings (such as floor

---

2 Duffy F (1983) *The Orbit Study: Information Technology and Office Design* DEGW/EOSYS, London.

size, depth, sectional heights and servicing capacity) to their ability to accommodate the emerging information technologies — both desk-top services such as personal computers and, critically, building automation systems. The fact that the study was a multi-client study, carried out with a number of companies involved in the office supply process, meant that the results got into the bloodstream of the industry very quickly.

The main findings of the research focused on the conclusion that information technology would have a profound effect on the design, management and occupation of buildings in coming years. *ORBIT* recognised both the direct and indirect effects of technology on design. Direct effects included, for example, that technology equipment would require novel forms of servicing, with an obvious impact on design in areas such as heating, cooling, ducting and so on. Indirect effects concerned the ways in which information technology would change organisations by, for example, changing the mix of skills required; introducing different forms of decision-making, and changing work patterns and locational imperatives. The report drew 10 key conclusions.[3]

- Most IT expected to have the greatest impact over the next 10 years already existed.
- IT was not easy to assimilate into office buildings.
- Demands of IT on new buildings were more stringent than assumed.
- Problems in accommodating computer equipment were not short term.
- IT would change the way in which organisations used buildings.
- IT changes patterns of space use in buildings.
- IT was changing the rules of office choice.
- Buildings vary greatly in their ability to absorb IT.
- Many existing buildings were in danger of premature obsolescence.
- Extensive and premature renovation of existing buildings would be expensive but inevitable.

Academia also produced some notable work around this time. In 1983, the Centre for Advanced Land Use Studies (CALUS) published a high-quality piece of research entitled *Property and Information Technology —*

---

3 Duffy (1983) *op cit* pp4–8.

the Future for the Offices Market.[4] The report demonstrated how IT would call into question many of the traditional beliefs upon which investment criteria were based. CALUS found that investors would need to be concerned with providing the flexibility to arrange office areas in different layouts, and in providing tenants with flexibility through the provision of a basic office shell. Also, they would have to pay increased attention to the quality of their offices because the standard of development was likely to become increasingly dictated by tenants. Anticipating the demand for business park space, the report found that office parks were one form of development for which there was likely to be increased demand, due to an increasing demand for property that is interchangeable between office and non-traditional office activities, including light assembly, research and development, and product testing.[5] Also from the same stable, in 1983, appeared a book by Anthony Salata entitled *Offices Today and Tomorrow*. Referring to the growing numbers of tenants dealing with "sophisticated products", Salata rather quaintly observed that they will "increasingly demand at least a modest degree of sophistication from the buildings that they are to occupy" and that those "in the property professions must be mindful of their needs."[6]

ORBIT was followed in 1985 by *ORBIT 2*,[7] which was placed in the North American context and was conducted by Harbinger Group Inc (a subsidiary of the Xerox Corporation) and Facilities Research Associates Inc. The report was published by Harbinger under the joint authorship of Gerald Davis, Franklin Becker, Frank Duffy and William Sims. The focus of *ORBIT 2* was on the growing interface between people, places and technology and it described the links between them giving guidance on how their interactions should be managed. The breakthrough of the report was that it developed a systematic and comprehensive building appraisal methodology that either consultants or occupier organisations themselves could use to rate the suitability of different buildings for specific organisations, or groups within organisations.

The overriding theme of the ORBIT research was that it set out consciously to address those technological forces of change that were

---

4 Centre for Advanced Land Use Studies (1983) *Property and Information Technology* CALUS Research Report, College of Estate Management, University of Reading

5 CALUS (1983) *op cit* pp1–2.

6 Salata A (1983) *Offices Today and Tomorrow* College of Estate Management, Reading p85.

7 Davis G, Becker F, Duffy F and Sims W (1985) *ORBIT 2* Harbinger Group, Norwalk.

acting on occupier businesses, and to understand these changes for their implications on building design. There were, however, a host of non-technological or technologically enabled changes that were also growing in importance. For example, the City was becoming more international and was beginning to confront the prospect of deregulation. Competition was driving a reorganisation of businesses through mergers and acquisitions. And the economy as a whole was being transformed, as traditional industries were eclipsed in their importance by the burgeoning office economy. From these big issues, it was apparent that the businesses that occupied office buildings would begin to make radical demands on their premises, and this justified a closer look through customer-focused research. Following the success of Finsbury Avenue, Stanhope led the way, this time through its joint venture with Rosehaugh, and largely through a unique collaboration with design and research practice DEGW. Together, they undertook some of the most important work that led to the transformation of property development into a more customer-focused and innovative process.

The first stream of work was a series of focus groups involving individuals from City companies. The discussions provided a forum to explore the pressures that were being faced by City businesses, how they were changing as a result, and how this change was having an impact on their use of buildings. The findings of the research were fed directly into the architectural briefing process for the buildings being developed by Rosehaugh Stanhope at Broadgate. A number of interesting facts emerged from the groups. First, it became quickly apparent that the individuals attending the workshops were unaccustomed to talking to each other about their premises. Despite the fact that they worked in a tightly knit community in the City, there was no evidence of a shared property experience, and the idea of gathering a group of people together for this purpose was an entirely novel concept.

Second, once gathered together, it also emerged that many of the participants actually had common concerns. Those involved were specifically selected because they were involved in some way with the business of the City, so there is no great surprise in this. But what emerged was a consensus around a set of building issues that would have to be addressed and resolved if City businesses were to avoid being hamstrung in their ability to respond to a changing financial services industry by inappropriate buildings.

Third, it became clear that the scale of change that the participants' businesses were beginning to confront was enormous. Many of the participants were not specialist facilities managers. A number were directly involved in their companies' core businesses and were able, through the focus groups, to bridge the gap between what was happening to their businesses and the issues that the focus groups were set up to explore. The focus groups revealed a deep-seated feeling among the participants that the buildings they occupied were inadequate to meet their operational needs in a rapidly changing business environment.

The results of the work were summarised in *Accommodating the Changing City*.[8] The report pointed to three trends changing the way business was done in the City: internationalisation of financial trade; increasing competition from large US and Japanese integrated merchant banking and securities houses; and proposed changes in the Stock Exchange rules and in the Bank of England. The report argued that these trends would have a profound effect on the organisational structure of the City institutions,[9] and that autumn 1986 would be critical because this was to be the time of Big Bang, when fixed commissions would end and single capacity would begin.[10] The key conclusions of the report suggested the emergence of profound changes in the demands of occupier businesses:

- shifts in the financial structure of the City being compounded by advances in technology
- growth and restructuring resulting in size and servicing constraints of many buildings
- larger floors, lower occupancy costs and flexibility to cope with change
- getting the right space becoming more critical than location and image
- the conservation policies of the draft City plan forcing companies to consider a location beyond the City boundaries.

A number of specific building requirements also emerged:

- floors of at least 929 sq m (10,000 sq ft) and up to 2800 sq m (30,000 sq ft), with uninterrupted space
- structural floor heights of at least 3.9m (12ft, 9 inches)

---

8 DEGW (1985) *Accommodating the Changing City* Unpublished report DEGW, London.

9 DEGW (1985) *op cit* p6.

10 DEGW (1985) *op cit* p8.

- finished floor-to-ceiling heights of 2.7m (9ft)
- highly serviced buildings with adequate vertical ducts, raised floors and zoned lighting, power and air-handling
- dealing floors of 18m (60ft) depth, very deep raised floors, support space to cope with data/telecoms needs, and boosted air-conditioning.

In 1985, these were radical demands that lay well outside the institutional specifications. They were also, as we saw in chapter 6, completely missed by the Corporation of London as it prepared to release its *Draft Local Plan* in November 1984. The focus groups were an enormous success, with a direct causal link being established between a changing business context and novel demands on buildings.

Such was the success of the work that Rosehaugh Stanhope and DEGW went on to investigate other parts of the office economy. Typical of the work was *The Space Requirements of Professional Firms in the City of London*.[11] Semi-structured interviews supported by industry analysis were used to investigate the business context of the leading firms, before implications for premises requirements were elucidated. Following deregulation of the financial services industry, professional firms were undergoing their own "little bang", although this was barely recognised within the property industry. The report began with some observations on generally held perceptions on the premises needs of professional firms:

- they generally share the same premises requirements
- they are not demanding space users
- they do not use much information technology
- the typical professional firm is slow to change.

The research found that professional firms had their own sub-set of requirements within the occupational market; that they were growing rapidly — often through merger, and that their needs were changing rapidly, especially in terms of location criteria, image and the uptake of information technology. More specifically, the work found that:

- they were being squeezed by the demand for office space from financial services, and would consider more fringe locations

---

11 DEGW (1987) *The Space Requirements of Professional Firms in the City of London* Unpublished report DEGW, London.

- they were growing at an average of 13% per year; diversifying and internationalising
- the amount of space they required had grown by around 40% since 1981
- they needed larger buildings and deeper floors to allow for two- and three-zone planning
- they needed more sophisticated provision of support space
- they were beginning to adopt much more intensive use of technology, both desk top and centralised, with implications for mechanical and electrical servicing.

The research painted a picture of change and upheaval within a sector that had previously exuded an image of stability and conservatism. For example, the report found that the use of IT by fee earners in legal firms was projected to increase markedly, and that their offices would be networked for electronic mail and to allow access to common data. The main implication of such a development was that cable management and raised floors would become more important to deal with highly cellular space and a high take up of IT. And this would mean significant changes to the institutional specification.

Some of the mechanics and findings of the research might seem a little naive in today's market. For example, it is difficult now to imagine a City legal practice without electronic mail and "access to common data". But, at the time, it represented a mind shift. The shift that was taking place was a fundamental one: from a position where for three decades buildings had been designed and built to institutional standards in a kind of "one size fits all" regime, to a position where product innovation through understanding and responding to customer needs became an acceptable means of developing buildings. The importance of the research also lay in the fact that it sought to discover what was happening within the businesses that occupied buildings and worked outwards to the implications for their occupancy needs and, ultimately, to the changing morphology of the city.

As well as pioneering product development through customer research, the Stanhope and DEGW collaboration also resulted in the first rigorous approaches to evaluating the qualities of buildings in a consistent and comparative manner. The earliest work, *Four Properties Compared*,[12] was also undertaken for the Finsbury Avenue project, and

---

12 DEGW (1983) *Four Properties Compared* Unpublished report DEGW, London.

compared its physical and design attributes with three other projects. The report covered areas such as floor efficiency; servicing (electrical and mechanical); parking and amenities; fitting out costs and service charges. The report was followed in 1986 by an altogether more ambitious project and perhaps the most influential report of the genre: *Eleven Contemporary Office Buildings: A Comparative Study*.[13] This unpublished report from 1986 set the benchmark for building evaluation but, more importantly, gave Rosehaugh Stanhope the ability to demonstrate how their user-led research had resulted in buildings that had a demonstrable set of advantages over competing projects.

The style and format *Eleven Buildings* were simple to use and visually pleasing, and the method gained widespread acceptance within the London property market in a very short time. The report itself made very clear:

> The purpose of this comparison of eleven contemporary office buildings in the City of London is to remedy the damaging lack of information about building performance. The data presented here are not about how buildings are constructed but what they can do — [but] what capacity they have to accommodate the new kinds of City organisations.[14]

The report suggested that the design community needed this comparative information in order to:

> put together building blocks based on user requirements in ways which are inventive and which will perform far better than the fragmented, under-serviced, poorly engineered, ugly structures, which were typical of developers' architecture in the City of London.[15]

At the time, Broadgate was the largest development in the City, but soon most developers were having their projects evaluated. The effect of the building appraisal techniques was to generally raise the quality of building specification in the City, as competitive pressures between developers led to a widespread adoption of comparative studies. Combined with the customer research described earlier, there emerged a general consensus that product development was a positive force in

---

13 DEGW (1986) *Eleven Contemporary Office Buildings: A Comparative Study* Unpublished report DEGW, London.

14 DEGW (1986) *op cit* p4.

15 DEGW (1986) *op cit* p4.

the market. Perhaps more significantly still, for the first time in commercial property development, there was feedback from users to the development and design process. Market gossip and the received wisdom of the agency community were dramatically relegated to irrelevance by a user-informed, research-led and systematic approach to design and development by a new kind of developer with a new kind of product.

Market research

Much of the research discussed thus far emanated from a new breed of developer and a new breed of research organisation with its roots in design. But, in parallel, the mainstream property industry also embarked upon an expansion into research, which grew quickly into a recognised and established sub-discipline of the property process. What brought this dramatic change about? What did property market research look like? And what impact did it have on the buildings that the industry produced?

Although the origins of property market research can be traced back to the stock broking houses of the 1960s, much of this research was on the indirect market, or property companies. As noted in chapter 5, these companies expanded rapidly during the 1960s, reinforcing the perceived security of property as an investment. Consequently, there was a growing interest in the companies responsible for its delivery, and there was a growing appetite for information that might throw light on the prospective fortunes of these companies. It was in the later-1960s and early-1970s that the first research teams were set up within the industry. The earliest were at Debenham Tewson & Chinnocks (now DTZ Tie Leung), Richard Ellis (now CBRE) and Hillier Parker May & Rowden (now also CBRE). However, these teams were, essentially, information providers: they collected data on market trends, such as rents, take-up and development activity, and they soon began producing market reports. Two of the longest-running publications, DTZ's *Money into Property* and *Office Rents and Rates*,[16] were both first published in 1975, with the former focusing on the sources, destination and allocation of investment, and the latter

---

16 DTZ (various) *Money into Property* and *Office Rents and Rates* published annually since 1975 by DTZ, London.

presenting data on prime rents and rates in the main office centres of the UK. Richard Ellis' *City of London Office Accommodation Survey* in 1976[17] was one of the earliest market-specific reports and set the general format for many to follow.

It was because of this origin in the surveying firms that property market research evolved in a particular way. Researchers, quite understandably, researched those areas that were of interest to the people who employed them. Thus, collecting data on rents, take-up and development activity provided the brokers who dominated the firms with metrics for the activities they were dealing in, literally, on a daily basis. The problem was that there was no room for independent commentary. It was not possible for researchers to make independent or objective statements on the fortunes of the market, especially when such statements might involve saying that the market was turning down. Consequently, property market research at this time involved the industry in "talking" to itself, having evolved a style of research that suited its established structure and process. The fact that none of this informed the industry about the evolving requirements of its customers failed to register any irony on those involved.

The next major step in the development of research took place following a report published in 1980 by the Property Advisory Group (PAG), the quango set up to advise the government on matters relating to the property industry. The report argued that:

> numerous developers and investors are in competition with each other, but with no common picture of the size of the market for new development or of all the schemes with planning permission or under development.[18]

The report went on to suggest that during the coming decade there would be "the need for greater spread and depth of information"[19] and that "the application of research effort to the information must be undertaken by the development industry itself."[20] The onus for more market research was thus categorically placed on the supply industry, and implicitly with those who had the resources to undertake such work: the large surveying firms. Richard Barras, one of the pre-eminent

---

17 Richard Ellis (1976) *City of London Office Accommodation Survey* Richard Ellis, London.

18 Property Advisory Group (1980) *Structure and Activity of the Development Industry* HMSO, London para 3.2.

19 PAG (1980) *op cit* para 4.9.

20 PAG (1980) *op cit* para 4.11.

research analysts, underlined the need for more detailed research: he argued that better and more up-to-date information about market conditions would help to moderate the inherent instability of the development cycle by encouraging a closer match between supply and demand.[21] The dearth of analysis in the development process was well-known. David Cadman and Leslie Austin-Crowe argued that: "too many projects have been undertaken entirely on hunches ... All too often development projects have been undertaken on the basis of superficial knowledge of the market."[22] The same authors recommended that "no development should be undertaken without proper analysis of the market for which buildings are constructed."[23]

Jones Lang Wootton (JLW), now Jones Lang LaSalle, set up the first research team with a broader remit in 1979, under the stewardship of Honor Chapman, and it was from this team that one of the earliest research reports to take up the challenge for more comprehensive analysis emerged.[24] Published in the same year as the PAG report, and like so many that followed, it focused on the City of London, but was important because it was the first report to take a more holistic view of the market. The report was expansive, ranging over the Blitz, post-war planning, floorspace and rental trends, future changes to floorspace, and, crucially, factors affecting future demand for space. The report involved a survey of 244 City firms and reported on their space standards, office sizes, tenure, floorspace requirements, location preferences and future building requirements. The location analysis exemplified the innovative nature of JLW's report in the context of supply-dominated research. It examined the spatial patterns of sector take-up; the type and quality of space both available and planned; and it asked questions about the requirements of users.

Incorporating the findings of a survey commissioned from Industrial Market Research, the report made many prescient comments. For example, on the unfolding impact of information technology the report suggested that the office of the future "will provide all the services that each individual needs in one integrated computer system with one

---

21 Barras R (1982) *An Office Development Information System for London* Centre for Environmental Studies, Paper 18, London.

22 Cadman D and Austin-Crowe L (1983) *Property Development* (2nd Edition) Spon, London p30.

23 *Ibid*.

24 Jones Lang Wootton (1980) *Offices in the City of London* JLW, London.

terminal at which he [sic] works."[25] Going on to note the relevance of this insight to the future demand for office space, the report noted that forecasts for future demand "range from massive reductions to little if any reduction overall, and continuing demand for modern up-to-date space."[26] This seems a little naive today and yet at the time — a year before IBM launched and legitimised its PC — and in a context where understanding the changing needs of customers was an entirely alien concept, the comments were indeed a major step forward.

It was this insight into the potential impact of information technology that was to provide market research with its first opportunity to become more demand-driven. The potential impact was seen to be sufficiently great that the industry simply had to get to grips with what it all meant in terms of changing property requirements. Herring Son & Daw (HS&D)[27] and Richard Ellis[28] quickly produced reports on similar themes. While HS&D called for changes to the Town and Country Planning (Use Classes Order) to recognise the need for "hybrid" (later B1) buildings, Richard Ellis drew, from its point of view, some comforting conclusions about the effect of technology on city centre office space:

> There is no evidence that floorspace requirements will be reduced over the next five years because of the usage of new equipment .... No link can ... be established ... between the application of microchip equipment ... and a reduction in demand for accommodation.[29]

In 1983, surveyors Savills published its *City Office Demand Survey*, in which it broadened the demand debate, and drew attention to the emerging needs of occupiers. It argued that new developments should recognise the need for large floors and services infrastructure, and provide "flexible accommodation with readily demountable features and low maintenance costs."[30]

Alongside this nascent demand research, data collection continued to grow. Within two years of the PAG report, JLW had set up its *Central*

---

25 Jones Lang Wootton (1980) *op cit*, p42.

26 *Ibid*.

27 Herring Son & Daw (1982) *Property and Technology* Herring Son & Daw, London.

28 Richard Ellis (1982) *The Impact of the Microchip on the Demand for Offices* Richard Ellis, London.

29 Richard Ellis (1982) *op cit* p12.

30 Savills (1983) *City Office Demand Survey* Savills, London p8.

London Offices Research (CLOR) monitoring reports (which were later followed by their *Greater London Office Research* reports). These sought to "provide a complete inventory of the office development supply pipeline in central London.[31] Published at six-monthly intervals, the reports met in full the need identified by PAG for a comprehensive picture of all the schemes with planning permission or under development. This new database added to those already available in the industry, and was to be followed by several more. However, what is evident from the frenetic activity of the early-1980s is the failure of the industry to respond to the spirit of the PAG recommendations. Despite notable examples, exploration of demand dynamics was a fringe activity, and there was no "common picture".

The need for more detailed research on the property market was underlined in 1982 by Richard Barras,[32] who suggested ways in which information on the office development market could be more efficiently co-ordinated, analysed and disseminated. He argued:

> Better and more up-to-date information about market conditions and the current and future level of development activity would make a crucial contribution to moderating the inherent instability of the development cycle, by helping to ensure a closer correspondence between supply and demand for new floorspace.[33]

In Barras' terms, "market conditions" relates to rental levels and it is significant that the proposed information system related specifically to the supply of space. The need to examine the structure of demand was not addressed at this stage. Barras' work was undertaken in conjunction with the Greater London Council, which was expected to be responsible for running the system. The proposals met their demise with the abolition of the GLC in 1986.

The growth of market research continued apace during the 1980s, with a number of specialist research firms springing up to help fill the gaps in knowledge, and market briefings became a regular feature. This was, of course, boom time in the market, and several mega-schemes were under way in the City, through London and beyond.

---

31 Jones Lang Wootton (1982) *The Decentralisation of Offices from Central London* JLW, London p1.

32 Barras R (1982) *An Office Development Information System for London* Centre for Environmental Studies, Paper 18, London.

33 Barras (1982) *op cit* p1.

There was suddenly an insatiable desire for information and developers were hungry for research that would give respectability to their own hunches. Of course, the party was not to last, and, in 1990, the economy fell into recession, changing the fortunes of the market researchers dramatically. As vacancy rates soared and property companies crashed (see chapter 4), fee income shrunk in the surveying firms and cash to support in-house research teams began to dry up. Many researchers in surveying firms at this time were supported within their businesses as non-fee earning resources and suddenly, teams that were marketed previously as providing "cutting edge", were highlighted as part of the dispensable overhead. Independent firms also struggled as many clients slashed their spending on research and fought for their own survival. Of course, the whole property process suffered and it was to be expected that research would absorb its fair share of redundancies. However, the recession revealed an underlying weakness of property market research. This was that its scope suffered from a narrow base, and it had not been absorbed into the mainstream culture of the property process.

Despite the positive lessons from the type of demand research outlined above, the property industry as a whole continued to undertake a style of research that suited its established structure and process. It is perhaps true that the 25-year FRI lease encouraged a culture in which the needs of customers were regarded as secondary to measuring the performance of the industry itself, which was deal-driven. The supply-led interpretation of the development process was encouraged by the view that "an office is an office" ...

> the suppliers of office space have generally been confident ... that, provided a building were reasonably located, space of any quality would eventually let. So they have not taken much interest in how occupiers use and run buildings.[34]

This static, homogenous view of the office was itself nurtured by the investment criteria of institutions whose priority was to appeal to as wide a segment of the demand market as possible. The problem with this institutionalisation of supply was that it "militates against innovation in research and the broader application of techniques to

34 Duffy F and Henney A (1989) *The Changing City* Bulstrode Press, London p29.

examine demand dynamics."[35] But the evidence of an emergent market dynamic was available for all to see. While the surveying community continued to publish numerous market commentaries, they failed to address externalities. But recession, continued technological advancement and its potential impact on working practices; political influences ... corporate management change and environmental pressures would all ultimately feed through to the demand market.[36] It was clear that research would need to:

> move from a retrospective mindset to a prospective, anticipatory framework, to get to grips with the demand side of the market. It must change its approach from a deterministic, linear ... supply-led framework, to one that allows for the full breadth of exogenous factors to be examined.[37]

The fact that market research had failed to integrate fully into the mainstream property process did not go unnoticed. A full 11 years after PAG, Sir Nigel Mobbs, a leading figure in the property industry and then chairman of Slough Estates, went on record as saying that researchers relied too much on anecdotal commentary rather than structural analysis. Choosing the first national RICS research conference to make his remarks, Mobbs went on to claim that research work failed to provide standardised, comparable information and too often reflected vested interests.[38] This latter comment was an observation on the practice of property research being used by its paymasters to talk up markets, rather than supplying rigorous appraisal. Mobbs was followed by no less than the Governor of the Bank of England, Robin Leigh-Pemberton. He was moved to comment, a full 13 years after PAG, that he was "surprised at the relative lack of consistent comprehensive data on the property markets and the apparent lack ... of research into the functioning of those markets."[39]

Notwithstanding these concerns over the direction of research, the

---

35 Guy S and Harris R (1995) *Property in a Global Risk Society: Towards Marketing Research* University of Newcastle, Dept of Town & Country Planning, Working Paper 47 p132.

36 Harris R and Cundell I (1995) Changing the Property Mindset by Making Research Relevant *Journal of Property Research* Vol 12 p77.

37 *Ibid.*

38 Cited in: Shrouder S Mobbs: Researchers Retaliate *Chartered Surveyor Weekly* 24 January p12.

39 Bank of England (1993) The Role of Property in Our Economic Life *Bank of England Quarterly Review* February 1993 Vol 33 No 1 p108.

depth of the property recession led many of the larger investment institutions to commit resources to the search for more predictive modelling techniques. This was an attempt to make property more transparent and comparable to other investment vehicles, such as gilts and equities. However, its impact was to reinforce the predominant supply-driven view within the property industry that it was somehow distanced from the dynamics of demand.[40] It failed to address the *functioning* of the property market and it fed the notion that that if enough variables were collected and analysed, then eventually the market's behaviour could be modelled. As funding poured into econometric modelling so research began "the pursuit of an unobtainable science of property analysis."[41] In doing so, it bore a striking resemblance to the drive towards quantitative techniques that swept through the social sciences during the 1960s and 1970s. It was at this time that geographers, for example, discovered *scientific method* and a near religious faith was placed in its explanatory powers.[42] However, as multivariate analysis and model building were adopted to explain urban form, settlement patterns and such like, so it became clear that increasingly sophisticated tools did not necessarily mean better understanding:

There is a clear disparity between the sophisticated theoretical and methodological framework which we are using and our ability to say anything really meaningful about events as they unfold around us.[43]

And just as the use of quantitative techniques in geography "failed to advance our understanding of the interconnectedness of the world,"[44] so econometric techniques in property largely failed to advance our understanding of the dynamics of the real estate market. This failure to explain was largely because such techniques cannot capture the way in which phases of development are "contingent upon contemporary circumstances — the key players, the planning framework, technical change" and their inability to project them forward.[45] The concern of

40 Guy S and Harris R (1997) Property in a Global-risk Society: Towards Marketing Research *Urban Studies* Vol 34 No 1 pp125–140.
41 Guy and Harris (1997) *op cit* p130.
42 Harris and Cundell (1995) *op cit* p76.
43 Harvey D (1973) *Social Justice and the City* Arnold, London pp128–129.
44 Harris and Cundell (1995) *op cit* p76.
45 Harris and Cundell (1995) *op cit* p76.

property research with cyclical phenomenon was symptomatic of a deterministic outlook in its fundamental thinking that restricted its ability to absorb an activity-based approach.

Econometric models are mathematical representations of economic relationships using linear equations. They use variables that have little to do with the internal dynamics of the market, thereby reducing their ability to identify causal relationships and therefore their usefulness in generalising trends. Formal forecasting methodologies, while very strong at identifying regularities in the patterns of property market behaviour, offer little scope for gaining useful insights into the underlying processes.[46] The context-free world of econometric forecasting, therefore, fails the basic test of improving our understanding. Like its parent discipline economics, it pursues a mechanistic and deterministic interpretation of the market. Its tools convey linear relationships when the system they are seeking to model is in fact a non-linear one. Just as classical economics relied on assumptions about the behaviour of the rational individual and the aggregated behaviour of individuals to arrive at a model of competitive equilibrium, so too with property forecasting. As long as the underlying assumptions hold, then everything is fine. But the property market is notorious for its sudden and violent swings brought about by exogenous factors.

The effort that was expended on the search for more predictive models reinforced this dysfunction at the expense of a framework for a better understanding. The market is not simply a set of rules waiting to be discovered, but numerous interactions and events engaging each other in a perpetual process of adjustment and realignment. It is constant change. One of the reasons for the rapid adoption of econometric modelling was that it was relatively straightforward. The alternative, activity-based approach was somehow too vague, too uncertain, and too difficult to contemplate. Yet, it is into this maelstrom of change that the industry places built structures that are expected to last for several decades.

None of this is to argue that econometric techniques are irrelevant, but rather to recognise their limitations. Such techniques "should not be accepted at the expense of proper analysis of the demand side, or the market as a system."[47] Commitment to property research that is rooted

---

46 Cundell I and Harris R (1995) In What Sense a Forecast? *Estates Gazette* Issue 9501 7 January p32.

47 Harris and Cundell (1995) *op cit* p76.

simply in a set of determining absolutes, the iron law of economic indices, encourages an elevation of short-term market conditions to universalised, fixed co-ordinates. This conceals the dynamism and specificity of property markets,[48] and reduces the ability to explain.

While the scope of market research was beginning to spread, its role remained largely a backroom one, and activity-based research remained a fringe activity. Even though a small number of specialists had generated some insightful work into the changing nature of demand, and although a few surveying firms had produced some prescient work, the focus of most research activity was on transactional information. More specifically, it focused on the balance between supply and demand — with demand defined as take-up. As seismic changes were taking place in the organisations that occupied the industry's buildings, and as they increasingly struggled to make their buildings work, the obsession with data in mainstream property firms continued and market data reports proliferated.

Why was it that the industry as a whole failed to absorb activity-based research against the backdrop of a rapidly changing customer environment? There are, it seems, two possibilities. Either the researchers failed to make their role relevant or no one was prepared to listen. The reality is probably a mixture of both. Because the locus of research was in surveying firms, it was difficult to create a "client culture" for research: the firms were deal-driven, and that set the tone for the research. Added to this, research grew most quickly in the heady market conditions of the 1980s. The speed of growth during this period was such that little attention was given to the opportunities presented by a more structured approach to research. Buildings were letting quickly and the industry as a whole cared little to do anything other than that which fitted the traditional supply-driven approach to property.

Building performance

While the market research of the mid-1980s outlined above correctly read many of the signals, research in the 1990s was different. Economic turbulence; corporate failure; the impending millennium and the rapid changes brought about by ICT induced a sense of fear and uncertainty

---

48 Guy and Harris (1997) *op cit* p126.

in society generally, and the specialist world of property research was not immune from the prevailing mood. It is during such periods of great change that a general sense of uncertainty can lead to the questioning of long-accepted truths; but it is also during such times that short-term fads can be accepted as long-term truths. The danger for research, especially in a commercial environment, is that it can get caught up in the momentum of the latest fashions, and fail in its role of sifting signals and sorting the real from the ephemeral. Contemporary changes can be taken out of context and treated as somehow unique, with fashionable theories distancing themselves from even the recent past. The sobriquet "post-modern" as applied to architecture and art is a classic of its kind; no matter what went before; today is different. So it was that a number of questionable streams of thinking took hold in the real estate market. For example, the sharply increased focus on cost reduction was taken as a cue for predicting massive reductions in the need for offices, and the new or "post-modern office" came into vogue. The following example illustrates the approach to the new office well.

For a variety of reasons, many desks are empty at various times during the average working day. For example, people leave their desks to attend meetings; to have lunch; to visit clients. They also take holidays, sick leave and go on training courses. Typical estimates put this vacancy figure at 40%, and in some organisations or parts of organisations it is said to rise to as high as 60%. Surely, the argument went, this must represent waste that can be turned to corporate advantage? One of the earliest proponents of this approach was consultant and writer on strategic planning, Bruce Lloyd.[49] He contrasted what he thought of as the cavalier use of office space with the pressure to utilise "major capital assets" such as coal mines and car assembly lines 24 hours a day, 7 days a week and nearly 52 weeks a year. He said of office buildings: "they stand empty and unoccupied for longer periods as the white-collar working week shortens and holiday periods lengthen."[50] He then went on to attack utilisation specifically.

Starting with 365 days as a notional 100% usage, Lloyd immediately reduced this to 260 days (71%) to allow for a five-day working week.

---

49 Lloyd B (1990) Office Productivity — Time for a Revolution? *Long Range Planning* Vol 23 No 1 pp66–79.

50 Lloyd (1990) *op cit*, 1990 p66.

He then took annual leave (25 days) and bank holidays (seven days) to reduce this figure to 228 days (63%). After allowing for the eight-hour day (a utilisation rate of one-third), the 228 days falls to 76 (21%). To this calculation is then added an allowance for lunch periods; illness; lateness and early leaving. For these, Lloyd deducted another 20% to bring effective use down to 57 days (or 16%). As if this wasn't enough, Lloyd went further. He took account of time spent by people organising their social activity, time spent on organisational issues; time spent "on the road" and time lost due to people operating at "little more than 50% efficiency". After all this, Lloyd concluded that the real utilisation figure could be closer to 2–3%, suggesting that not many "factories or power stations are allowed to waste assets on such a prolific scale."[51]

The timing of the article could not have been better. It fitted the cost-cutting agenda of the early-1990s perfectly and was seized upon with gusto by eager consultants and real estate managers. But it was also a poorly reasoned argument. There was, for example, no recognition of opportunity cost, and the basic premise was that cost-reduction strategies would lead to cost-elimination strategies. But it encouraged a more alarmist fringe that predicted the demise of the office altogether. Typical of the genre was the "post-Fordist" agenda.[52] Laing suggested that business organisations and the world economy were being transformed from the mass production systems of Fordism "to a new world of post-Fordism."[53] This sweeping statement was followed by the claim that businesses would have to resolve an acute contradiction: the need to minimise costs while maximising added value and creativity. However, cost cutting and value creation do not have to be contradictory. They can simply be twin elements of an integrated business strategy. But the logic led to the claim that the "conventional office now inhibits the more creative and innovative patterns" of work that have "emerged out of conventional Fordist organisations."[54] Laing pushed the logic to suggest that "the fetters of the conventional office workplace are frustrating the demands of new uses of information technology and creative forms of organisation".[55]

---

51 Lloyd (1990) *op cit*, 1990 p67.

52 Laing A (1991) The Post-Fordist Workplace: Issues of Time and Place *Facilities* Vol 9 No 8 pp13–18 MCB University Press.

53 Laing (1991) *op cit*, p13.

54 *Ibid*.

55 *Ibid*.

This analysis was then used as the basis for a wholesale assault on the very existence of offices: "the office workplace is an anachronism".[56] Such dramatic writing detracted from what was in fact a sound underlying observation, ie that as organisations became more focused on squeezing out costs they would need to become more flexible in the way that they used real estate. Laing's error, in common with many others, was to focus on the physical resource as the inhibitor of change. This error, design determinism, was widespread, and was driven by the notion that the answer to business' desire for organisational flexibility and cost efficiency could be delivered through a new workplace design agenda. What was needed, and later proved to be the case, was a far more sophisticated approach to the delivery of integrated people, space and technology services within organisations and across space: one that also addressed the undercurrent of change that was driving change in corporate organisations for the long term.

However, in the short term, alarmist writing such as that above helped to set the tone for an approach to the design of office environments on a more general level. It took a single aspect of management focus, ie cost reduction, and built a design philosophy around it. Before long, design firms were sending teams of researchers into clients' organisations to undertake "time utilisation surveys". Ironically reminiscent of Fred Taylor's early methods, such studies "proved" that a certain amount of space was vacant at any one point in time and, therefore, the client could reduce its space commitment. Companies began to implement ambitious schemes to reduce the amount of space they occupied by reducing the number of desks they occupied.

But the approach was based on three false premises:

- first, that cost cutting would lead to cost elimination
- second, that technological gadgetry would itself drive change
- third, that offices performed a one dimensional, single functional aspect to individual and corporate life.

The premises were wrong. And they remain wrong. They demonstrate the dangers of context-free, future-watching from highly specialist perspectives: in short, reductionism. This is the tendency to divide the world into ever smaller boxes until finally we find one that helps to confirm our expectations. This process of description and categorising

---

56 *Ibid.*

is comforting because it gives us a level of simplicity that is not otherwise there. The danger comes when we use these specific tools to generate prescriptive models that claim to provide a more general understanding. And this is precisely what the property industry did with the "new office" agenda.

As the economy recovered, the focus of attention in research shifted again, this time towards understanding the performance of buildings in use, rather than simply their physical parameters. The context for this shift included a more structured approach to evaluating overall business performance. For example, Robert Kaplan and David Norton[57] undertook a year-long research project with 12 companies at the leading edge of performance measurement to devise a "balanced scorecard". This scorecard comprised a set of measures to give top managers a fast but comprehensive view of their businesses. The authors argued that it provided the answers to four basic questions:

- How do customers see us? (Customer perspective.)
- What must we excel at? (Internal perspective.)
- Can we continue to improve and create value? (Innovation and learning perspective.)
- How do we look to shareholders? (Financial perspective.)

It was but a small step to translate these business-wide questions into a framework for setting down the objectives of a real estate function. And this is exactly what happened. For example, Deloitte & Touche's 1997 survey[58] of the impact of business re-engineering on real estate made six recommendations for real estate executives facing re-engineering:

- Understand your company.
- Understand the company and its products' life cycles.
- Align real estate with the company's business planning and strategy development processes.
- Develop performance metrics and show value.
- Move to a customer service focus.
- Learn more about re-engineering.

---

57 Kaplan R S and Norton D P (1992) The Balanced Scorecard — Measures that Drive Performance *Harvard Business Review* No 92105 January-February p71.

58 Deloitte & Touche LLP (1997) *Impact of Reengineering on Corporate Real Estate* Deloitte & Touche pp13–14.

Joe Akinori and colleagues[59] referred to a new and strong focus on value-added service in corporate real estate. Specifically, the focus was on what corporate real estate was contributing to the company's bottom line or what value it was adding to the organisation. In other words, how does real estate management contribute to better products or services? How does it help the company focus on its core competencies? What does real estate have to do with staff productivity? And how does it help the company to strategically position itself to take advantage of the changing marketplace? To answer these questions, innovative approaches to measuring "value" were required.

Value assessment in real estate took the form of benchmarking and measurement. Edward Noha[60] identified four principal benefits of benchmarking in real estate.

- Identifying and measuring superior performance, which "allows companies to quantify real estate performance [and] set specific targets". This can then be communicated to "senior management in the businesses' own language: earnings per share, return on assets, cash flow, and so forth".
- Prioritising opportunities, allowing real estate managers "to focus scarce personnel resources on the areas of greatest value".
- Identifying solutions through best practices and processes by "examining the qualitative information collected to support quantitative performance data".
- Empowering the real estate function by focusing the attention of senior management "on past and future contributions of the real estate function", thereby significantly enhancing the status and credibility of the real estate function.

Hugh Nourse studied 11 corporations in an attempt to "compare how firms measure and monitor real property performance to achieve strategic goals." [61] He observed that the results of his work confirmed

---

59 Akinori J, Darwish A and Young J D (1993) Reinventing Corporate Real Estate and Facilities Site *Selection and Industrial Development* June pp769–775 IDRC, Atlanta.

60 Noha E A (1993) Benchmarking: The Search for Best Practices in Corporate Real Estate *The Journal of Real Estate Research* Vol 8 No 4 Fall pp511–523 American Real Estate Society, Austin, Texas.

61 Nourse H O (1994) Measuring Business Real Property Performance *The Journal of Real Estate Research* Vol 9 No 4 Fall pp431–444 American Real Estate Society, Austin, Texas p431.

findings from earlier surveys, which concluded "creating a separate information system for real property is associated with a tighter linkage between corporate strategy and real property operations". The "customers" of a real estate function are themselves varied. They include senior management (typically the Board); heads of business units; direct users (people who occupy space during the working day and, indirectly, customers of the business. The benchmarking process needs to address the needs of each of these disparate audiences.

One of the greatest proponents of benchmarking in the UK, Barry Varcoe, sought to ensure the management of value and outcomes rather than the more commonly measured and easily understood property-related metrics, such as cost per unit of space. Varcoe identified cost as an important yet inevitable side-effect to the main purpose in hand and suggested:

> In terms of achieving success from an operational perspective it is more important to measure the efficiency of the resources as they get used in processes (which itself will be a big influence on economy or cost anyway), the outcomes achieved by the processes, and whether those outcomes meet the needs of the consumers.[62]

On this basis, Varcoe proposed the "Four Es of property performance" (figure 7.1). Efficiency is a measure of making the best use of resources. Effectiveness refers to the degree of achievement of the outcome. And efficacy refers to the degree of relevance of the outcome. The diagram shows that economy, or cost minimisation, is a side-effect of achieving efficiency, effectiveness and efficacy.

What Varcoe and others had begun to do was to measure and evaluate the performance of real estate in the context of its contribution to the overall performance of the organisations that it accommodated, and in the context of its life cycle. These new approaches mirrored the growth in outsourcing and corporate PFI grew during the late-1990s (see chapter 8), when the need for a more holistic understanding of occupancy performance increased. The key driver for this was that in tendering, selecting and monitoring the provision of externally provided services, it became ever more critical to reach service level agreements, by which the quality of service provided could be objectively evaluated. Equally, those tendering for

---

62 Varcoe B J (2002) The Performance Measurement of Corporate Real Estate Portfolio Management *Journal of Facilities Management* Vol 1 No 2 p119.

Figure 7.1 The four Es of property performance

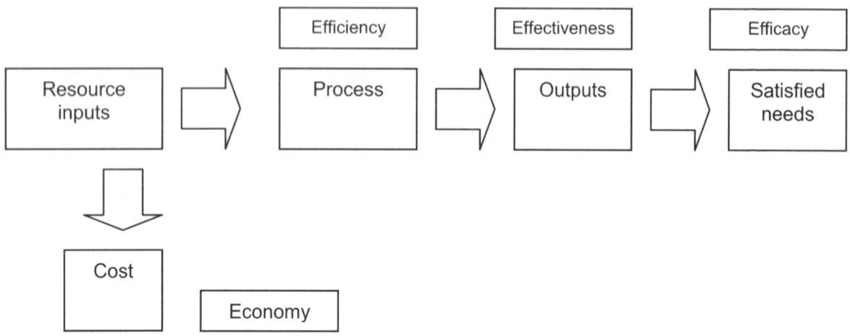

Source: Varcoe[63]

the long-term contracts needed a more accurate means of estimating what their cost base would be during the life of the contract. This need is explained when it is understood that the capital cost of providing a building, or upgrading it during its life, is dwarfed by the actual cost of operation — perhaps by a factor of 10 over a 20–25 life span.

The drive to whole life benchmarking led to the creation of companies whose specialisation was the development of databases for performance measurement. The most notable of these is the Occupiers Property Databank (OPD), a subsidiary of the Investment Property Databank (IPD). In the mid-1980s, the IPD had established itself as the industry standard for recording and publishing data on the performance of investment property against criteria such as capital returns, income returns, rental growth and capital growth. The OPD set out to repeat this success by setting up a standard method for measuring the performance of occupied property. The new database provides occupiers with reliable and objective benchmarks of their property's performance. It works on the same principals as the IPD in so far as clients are invited to submit data on their own organisation's occupancy characteristics, which are then pooled for broader analysis. Detailed results are made available to sponsoring organisations; while more generic results are released to the public. By 1999, the OPD was in a position to release the OPD Total Occupancy Cost Code.[64] The

63 Varcoe (2002) *op cit* p119.

64 OPD (1999) *The Total Occupancy Cost Code*, OPD, London.

report presented a comprehensive set of cost measures covering property occupancy costs (eg rent and rates); adaptation and equipment costs (eg fitting-out and furniture); building operation costs (eg maintenance and cleaning); business support costs (eg catering and telephony) and management costs (eg facilities management fees). The report was hailed in its introduction as being a step forward to helping occupiers track the totality of their costs using practical definitions. The drive to improve the performance of office property was also recognised in public sector offices.

The significance of the trend towards better measurement of space use and towards more formal feedback in the occupancy life-cycle is that it signified a new transparency in the use of information in the property market. Until the mid-1980s, a great deal of the market process relied for its success on the lack of information; it was the perfect imperfect market. Publishing research (as distinct from market commentaries) was frowned upon for its tendency to give competitors information that they might use to advantage. Even in these dark days, many years before the internet made the concept of "knowledge is power" redundant, it was obvious to many that releasing information improved the overall level of debate. Anyway, once the genie was out, there seemed little prospect of putting it back in the bottle. It is perhaps also significant that Rosehaugh Stanhope turned to a UK design practice that was heavily American-influenced in its approach for advice on product design. It is probably fair to say that at the time there was not a single surveying firm with the necessary skills to respond.

This chapter began by describing an industry that was working in a knowledge vacuum. The industry worked in an entirely opaque manner; it was untroubled by a concern to satisfy customer needs and it provided a product that was designed and priced to meet the requirements of the investor market rather than the occupier market. For much of the period after the war, the economy was space hungry: there was an overall shortage of space and it was a sellers' market. But, as we have seen, during the past 20 years much has changed. In the early years of this period, the product was much improved through better intelligence on the needs of occupiers. And more recently there has emerged a more sophisticated understanding of how buildings perform, and how they contribute to the efficiency and effectiveness of the organisations that occupy them. These are all welcome trends, but they are only steps along the way. One of the key problem areas remaining is a symptom of one of the industry's structural weaknesses referred to in chapter 4 — knowledge fragmentation. Research and knowledge continues to advance in the area of product development; and the same is happening in the area of building occupation through building performance research and metrics. But practitioners in each field continue to work in isolation, and there remains a highly fragmented feedback mechanism that limits the ability of the supply process to anticipate change and respond through product and service adaptation.

The Office as a Business Resource

8

Long-term planning, short-term change

In the midst of the Industrial Revolution, Benjamin Disraeli observed that change is inevitable, and in true Victorian style he added, "In a progressive country change is constant."[1] He was speaking at a time when western society was undergoing immense change and on the threshold of major advances, such as the introduction of electricity, the motorcar and the skyscraper, to mention but three world-changing innovations. Similarly, the notion of change within the office economy has come to take on similar qualities. Certainly the past 30 years have seen more or less constant change in the office environment and the organisations accommodated within them. It could not be otherwise given the changing technological, economic and social context that gives rise to its physical expression. Against such a background, how do organisations plan ahead? How can investors, for example, begin to decide what product to buy when future consumers are so ill-defined? Similarly, how can designers design buildings that won't be obsolete before they leave the drawing board? And what about the occupier? How does a business make a long-term commitment to real estate when it does not know what changes next year will bring to its business, let alone five to ten years' time? How can organisations possibly plan for the future and have any hope of being in control of their destiny when

---

1 Benjamin Disraeli Speech in Edinburgh, 29 October 1867, cited in: *The Times* 30 October 1987.

change is relentless? The law of initial conditions prevails, and nowhere have the implications of this situation been seen more clearly than in the dot.com boom during the late-1990s and its inevitable fallout.

During the 1990s, expectations for the internet soared higher and higher. It would, we were told, do little less than change the way we lived. It would revolutionise our patterns of work and consumerism; redefine the relationships between business and consumer and between business and supplier; and open up undreamt of opportunities through access to unlimited information, enmeshing individuals, companies, communities and societies in a virtual, global network. This new economy would release us from the shackles of locational friction that the old one imposed on our businesses, and create a foot-loose economy where innovation replaced profit as the main goal of business. Wanting to forget the lean times of the early-1990s and buoyed by a more recent stock market boom, City analysts jumped on to an already dangerously overloaded bandwagon. The stock market valuations of technology, media and telecoms businesses have since become legendary.

> The market capitalisation of Yahoo!, the leading internet company, has appreciated by 3,800% since 1996 and is now 480 times expected earnings for 1999. Yahoo! is worth more than Texaco or Merrill Lynch. America Online, the largest internet company, has risen by 34,000% since 1992 and is now worth more than 273 times expected earnings for the year to June. That makes it bigger than Ford or Disney. Both companies would be in the Japanese top 10, and AOL would be in Europe's top 10, ahead of Nestlé, Shell or UBS.[2]

The stampede for technology stock was so great that there was a hidden crash in the stock value of "old economy" companies. In the latter half of 1999 and the first quarter of 2000, when the dot.com hype was at its maximal phase of growth, £150bn was wiped off the value of Britain's leading industrial companies. This compared to the £50bn wiped off by Black Monday in October 1987.[3] Amid all the hype there was, again, the promise that technology would reduce our dependency upon real estate as businesses and consumers conducted their transactional activity across the internet. Retailers and "e-tailers" were seen to be locked in a battle for customers with only one possible outcome. Banks, insurance companies, travel firms, supermarkets — all manner of providers of goods and services — were widely

---

2 Taylor R and Labate J (1999) Age of the Day Trader *Financial Times* 9 February p23.
3 Waples J (2000) The Hidden Crash *Sunday Times* 5 March p5, business section.

predicted to become internet-based and, in the process, shed great swathes of unwanted retail outlets. Under such a scenario, who would need all those armies of "paper pushers" at head office?

Yet, by 2001, the rubble of the dot.com boom lay all around. Established companies joined the list of casualties, alongside new dot.coms, such as Amazon.com; Boo.com, Buy.com, Etoys.com and Letsbuyit.com. In May 2002, the directors of WorldCom, America's second-largest, long-distance telephone company disclosed a massive accounting fraud, in which nearly $4bn of the company's expenses were reclassified as capital expenditure. Once valued at $180bn, the business was pushed to the brink of extinction. AOL's all-share take-over of Time Warner marked the summit of the dot.com boom. Afterwards, shares plummeted; advertising collapsed and huge debts were racked up. Shares fell from a high of around $56 in mid-2001, to around $12 by late-2002. Similar fates befell Adelphia Communications, Cisco Systems, Global Crossing, NTL, Qwest Communications, Tyco International and Xerox Corporation. It was an extraordinary chain of events that saw so many companies lose 90% of their share value in the space of two years. Yet, within this hugely volatile environment, the businesses had to first acquire the physical environments to accommodate their expected growth, and then dispose of the space once it became clear that their growth expectations would not materialise.

While the dot.com bubble was an extraordinary event, it demonstrates clearly the rapidly changing business context within which office space has to be planned, procured and occupied. It also demonstrates the heightened sense of uncertainty that now pervades business planning compared with earlier times. In this sense, the way in which offices are planned and managed has begun to change dramatically in recent times. Offices are no longer regarded simply as inert, physical environments within which office processes take place. Rather, they have become part of the business infrastructure of the organisations that occupy them, and are increasingly planned and managed as one facet of corporate resource planning. Technology has driven this fundamental change in two ways. First, as buildings and the IT systems required to support them have become intertwined, so they have become critical to business continuity. Consequently, the office environment has assumed a complexity that demands a far more sophisticated management approach. Second, technology has fundamentally changed the way in which businesses organise themselves through space and time, bringing with it new structures and work processes to respond to competitive pressures and changing market opportunities. As a result, offices must be planned and delivered in a far more responsive manner. This chapter examines the evolution of new thinking in real estate management and speculates on the increasingly important role of integrated business resource management.

Building complexity and a new profession

At one level, an office building provides the physical environment within which occupiers undertake their work. Whether the occupier is a bank, an advertising agency, a local authority or a university, the built environment provides the envelope within which to accommodate the activities that define the organisation's *raison d'être*. In addition to the envelope, the building is expected to provide comfort and safety in the form of clean air, fresh water and sanitation, heating and lighting. Then, it is expected to provide the equipment necessary to undertake the work: furniture, computers, telephones, photocopiers, printers, equipment, and all the other paraphernalia that makes the modern office work. Finally, it provides the services to people's needs, such as vending, catering, meeting facilities and so on. All this comes together, every day, in the seamless provision of environment and services. Until it goes wrong: the hot summer's day when the air-conditioning fails; the morning rush when the lift fails; the day when the server goes down and there is no means of communicating with the outside world; or simply the ongoing niggle of a back pain caused by a badly designed chair or a poorly configured workstation.

Space should be a commodity, a resource, and an aspect of production. It should be available as and when needed; and it should enable productivity. This message has been emphasised throughout this book. It has been referred to as part of the activity-based approach to understanding real estate in so far as it focuses on the activities that buildings support, rather than the buildings themselves as financial instruments. Of course, we know that it is unrealistic to treat the activity-based approach in a vacuum because real estate has its own peculiarities that make it unique and, indeed, which have a profound impact on how it is delivered, managed and used. However, the activity-based approach provides a perspective from which to view the purpose of buildings, which can then inform the supply process. It is in this respect that we turn to examine the way in which occupiers engage with the property that they occupy.

During the post-war period, and particularly during the past 25 years, office buildings have changed from relatively simple structures to hugely complex items of business infrastructure. In the mid-1970s, only 15% of office units in the City of London were larger than 1000 sq m (10,760 sq ft) and over 60% of units were smaller than 300 sq m (3230 sq ft); the buildings themselves were uncomplicated and the demands placed upon them by the businesses that occupied them were relatively light. At this time, the City comprised predominantly small-scale offices, often in buildings that were built for different purposes. Only one-third of the floorspace was air-conditioned and the PC had yet to be invented, let alone occupy every desk. As was shown in chapter 7, rapid developments in the economic, organisational and technological landscape of the 1980s brought many of these buildings to premature obsolescence. By the late-1980s, technological capability and technology adoption proceeded in a kind of arms race in which more capability served only to increase the appetite of occupiers for more and more technological capability. As the bulk of occupiers caught up on one innovation, so there seemed to be a dozen others to succeed it. The knock-on effect for buildings was profound. The amount of cabling, the capacity and demands on heating and cooling, the power loadings and the proliferation of kit all increased greatly. As part of the arms race, entirely new building forms emerged, designed specifically to cope with this new Star Wars approach to office technology. The purpose-designed dealing floor was born. And it was not just the financial services companies that caught the bug. The traditionally staid environment of the accountants was changed forever when the leading firms began to intensify the use of their buildings, issue laptops to all fee earners and take away personal desks to introduce "hot-desking".

The market shifted almost overnight from no raised floors, to floors sometimes a metre deep. Air-conditioning became *de rigeur*. New spaces appeared in buildings — technology rooms, for example, where the kit was created, tested and monitored. And the buildings themselves took on new forms. The "groundscraper" was born at Broadgate in the City — huge (by historic standards) buildings with floors the size of football pitches yet relatively low-rise at around 8-10 storeys. As this revolution in building design was taking place, the buildings themselves began to assume a less passive role in the lives of their occupiers. Up to this point, there was little recognition that real estate had any impact whatsoever upon the performance of a company, or if there was recognition, the restrictions on the supply side meant there was little to be done about it: the "take it or leave it" approach of the development industry was uncompromising. In general terms, property was regarded as a necessity in the process of conducting business. It was often the role of the company secretary or finance director to pay the rent and deal with the managing agents on issues such as repairs, maintenance and security. In large organisations, such as the clearing banks and insurance companies, it often fell to line managers who had reached the extent of their potential in the core business, to move across and look after property. Sometimes there would be a "building manager" — whose responsibilities included managing the cleaners, making sure catering and vending were delivered, ordering supplies, such as paper, pens, and the other paraphernalia of office life at the time.

But the growing complexity of buildings was increasingly calling for more specialist skills and dedicated responsibility. The buildings were becoming business critical, in that if the building services failed, then so would the business: a one-hour failure in the systems inside an investment bank could be catastrophic. Unlike earlier times, when the building was simply the three-dimensional space within which the work process took place, now there emerged a critical inter-dependency between the space and the business. A new approach to the management of space was called for.

Real estate management first became a recognisable stream of business management in the US in the late-1970s, where it emerged in the industrial sector, before becoming established in the office sector during the early-1980s. It became recognised and practised in the UK in around 1983. In these early days, it was known as facilities management, taking more than 10 years to mature into a more broadly based and professional real estate management profession. Several other terms have been used, reflecting the various professional roots and career paths of the early adopters: property or estate management; fixed or operational property asset management; real property or real estate asset management, and real property portfolio management.[4]

Various elements of real estate management had existed before the collective label arrived, but its newness and achievement lay in a growing recognition that an integrated and co-ordinated approach to the management of occupied space could add significant value to the operational performance of businesses. From the outset, therefore, real

---

4 Bon R (1992) Corporate Real Estate Management *Facilities* Vol 10 No 12 p13 MCB University Press.

estate management was, functionally, "concerned with the integration of property management, with the management of its utilization and with the full range of services provided to support a business operation."[5] Perhaps another way of looking at it is as the drive to stop property holdings getting in the way of doing business and instead get them to actively support the business rather than simply be a passive box.

The evolution of real estate management during the past 20 years has taken place in overlapping but distinctive phases. To some extent, these phases reflect changes in the macro economy. An expansionist first phase occurred during the boom of the 1980s. Led by the large financial and business services companies in London, specialist facilities managers began to emerge and bring some coherence and profile to the various activities that were bundled together as "property matters". Phase two arrived with the recession of the early-1990s and had a focus on the core business agenda. As with every other resource area in corporate organisations, property came under the spotlight, and was expected to make its contribution to bottom line savings. Cost saving quickly spread to outsourcing as managers realised the benefits of externalising services. This was another form of cost cutting, but it also had broader drivers and entailed new approaches to management. Benchmarking became popular as the economy began to improve in the mid-1990s, and as value assumed more importance than the crude measure of cost. Real estate managers strove to demonstrate that the kind of business management tools used to make other areas of corporate accountability transparent could be applied to property with the same effect. The third phase, still in its early stages, began as the economy buoyed in the late-1990s. In this phase, the notion of integrated workplace solutions was established, in which the traditionally separate disciplines of real estate management, human resources and information technology began to converge.

The significance of this professionalisation of the real estate management process lies in its effect on the wider property supply chain and in its impact on the pattern, or profile, of demand. It has meant that the supply process now has a sophisticated client that is no longer prepared to simply accept the product that it is offered by a supply process that see its customer as the owner of the building. Also, it has

---

5 Alexander K (1992) Facilities Management in the New Organisation *Facilities* Vol 10 No 1 p7 MCB University Press.

meant that a far more sophisticated approach to real estate management has led to changes in the kind of space that is now in demand.

Getting real estate on the corporate agenda

The 1980s was a period of rapid growth and change for business generally. Expansion and diversification spread as the "bigger is better" philosophy grew; planning and decision-making were short term; overcapacity grew and corporate emphasis was on short-term growth rather than on long-term strategy. During this period of economic growth, John Renzas observed that:

> companies often entered new business areas that were poor strategic fits with their core businesses ... The financial terms under which these new acquisitions were made were often predicated upon continuation of aggressive rates of growth, which may seem unrealistic in today's environment.[6]

More specifically, rapid growth meant that businesses could subsidise the property industry; they could afford the escalations in rents demanded by landlords, and the mistakes in the construction process that meant too much money was being spent unnecessarily on the product. Few questions were asked of the long-term utility of the buildings (either by providers or occupiers), and the role of property in corporate planning was poorly understood.

The genesis of a new way of thinking can be traced back to the US, where a Harvard University study in 1981 highlighted the low priority afforded to property in the public and private sectors, and the continuing failure to manage real estate as a resource.[7] These findings were confirmed and expanded on in a later study at Massachusetts Institute of Technology.[8] The public sector in the UK showed, not for

---

6 Renzas J H (1992) Corporate Restructuring: Evaluating the Real Estate Component *Area Development* January pp33, 50, 54 and 57 S/H Publications Inc, Easton, Philadelphia.

7 Zeckhauser S and Silverman R (1981) *Corporate Real Estate Asset Management in the United States* Harvard College, Cambridge, Massachusetts.

8 Veale P (1987) *Managing Corporate Real Estate Assets: A Survey of US Real Estate Executives* The Laboratory of Architecture and Planning, Massachusetts Institute of Technology, Massachusetts.

the first time, that its thinking was ahead of the corporate sector. A report from the Department of Health and Social Security in 1982 expressed concern over the management of property within the NHS.[9] Further public sector reports were to follow from the Audit Commission;[10] and the National Audit Office,[11] all addressing the role of property in operational efficiency within the public sector.

In the first work of its kind in the UK, Martin Avis, Virginia Gibson and Jenny Watts[12] made an extensive study of the way in which major corporate occupiers managed property. They uncovered a profound lack of understanding of the role of property and could find little evidence of understanding of the contribution it made to the organisations. They found that the majority of organisations did not clearly establish property objectives as part of their overall organisational objectives, and that, in many cases, the more general organisational objectives were neither clearly expressed nor conveyed widely through the organisation.

These findings were despite the fact that more than half the organisations interviewed for the study claimed to have property assets worth 30% or more of their total asset value. In part, the lack of a proactive approach to premises management was caused by the mismatch between business planning horizons and those of property:

> The business and political decisions tended to have shorter lead times than property decisions. The majority of organisations' planning period was between 1 and 5 years. These two factors made it difficult to incorporate property into the strategic planning process.[13]

However, as real estate managers became more organised and more vociferous, and as the building implications of technological advances

---

9 Department of Health and Social Security (1982) *Underused and Surplus Property in the National Health Service* HMSO, London.

10 Audit Commission, The (1988) *Local Authority Property — A Management Overview* HMSO, London.

11 National Audit Office (1989) *Home Office: Control and Management of the Metropolitan Police Estate* HC 455 HMSO, London; National Audit Office (1988a) *Estate Management in the National Health Service* HC 405 HMSO, London; National Audit Office (1988b) *Property Services Agency: Management of the Civil Estate* HC 507 HMSO, London.

12 Avis M, Gibson V and Watts J (1989) *Managing Operational Property Assets* Department of Land Management, University of Reading.

13 Avis *et al* (1989) *op cit* pii.

became more widely understood, so property began to appear on the corporate agenda. Although it remained very much the Cinderella of corporate management decision-making, attention increasingly focused on property and its role in overall operational performance. Generally, a much closer relationship between business strategy and premises strategy began to emerge. This was reflected in an increasing concern to maximise the utility of property. Frank Duffy and Alex Henney observed that:

> Historically companies have focused their attention on the "sharp end" of their businesses, such as marketing, controlling costs, and finance. Few have paid much attention to using and operating buildings efficiently and to providing an agreeable environment within which people will work efficiently.[14]

The authors argued that such attitudes were changing because:

> Some modern office buildings in the City are now very large and expensive, and for that reason alone demand more care. In addition buildings have become technologically far more complex.... If such buildings are not looked after carefully ... then they will not perform properly.[15]

But progress was slow. Well into the 1990s, surveys consistently found evidence of real estate remaining low on the corporate agenda. Debenham Tewson and Chinnocks found that "only around 10% of *The Times'* top 1000 have a property director responsible for real estate."[16] These findings were consistent with those of Graham Bannock & Partners;[17] Ranko Bon;[18] and Arthur Andersen.[19] Real estate management continued to be the poor relation of other corporate resources. Virginia Gibson highlighted the low priority

---

14 Duffy F and Henney A (1989) *The Changing City* Bulstrode Press, London p72.

15 Duffy and Henney (1989) *op cit* p73.

16 Debenham Tewson and Chinnocks (1992) *The Role of Property: Managing Cost and Releasing Value* DTC, London piv.

17 Graham Bannock and Partners (1994) *Property in the Boardroom* Hillier Parker, London.

18 Bon R (1995) Corporate Real Estate Management Practices in Europe and the United States: 1993 and 1994 Surveys *Facilities* Vol 13 No 7 pp5–13 MCB University Press.

19 Arthur Andersen (1993) *Real Estate in the Corporation: The Bottom Line for Senior Management* Arthur Andersen & Co, South Carolina.

Table 8.1 Importance of resources in terms of future success (%)

	Critical	*Very important*	*Moderately important*	*Not relevant*
Info/data	32	48	13	7
Finance	23	52	26	0
People	84	10	3	3
Property	3	20	74	3
Technology	32	45	13	10

Source: Gibson[20]

given to property. Referring to the results of a survey (see table 8.1), she found that the "vast majority" of organisations considered property to be only moderately important or not relevant to their future success, compared with other resources that were considered critical or very important.[21]

Gibson concluded that property resources still appeared to be "considered a less important and less dynamic resource than the other main resources" and therefore likely to receive less attention by senior management.[22] Despite this rather gloomy finding, some changes had taken place. For example, Avis and Gibson reported in 1995 that in the previous six years the representation of heads of property at senior management team level had risen from 40% to 69%. Of these, 13% were the equivalent of board level in their organisations, whereas none had been in 1989. Avis and Gibson observed that this improved representation of property at a senior level indicated increased perception of its importance and a greater consideration given to it in strategic decision making."[23]

Barry Varcoe made a persuasive case for the strategic role of property in corporate planning. He conceded that because staff usually represent the majority of a business' cost base, premises are

---

20 Gibson V (1995) Is Property on the Strategic Agenda? *Property Review* May pp104–109 Eclipse Group, London.

21 *Ibid.*

22 Gibson (1995) *op cit* p107.

23 Avis M and Gibson V (1995) *Real Estate Resource Management* Oxford Brookes University, Oxford p33.

usually seen as relatively unimportant, which, in turn, often gives rise to the corporate attitudes that regard premises as an overhead cost that has to be kept as low as possible.[24] He then argued that such an approach underestimated two critical factors. First, that business premises often represent more than 30% of an organisation's total asset value. And second, that premises have a fundamental effect on the people who occupy them — the business's most important asset. This led him to conclude that the primary role of property has to be:

that of supporting at all levels, from the individual to the strategic, the goals and aims of the businesses and organizations which occupy them. They must be as ready for change as any other business component, if not more so, being able to adapt to or absorb its effects with speed and efficiency.[25]

All of which means premises meant a more proactive approach to property management. Varcoe concluded that an agreed premises policy, and its use in building and maintaining business models would enable the proactive management of property, because corporate premises needs:

are established in a manner which promotes the optimisation of the property resource, and instils management disciplines which predict change and are ready to accommodate it, rather than react hastily to it in an unco-ordinated ad hoc manner that is unlikely to meet the constraints of time, quality and cost.[26]

In a similar way, Keith Alexander argued that the mission of real estate management should be "to improve the quality of the operating environment, to add value to the business and to minimise the exposure of an organisation to risk".[27] He went on:

Facilities management is concerned with managing the quality, value and risk associated with the occupancy of buildings and the delivery of quality customer services.[28]

---

24 Varcoe B J (1992) Premises of Value *Facilities* Vol 10 No 3 p14 MCB University Press.
25 *Ibid.*
26 Varcoe (1992) *op cit* p20.
27 Alexander (1992) *op cit* p7.
28 *Ibid.*

In the early-1990s, two large, competing, American real estate management organisations established "chapters" in the UK. Both the International Association of Corporate Real Estate Executives (NACORE) and the Industrial Development Research Council (IDRC) sought to place real estate within a more strategic context. The two organisations co-existed until they merged into CoreNet Global in 2003. Both organisations pursued an explicit agenda of connecting real estate management to corporate planning, thereby empowering the real estate manager. They quickly became lobbies within the property industry, espousing the interests of the occupier. Coinciding as their setting up did with the deepest property recession in post-war years, both organisations began to exert effective pressure on landlords to re-appraise the 25-year, FRI lease. As vacancy levels soared to all-time highs, the supply industry met, for the first time, a vocal, well-informed and organised opposition.

Two highly influential research reports were published in 1993, significantly both in the US, which helped to move the real estate agenda on to the next phase. Michael Joroff and colleagues encapsulated the task for real estate managers in their report *Strategic Management of the Fifth Resource: Corporate Real Estate*. They said in the preface that:

> In the 1980s, corporate managers, consultants, and researchers transformed the role of four corporate resources — capital, people, technology, and information. As a result these four resources now support their core businesses far more effectively than before.[29]

They then set out a number of ways in which real estate managers were transforming their own resource area into more effective alignment with prime corporate concerns by moving from:

- real estate orientation to business focus
- transactional to a process orientation
- control-oriented to service-oriented
- reactive to proactive
- decentralised to centralised

---

29 Joroff M, Louargand M, Lambert S and Becker F (1993) *Strategic Management of the Fifth Resource: Corporate Real Estate* Industrial Development Research Foundation, US.

- in-house experience to collaboration
- hiring experts to inviting experts to join the team
- automating to informating
- real estate skills to general management capability.

In short, their vision was of real estate transformed into a strategic corporate resource, lying at the heart of business planning, and making a direct positive contribution to the performance of the business. To this end, they argued that the under-management of corporate real estate was no longer acceptable, and that:

> The challenge for corporate real estate executives is to learn the needs of the corporation as a whole and the needs of business units in particular and then to devise a strategy to satisfy them even when the answer may not involve traditional forms of real estate.[30]

In this sense, the real estate plan had to integrate disparate workplace disciplines (for example, the impact of space planning on productivity), but also it had itself to integrate into other parts of the corporate plan (for example, by contributing to corporate asset management objectives).

In the same year as the Joroff study came a report from Arthur Andersen.[31] This study was sponsored by NACORE and the Commercial Investment Real Estate Institute. *Real Estate in the Corporation: the Bottom Line from Senior Management* set out to examine how corporate real estate (CRE) assets could be managed to support businesses that were experiencing structural changes. The key conclusions emerging from the research included the need for efficient and innovative work environments, and for flexibility. It concluded that meeting the needs of business units was the most important real estate management activity, and that while cost per square foot was the primary measure of real estate activity, business return on assets was the most meaningful indicator of corporate performance.

Real estate executives cited corporate downsizing and restructuring as their biggest challenge; while changing business practices was the most important trend shaping their future roles. A non-involvement in

---

30 Joroff *et al* (1993) *op cit* p21.

31 Arthur Andersen (1993) *op cit*.

strategic planning and lack of access to senior executives, together with a poor understanding of real estate by senior management, were seen as impediments. For many, benchmarking was the top planned activity. The research team drew a number of important implications from the study.

- CRE organisations should evolve to respond to emerging needs of business units.
- CRE activities should support the top corporate challenges of profitability, quality, productivity and market share.
- CRE executives should bring proactive solutions and innovations to their customers.
- CRE performance should be cast and communicated in terms of business returns.
- CRE organisations would need to develop new skills and management capabilities.[32]

Real estate management had matured considerably. Leifer encapsulated the nature of the change well:

> The role of corporate real estate has evolved from co-ordinating real estate transactions and maintaining properties to designing a real estate strategy that ties directly into the business plan of the corporation.[33]

Real estate was now increasingly being managed as a corporate resource within the office economy. It was being managed to support and reinforce broader corporate imperatives and to enable businesses to respond to a rapidly changing business environment. However, events in the economy more generally during the 1990s added a further focus to the already crowded real estate agenda.

Towards a focus on the core business

By the end of the 1980s, real estate management had become established as a credible profession in its own right. The British Institute of Facilities Management (BIFM) was set up; several universities

---

32 Arthur Anderson (1993) *op cit p*8.

33 Leifer W (1998) A Primer on the Evolving Role of Corporate Real Estate *Corporate Real Estate Executive* Vol 13 No 5 June p39 and p43.

offered specialist facilities management courses and industry journals, such as *Facilities*, were established. Then the recession struck: the excesses of the go-go 1980s disappeared, seemingly overnight, and the corporate community fell precipitously into recession. This set in train a cost-cutting agenda that was to dominate real estate management for the next 10 years. Suddenly, large corporations were being caricatured as oversized, slow moving and inefficient. Their response was to seek flexibility to allow them to respond to changes and uncertainty in their markets, which were being dramatically changed by the twin forces of technology and globalisation. Senior management sought to shrink to core activities, relieving their organisations of the overhead burdens associated with support activities.

As the white-collar recession focused management attention on the need to reduce costs, improve efficiency and increase productivity, so decision-making and planning focused on those issues that would help to equip companies with the ability to adapt and succeed in increasingly competitive and uncertain markets:

> the primary organizational need is for greater adaptability, to anticipate differential rates of change, to accommodate expansion and contraction and to enable rapid response to business opportunities.[34]

Inevitably, the spotlight fell on property. For most organisations, accommodation costs are the second-highest outgoing after salary costs. Today, it costs around £12,000–14,000 per year to accommodate every office worker in central London. This includes the costs of the premises (rent, property tax and service charge), utilities (electricity, gas and water), and services, such as catering, cleaning, maintenance, reprographics, security, telecoms and so on. At the higher end of this cost range, a modest 100-person organisation will have to earn at least £1.4m simply to pay its annual occupancy bill, and a larger 500-person organisation will have to earn at least £7m. During the recession in the 1990s, the cost of property began to register with financial officers who had sanctioned rapid growth and expansion of physical assets during the heady years of the 1980s.

In further evidence of the commitment of companies to office premises, property advisor Debenham Tewson and Chinnocks produced the results of research showing that among the 29 largest real

---

34 Alexander (1992) *op cit* p6.

estate-owning companies, only eight were property companies. The 10 largest non-property companies were, in descending order: Hanson Trust; Trust House Forte; National Westminster Bank; Marks & Spencer; British Gas; Ladbroke Group; Barclays Bank; British Telecom; Post Office and P&O. All of these had property assets in excess of £1.5bn, with Hanson owning over £4bn.[35]

The leaden weight of property on companies' balance sheets was thrown into sharp relief as businesses sought greater flexibility and a reduced cost base. If businesses were to become more flexible, more agile and more adaptive, then property would need to respond in kind. However, prior to the mid-1990s, there were only two real occupational options available: owner occupation or an institutional FRI lease of 25 years with upward-only rent reviews. In both cases, the commitment was long term and onerous. For most businesses, owner occupation was simply not an option, and for many others the FRI imposed obligations that acted as a drag on their businesses. For example, in renting space, occupiers took on full responsibility for all the internal repair and maintenance of the space. For the larger organisations, this often meant employing large numbers of people to manage and maintain the space and procure property services. In other words, the very act of occupying rented space led to the growth of a non-core activity to manage an inflexible resource.

Initially, corporate focus was simply on cost, and wherever possible businesses sought to reduce their overall commitment to property. Mahlon Apgar argued that rising occupancy costs impaired a company's earnings, share value and overall performance and that reducing these costs could "increase a company's profitability because every dollar saved drops straight to the bottom line."[36] Apgar went on to suggest that efforts to reduce occupancy costs had never been timelier:

> During the 1980s, the typical service business saw its ratio of occupancy costs to revenues more than double, its real rents increase by 50%, and its space use per employee grow by 80%.[37]

---

35 Debenham Tewson and Chinnocks (1992) *The Role of Property: Managing Cost and Releasing Value* DTC, London.

36 Apgar M (1993) Uncovering Your Hidden Occupancy Costs *Harvard Business Review* May–June p124.

37 Apgar (1993) *op cit* p124.

Such stark figures showed how the expanding office economy was driving an expanding real estate industry and ultimately increased demand for office space. They also hinted at the scope for making cost savings, and many organisations instigated severe cost-reduction programmes. However, the limitation of the cost-cutting agenda was its one-dimensional approach. What was being called for in business was the introduction of flexibility and agility to enable responsiveness to a rapidly changing business environment; equally, what was being demanded in real estate was a more radical approach to the basis of occupancy.

As the focus shifted towards more radical approaches to real estate management, inefficiencies in the supply chain itself were highlighted. It became clear, for example, that the highly fragmented nature of the traditional supply chain was inadequate to respond to the increasingly complex and comprehensive services required. Rather, the need was emerging for a more integrated process that focused on service and partnership, in which risk was transferred from the occupier to the supplier. Oliver Jones, CEO of outsourcing group Citex, set out the nature of the challenge:

> Traditional property and surveying firms and traditional FM operators will potentially face exposure in a more service-oriented, value-driven world as the leading outsourced service providers recognise the prospects ... The innovators in the market are recognising that property, as with so many other businesses today, is seen increasingly in the eyes of the consumer and purchaser as a service not as an asset.[38]

Jones' comments signalled the beginnings of a transformation, still under way, that would fundamentally alter the traditional relationship between owner and occupier, and lead to much greater choice in the form of contract between the two.

One of the earliest symptoms of the new approach was the spread of serviced offices. While serviced offices were a novel concept in the UK, they had been an established feature of the much more fluid US real estate market for many years. They were, in essence, a response to the increasingly fast-moving nature of much of corporate America that demanded a shorter-term approach to procuring real estate. The key

---

38 Jones O (2000) Facility Management: Opportunities, Scope and Impact In: Nutt B and McLennan P *Facility Management: Risks and Opportunities* Blackwell Science, London p32.

difference with more traditional approaches was that business centres were about providing space, or work environments, rather than real estate. Service contracts and licences replaced leases with short-term arrangements typically involving the provision of staffed facilities; shared meeting/conference space; fully equipped work environments and ICT infrastructure. In the early years, serviced offices were typically occupied by small companies looking to portray a large company image, but economic as well as corporate demands led to them catering for the sophisticated needs of fast-moving Fortune 1000 companies. By 1999, the business centre market in the US was estimated as a $2bn industry, with over 4000 centres.[39]

The recent history of serviced offices has been dominated by the high-profile financial restructuring that the major players have been through. However, that market is now an established and accepted subsector of the property-supply industry. The two largest players in Europe are Regus and HQ Global Workplaces. While Regus started as a European business, HQ was a US-franchised operation. The growth of companies providing serviced offices in the late-1990s was rapid and, as their success became more obvious, traditional providers of property began to look at ways in which they could add value to their assets through the provision of more intensive management, and the provision of the kinds of service support that would attract and retain occupiers who might otherwise consider the serviced office option.

One of the earlier entrants into this market for an enhanced landlord offer was property company Land Securities. Its LandFlex model involved a choice of lease structures, space configuration and service levels. It allowed for leases of between six months and 10 years, with the ability to cancel or extend. Occupiers could take more than one lease in a building to create a lease profile to align with their business plan. LandFlex included space that was finished to include power and data cabling, carpets and security, with options for furniture and partitioning — all traditionally the responsibility of the occupier. The offer also included unbranded business club areas, including meeting rooms, breakout areas and touchdown desks, thereby allowing occupiers to reduce their overall space requirement and therefore their financial commitment.[40]

---

39 Arenas J P (1999) The Disposable Office *Corporate Real Estate Executive* September pp29–31.

40 Gray S (2002) LandSec Lets Tenants have it their Own Way *Estates Gazette* 9 November pp146–147.

Other landlords launched similar products, and an increasing number identified the opportunity to sell services not only to the corporate occupier, but also to the individual office worker. In 2000, specialist business park developer and operator Arlington Securities launched an online property and business service for the 34,000 workers on its 18 business parks. The intranet service is designed to be a virtual community, offering its members access to information and a range of lifestyle and business-to-business services — from interactive facilities management to online shopping and information about local events.[41] In similar moves, developer MEPC launched an intranet site with an online order and delivery service, as well as information on local lifestyle support services[42] and Stanhope launched a service at its high-profile Chiswick Park in west London. These service-oriented approaches led to the gradual acceptance of new processes, and along with the new products came a new language in which the property supply industry started talking about customers rather than tenants.

A further variation in the market for enhanced service provision occurred where property owners combined with service providers to proactively offer integrated support services within their buildings. In 1999, developer MEPC and service office provider Regus created an offer for owner occupiers to sell all or part of their portfolios to MEPC, and then to lease them back with the required Regus services for as little as six months. The model involved the property being bought by MEPC outside of the JV, and then leased to the JV on a 20-year lease. Regus would provide the services for the space while MEPC dealt with the property management and refurbishment.

In May 2000, a partnership comprising MEPC, the Institute of Directors, Stonemartin Corporate Centres and Eurica launched a £500m programme to open IoD-branded office centres throughout the UK. The programme was launched as "a new way of managing property, breaking away from the inflexibility of traditional leases."[43] Recognising that most office units in the UK are small, the consortium targets the 900 sq m (10,000 sq ft) market, with a comprehensive business infrastructure management service.

Serviced offices and offices with enhanced landlord services are two principle means in which occupiers can reduce their exposure to real

---

41 Cooper M (2000) Tenants Offered Virtual Village *Estates Gazette* 11 March 2000 p63.

42 Cited in: MEPC Workforce Get Desk Top Shopping *Estates Gazette* 29 July 2000 p43.

43 Blackwell D (2000) IoD to Provide Business Centres *Financial Times* 5 May 2000 p5.

estate and achieve some flexibility through different forms of contract. They allow a business to relieve itself of unwanted, non-core activities and introduce some certainty into their corporate planning. There is, however, a further step that can be taken and that is to outsource property altogether.

It is one of the peculiarities of the real estate market that, having leased premises from a landlord, the onus is on the lessee source the various services to make the space work — cleaning, maintenance, security, catering and so on. These facilities services are normally procured on contracts that run anywhere between one and five years, and it is one of the real estate managers' key responsibilities to manage the contracts and secure best value. Traditionally, the contracts have been let either as single packages or bundled together for convenience and cost saving. Where service bundling occurred, specialist facilities management companies took on the responsibility of managing service contracts with multitudes of suppliers on behalf of the client company. In this sense, facilities services had been outsourced for many years.

Outsourcing had a major impact on real estate as senior management sought to shrink to a newly defined core of activities, relieving their organisations of the overhead burdens associated with support activities. Thus, companies strove for tighter control of their cost bases while increasing their flexibility, and the Holy Grail became "a lower cost source for the required service while maintaining or improving the quality of that service."[44] Table 8.2 summarises the key reasons for outsourcing.

The traditional role of outsourcing was simply the provision of services (such as cleaning, maintenance, security, reprographics, post room, reception services and so on). However, the system yielded to a more packaged approach as its acceptance grew, sometimes referred to as Total Facilities Management in which:

> a specialist facilities management company takes on the responsibility to manage the variety of contracts with the various service suppliers on behalf of the client company, who simply pays one cheque per month to the facilities management company.[45]

---

44 Connell C (1995) The Outsourcing Debate *Corporate Real Estate Executive* October pp28–29.

45 Conner J (1997) Outsourcing Facilities Management In: Worthington J (1997) *Reinventing the Workplace* Architectural Press, Oxford p137.

Table 8.2 The key reasons for outsourcing property

Top five strategic reasons	*Top five tactical reasons*
Improve business focus	Reduce or control operating costs
Access to world-class capabilities	Make capital funds available
Accelerated re-engineering benefits	Cash infusion
Shared risks	Resources unavailable internally
Free resources for other purposes	Difficulties in managing function

Source: Varcoe[46]

But as the recession of the 1990s took hold, and as real estate managers looked for ways of stripping cost out of their functions, attention switched to looking for more radical approaches to space and service provision. The seeds of a new approach lay in central government's Private Finance Initiative (PFI), a scheme that allowed a new approach to the funding of large capital projects through the use of private capital, particularly in the health, education and transport sectors. Although launched in 1992 by the then Chancellor Norman Lamont, it was not until his successor Kenneth Clarke outlined key details in the 1995 Budget Statement that it really came to the attention of property professionals. However, it was not long before the *principle* of PFI was transferred into the commercial sector, into what quickly became known as "corporate PFIs". This was a logical extension of the evolution of flexible occupation and ownership that began with packaged contract outsourcing.

Within a short time, corporate PFIs became the mantra of real estate management. The apparent benefits were manifold but, given the history of outsourcing as described above, clearly cost reduction was a major factor. Such contracts were said to allow savings to be achieved by offering economies of scale, price flexibility and so on. For example, the National Audit Office estimated in 1999 that the DSS PRIME contract (see below) reduced costs by 22%. But cost reduction is just one of a number of reasons for outsourcing. In fact, costs might even rise if the outsourcing is linked, for example, to speed of delivery or quality of service. A fuller list of benefits is shown below.

46 Varcoe B J (1996) Outsourcing the Work Environment *Flexible Working* August pp19–21 and p27 The Eclipse Group, London.

- Lower, fixed costs, with predictable cash flow.
- Transfer of overheads from fixed to variable and reduced headcount.
- Better value for money through, for example, economy-of-scale purchasing.
- Transfer of risk to third parties.
- Enhanced service provision through service level agreements.
- Flexibility through reduced exposure to long leaseholds/ ownerships.
- Release of fixed capital from the balance sheet through disposal of surplus assets.

All of these are measurable and, in some cases, can be reflected in the bottom line. However, in addition to these "hard" benefits, there are very significant "soft" benefits.

- Making operational needs paramount through the introduction of occupational flexibility and enabling corporate change.
- New types of relationship in the premises supply chain, releasing management time to core business.
- A strategic partnership approach, aligning the interests of client with supplier.
- A clear link between business objectives and property strategy.
- Impartial expertise and the breaking down of cultures that are resistant to change.
- Management of non-core functions to best practice standards, with access to skills; research; innovation and market awareness.

The use of the term corporate PFI is difficult not least because much of the activity to date has been with the public or quasi public sector. Also, close examination of the meaning of PFI makes use of the term difficult in the context of corporate outsourcing. It is for these reasons that the remaining part of this discussion uses the term *real estate partnership*, or REP. It is thought that this better reflects the intention of the arrangements between procurer and supplier.

In 1998, government set out the model for REPs when it released a portfolio of more than 650 DSS properties, comprising around 1.6m sq m (17.2m sq ft), to outsourcing specialist Trillium, with backing from Goldman Sachs. The deal, a 20-year partnership, involved the consortium in an upfront payment of £250m to the DSS for all their freehold and leasehold properties, and an annual payment of £250m, paid to the consortium for the provision of accommodation and related services. A similar deal was concluded in July 2000, when George Soros' Quantum Realty Fund backed Mapeley to win the contract to take over 723 properties occupied by the Inland Revenue and Customs & Excise. In this deal, an annual fee of up to £100m was to be paid for the management of a 130,000 sq m (1.4m sq ft) estate, valued at £2bn for a period of 20 years.[47]

In November 2000, Land Securities had bought Trillium. The contrast was stark. The UK's largest and, some would argue, most traditional of property companies had paid £160m in cash and £5m worth of shares to purchase a three-year-old upstart at the other extreme of the food chain.

> Trillium's tenant-focused strategy is at odds with that of most UK property companies, which have concentrated on tying tenants into long leases ...[48]

The news was swiftly followed by the announcement of property company Delancey's acquisition of services provider Mapeley. Both moves underscored the importance of what was happening and the growing recognition by the property sector of the need to introduce a service element into its traditional offering.

Once the dust had settled on Land Securities' and Mapeley's acquisitions, the question that arose was whether the apparent success of the DSS and Inland Revenue deals could be replicated in the private sector. Certainly, the market got off to a faltering start. Perhaps the first commercial occupier to go for a REP was ICL. When the original consortium backed by Nomura pulled out at the end of 1998, ICL started negotiations with another consortium, comprising Comex, Deutsche Bank and Regus.[49] This discussion also failed, and in March 2000 ICL pulled out of discussions with Integrated Workspace Solutions (backed by CSFB).[50] It then began discussions with another consortium called Prospero, including Bovis Lend Lease, Chesterton and Bank of

---

47 Blue Nelson R (2000) Priest's Prayers Answered *Property Week* 22 September p8.

48 Cohen N (2000) Land Securities Abandons the Traditional Way *Financial Times* 3 November p25.

49 Cohen N (1999) "Offices for Life" Philosophy Vanishing into Space *Financial Times* 5 July p20.

50 Jameson A (2000) ICL Hits Another Hurdle in £1bn Outsourcing Deal *Property Week* 3 March p5.

Tokyo/Mitsubishi. In August 2000, ICL announced that the plan was to be reviewed as a part of a rethink across the group's business.

It began to look as if corporate REPs would be difficult. This view was reinforced by the lack of progress being made by US-based investment bank JP Morgan. The bank had originally announced its interest in a REP in 1999, when it began to look for a partner to own and operate its 111,500 sq m (1.2m sq ft) in 11 buildings in the City of London and elsewhere. An article in the *Financial Times* underlined the novelty of the approach:

> It is the first time a financial services firm has adopted a private finance initiative-style approach to accommodation, in which ownership and management of property are transferred to a third party in exchange for rent and income. [51]

However, progress in the REP market was being made. In April 2000, it was announced that Abbey National had drawn up plans for a complex sale-and-leaseback of its 550,000 sq m (6m sq ft), 1700 property portfolio.[52] Then, in October, Mapeley Columbus Ltd acquired the portfolio for £457m. The contract saw Abbey retain control of facilities management responsibilities, such as security and cleaning. In the following year, both BT and the BBC announced major REPs, outsourcing 6m sq m (64m sq ft) and 400,000 sq m (4m sq ft), respectively. But the market was still dominated by public sector and quasi public sector organisations. The first significant, genuinely private sector REP had to wait until 2004 to happen. This was when JP Morgan eventually announced a deal, in which it was made known that outsourcing specialist Land Securities Trillium had been selected as the preferred partner. A few months later, insurance group Aviva announced that it had also selected Land Securities Trillium as its partner to take over the management of its 557,413 sq m (6m sq ft) portfolio. In summer 2004, Royal Bank of Scotland also announced plans to outsource the bulk of its 3000 properties.

Table 8.3 summarises the main REPs discussed here, and it can be seen that nearly 10m sq m (100m sq ft) has been subject to real estate partnerships. This is clearly a large number, but it remains that case

---

51 Cohen N (1999) JP Morgan to Recruit Property Partner *Financial Times* 8 December p32.

52 Jameson A and Barrie G (2000) Abbey Gets New Real Estate Habit *Property Week* 7 April p1.

Table 8.3 Summary of major REPs

Year	*Organisation*	*Sq m*	*m sq ft*
1998	DSS	1,600,000	17.2
2000	Inland Revenue	130,000	1.4
2000	Abbey National	550,000	6.0
2001	BT	6,000,000	64.0
2001	BBC	400,000	4.3
2004	JP Morgan	111,500	1.2
2004	Aviva	557,400	6.0

that only a small number of corporate organisations have pursued such an approach to its real estate management.

Whether JP Morgan and Aviva are models for other corporate organisations will become clear in the years ahead. But what is obvious is that the REP market has encouraged the property-supply industry to throw away some of its old rules and begin to embrace the notion that the businesses that occupy its buildings are in fact its customers, and that novel ways can and need to be found to secure value out of their continued occupation of its buildings.

The old real estate supply model has begun to break down. The fragmented supply chain, with single service purchasing and adversarial contracts, is beginning to yield to a more service-oriented approach. The relatively immature supply side of the outsourcing market will continue to evolve over the coming years and offer a broader range of commoditised solutions. Suppliers will become better at assessing and managing risk, and they will offer more innovative solutions, such as "pooled property", extranet services and "hotel" services. To date, most large-scale property and facilities outsourcing transactions have involved large property portfolios, often in complex sale and leaseback deals. The future, however, is likely to see the principles applied to a broader range of clients.

Integrated real estate management

Real estate management matured during the late-1990s. As a discipline in its own right, it was increasingly recognised by the property-supply industry as a force to be reckoned with: it became organised, vociferous and demanding. More rigorous approaches to the management of service suppliers and contracts, and better information and analysis of the characteristics of occupied portfolios increased the efficiency and effectiveness of real estate within the context of organisational performance. We have seen in this chapter how the dot.com bubble highlighted the increasingly volatile business environment within which most businesses now operate, and in which office space has to be planned, procured and occupied. We have seen how perceptions of the role of offices have begun to change, and that they are no longer perceived to be a passive, inert bi-product of doing business, but rather an active component of business survival that needs to be planned and provided in the same efficient and effective way as other organisational resources. We have seen also how the recession of the early-1990s led to different ways of procuring space as the property-supply industry sought to find innovative ways of attracting and retaining the occupiers of its buildings.

But despite this undoubted progress, the results have not been uniform. In 2003, economist Roger Bootle observed that across UK business, property was rarely on the boardroom agenda, and that around £18bn was being lost annually through the inefficient use of property. He stated that cutting out this waste would increase gross trading profits by up to 13%; that new working practices, such as hot-desking, could save £6.5bn a year, and a feasible 10% reduction in facilities management costs could save £1.3bn annually.[53] The figures suggested that there remained a long way to go before property within organisations could change from being simply a cost of doing business to a key input to production.

One of the reasons for the continuing inefficiency in the management of real estate is the separation that often exists between *property* management and *facilities* management. The former typically deals with acquisition and disposal of properties together with capital projects, while the latter, often seen as the poor relation, deals with the day-to-day management of service contracts and external service providers. While there are some notable examples where this *upstairs-downstairs* culture has been overcome, it remains the case that the prevalent model is for the two to operate independently. The distinction is often sharpened by the existence of different skill sets managing each area. Thus, typically, property will be the responsibility of someone

---

53 Bootle R (2002) *Property in Business: A Waste of Space?* RICS, London.

with the letters RICS after their name, while the person responsible for facilities is more likely to have a business management qualification. Again, these are generalisations, but they do help to explain some of the ongoing inefficiencies in the management of real estate.

The same separation of roles also occurs in the supply process. Thus, property companies will employ "managing agents" to collect rent and administer leases, and who, in turn, will enter into contract with service providers. This means that the provider of the space and the user of the space are in fact separated by layers of decision making, which, in turn, means that feedback is very inefficient. Yet, a more integrated approach is needed if real estate management is to successfully address the on-going changes affecting the office economy. Writing well in advance of trends in the UK, a team from Cornell University, led by Franklin Becker, summarised the need clearly:

> In no cases was it possible, or desirable, to try to understand the success or failure of a particular facility approach in terms of its constituent elements. Good facility design requires a systems or ecological view from the beginning. This means considering the nature of technology, management style and organizational practices, use policies, facility design and work practices as interdependent components. The system is not likely to prosper, or even survive, unless all these factors are working in harmony.[54]

In a more recent example, the benefits of a more integrated approach to real estate management were spelt out by Edmond Rondeau and colleagues. They argued that *integrated asset management* is "the sum of all those activities that result in appropriate infrastructure for the cost-efficient delivery of service", including the identification of the need for an asset; providing the asset, including its renovation; the operation of the asset, including its maintenance; and the disposal of the asset.[55]

This more integrated approach becomes critical in the context of growing levels of uncertainty, the unfolding impact of technology on patterns of work and the ever-present need for flexibility to respond to

---

54 Becker F, Sims W and Davis B (1991) *Managing Space Efficiently* Cornell University, International Facility Management Program p103.

55 Rondeau E, Stack T and Fox E (2000) Integrated Asset Management In: Nutt B and McLennan P *Facility Management: Risks and Opportunities* Blackwell Science, London p51.

market change. It might also be argued that the process of integration needs to go further yet. Real estate is only one aspect of an organisation's business infrastructure. The other key elements are people and technology. The three areas are increasingly interdependent, and changes in one area can have a dramatic impact of the others. For example, flexible work strategies cannot be successfully implemented without there being a clearly integrated approach to all three components. If a business wishes to introduce flexible working by providing a work hub, and allowing a high proportion of its workforce to be mobile or home-based, then real estate, HR and ICT all have roles to play in supporting such a strategy. It is more efficient and effective to have one plan with these different aspects integrated into a seamless approach, rather than to have three plans with contradictory policies and procedures. Wes McGregor argued that, to be effective, the work environment will need to result from the collaborative efforts of all aspects of business, "where IT and HR along with facilities management are combined to achieve an effective integrated support service for business operations".[56] McGregor went on to argue that this new agenda would call for much higher skill levels than traditionally evident in facilities managers who would:

> need to become "multi-lingual" in terms of their ability to interpret the needs of their customers (individual, group and corporate) and translate facilities related issues into a language that enables them to communicate effectively with managers of the business.[57]

Traditionally, these aspects of organisational planning have existed in silos with virtually no joined up approaches. All three disciplines have had their own "territories" or "empires". But organisational planning is demanding more flexible approaches to the deployment of resources, and there is an increasing need for a more co-ordinated approach to resource planning. For example, as corporate planners consider areas such as best practice, knowledge management, change management programmes and cost-control measures, so they will require integrated approaches and strategies for dealing with them. Figure 8.1 shows a

---

56 McGregor W (2000) The Future of Workspace Management In: Nutt B and McLennan P *Facility Management: Risks and Opportunities* Blackwell Science, London p85.

57 *Ibid.*

conceptual model of integrated business resource management. "Occupancy management" refers to an integrated property and facilities function, and knowledge management is included within the ICT function to recognise the increasingly important role that integrated systems have in linking resource areas in organisational planning.

Figure 8.1 Integrated business resource management

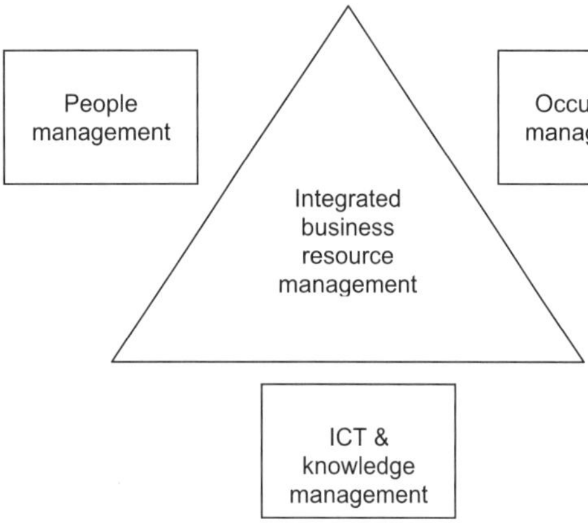

We have seen already that fundamental changes are taking place in the way in which work is undertaken. As this trend continues to bring greater complexity to the management of organisations, so it will become more critical to have joined up thinking in key resource areas. This means that those charged with the management of offices will have to take a far wider perspective on their role for its contribution to achieving organisational objectives than has traditionally been the case. As they do so, novel approaches are likely to emerge in the management of real estate to cope with new ways of working, which, in turn, will place demands upon the supply industry for more flexible forms of occupation, and even for more innovative approaches to their product offer. The implication here is that there is an opportunity for the supply industry to respond, for example, with more commoditised products, with different approaches to charging for space, and for a switch away from the landlord and tenant culture, which is based on an adversarial approach, to a business-to-business relationship in which the occupier becomes the customer.

9 New Economy, New Work, New Office

White-collar factories

Frederick Winslow Taylor was born in Germantown, Philadelphia in 1856. His father was a graduate of Princeton and a lawyer, his mother an abolitionist and feminist; both were Quakers. The family was wealthy, highly educated and liberal-minded: when Frederick was just 13, the family embarked on a three-year grand tour of Europe. Upon his return to America, the young Taylor enrolled into the highly respected Phillips Exeter Academy in New Hampshire. However, his health was poor and despite passing the Harvard entrance examination, he left Exeter prematurely. After several months of recuperation, and in his 18th year, he chose a vocation in engineering, joining Ferrell and Jones (later the Enterprise Hydraulic Works). Despite his social background and obvious intellectual strengths, Taylor followed the pure and principled nature of his upbringing and started his new vocation as a humble pattern maker's apprentice. On completing his apprenticeship in 1878, Frederick moved to the Midvale Steel Company, starting there as a machinist.

His inquisitive and innovative mind soon marked him out for greater things, and he scaled the corporate ladder rapidly, rising to research director and then chief engineer. His dedication was to be demonstrated by his ability to earn an engineering degree from the Stevens Institute of Technology in New Jersey, at age 25, while working full time. Taylor was imbued with a belief in the role of science and technology in the advancement of mankind: he was an innovator and a rationalist.

While at Midvale, Taylor studied industrial productivity and methods for measuring output. He introduced piecework, developing detailed systems aimed at maximising the efficiency of men and machines in the factory. His work involved time and motion studies to determine the best methods for performing tasks in the least amount of time. His basic thesis was that incentive-based wages were ineffective unless they were used alongside carefully planned and managed tasks, backed up by supportive and co-operative management. He argued for the careful selection and development of people, identifying clear goals and tasks, organising feedback, providing training and encouraging group support. His methods were successful and output rose significantly. Scientific management was born.

Taylor's formative years in industry coincided with the vertical integration of the US economy, when American business switched structural models. Up to the 1880s, the American economy consisted primarily of entrepreneurial, local, owner-managed businesses, and was characterised by many layers of production and distribution. The new model was to be dominated by large, vertically integrated businesses, which gained significant economies of scale and stripped out the add-on costs of intermediaries, brokers and distributors. Such change provided Taylor with the ideal environment to apply his inquisitive and analytical mind to scientific management.

The new businesses practiced centralised command and control management, and there was a consequential rise in white-collar work as the emerging behemoths generated a demand for process management, administration, sales, accounting and so on. The demand for new office buildings rose accordingly. For example, during the latter half of the 1880s, 400 office buildings were completed in central Pittsburgh.[1] Necessitated by the reorganisation of business and enabled by new technologies (such as lifts, telephony, sanitation and steel-frame construction), the skyscraper emerged and came to symbolise the new model of business. And it was into the skyscrapers that so many of the defining characteristics of scientific management in the factories was transposed. Work processes, for example, were physically organised on the principle of the production line. Early images of skyscrapers in the US show factory-style layouts with long, regimented rows of large, imposing desks arranged to allow a flow of paper.

---

1 Shlaes J and Weiss M A (1993) Evolution of the Office Building In: White J R *The Office Building: From Concept to Investment Reality* Counsellors of Real Estate, Chicago p9.

Taylor became a consulting engineer at the age of 37, often making enemies in the companies where his methods resulted in job losses aimed at increasing efficiency. His most important client became the Bethlehem Iron Company, but following various disputes with the management, he was fired in 1901. This was to be his last job. His most famous published work, *Principles of Scientific Management* (1909), was based largely on transcripts of talks given long after leaving employment. He contracted influenza in 1915 while on a speaking tour and died the day after his 59th birthday. Taylor's legacy was to influence management thinking, both in the factory and the office, for nearly a century, as offices came to resemble factories stuffed full of white-collar workers.

Large, inflexible, hierarchical and slowly moving businesses dominated by clerical, process-based work and with clear demarcations between grades and functions of work grew and dominated economic life through to the late-1980s. Anthony Sampson captured the essence of this phenomenon in his 1995 book *Company Man: the Rise and Fall of Corporate Life*.[2] He suggested that the corporate organisations that emerged in the late-19th century in the US, with their massive structures, rigid hierarchies and life-time employment, created the professional manager, or company man, thereby allowing the middle class to grow immensely. By the 1920s and 1930s, he argued, British corporations were emerging along similar lines with their own armies of loyal company men occupying managerial roles in corporate organisations typified by the likes of BP, Shell and Unilever: corporate leviathans that bestrode the economic landscape for much of the post-war period.

The office economy, as we saw in chapter 3, reached its maximal phase of expansion between the 1960s and 1980s. These, it now transpires, were the golden years for company man, because this stable, almost paternal corporate environment began to change in the mid-1980s when, as Sampson argued, the security of company man began to be undermined, and a changing economic landscape sounded the death knell for large, slumbering, multi-layered and complacent organisations. The scale of the change is shown by data from the US economy. During the 1980s, the Fortune 500 companies cut their workforces by 3.5 million, while small companies created more than 20

---

2 Sampson A (1995) *Company Man: the Rise and Fall of Corporate Life* HarperCollins, London.

million new jobs; and the corporate giants now employ only about 10% of the workforce, compared with 20% in the late-1960s and early-1970s.[3] The fact that the old model had lasted for so long was testament to its robustness, and it was therefore to be expected that its fate should be sealed by a change as equally profound as the reorganisation of the US economy in the latter part of the 19th century. Indeed, the change was to involve the wholesale reorganisation of the white-collar factories as they underwent their greatest change in 100 years.

The first symptoms of this impending change were to be seen in the economic restructuring of the late-1980s, with the rise of globalisation and the deregulation of markets in the US, and with geo-political changes, such as the dismantling of the Berlin Wall, which led to radical changes in trading patterns. But it was the computer, in particular, and communications technology, generally, that was to have the most profound influence on change in the office economy. The new technologies changed both the nature of the work itself and the nature of the physical surroundings in which office work was undertaken. We saw in chapter 7 how the *ORBIT* study highlighted the potential impact of organisational change and emerging technologies on building design.[4] This research was among the first empirical evidence to link the physical characteristics of buildings and their ability to accommodate the emerging information technologies — both desk-top services, such as personal computers, but also, critically, building management systems. At the heart of the research was the message that information technology would have a profound impact on the design, management and occupation of buildings in coming years.

Then, in 1985, an article appeared in the *Harvard Business Review* that was particularly prescient in its claims for the unfolding impact of technology on the nature of work. It was written by Philip Stone and Robert Luchetti, from Harvard's Faculty of Arts and Sciences, and was titled *Your Office is Where You Are*. The authors set out to "challenge the customary ways of thinking about offices" and to show how managers could "integrate physical layout, design, and communications to support organizational objectives ..."[5] These objectives were to

---

3 Stelzer I (1993) Transition to Save the American Dream *The Times*, 15 April p25.

4 Duffy F (1983) *The Orbit Study: Information Technology and Office Design* DEGW/EOSYS, London.

5 Stone P J and Luchetti R (1985) Your Office is Where You Are *Harvard Business Review* March–April p102.

emphasise informal exchange; reassign people to different work teams and study groups; provide employees with access to specialised equipment; value individual initiative and mobility; derive payoffs from serendipity; attract talented employees and increase productivity while reducing office costs. Stone and Luchetti proposed that managers should rethink how both information and people flow in an office, and adopt "activity settings" to provide a richer office experience with appropriate environments to suit the work in hand. Such thinking was a world away from the command and control systems that had been so dominant for so long. It was holistic, it was purposeful and it recognised technology as an enabler, not a driver. The newly emerging corporate real estate management profession started to recognise the growing implications of organisational and technological change for the delivery of support services to enable new organisational structures and new patterns of work.

The chill winds of the 1990s

In 1990, just as the new work agenda was gathering momentum, the economy slipped into recession — deep, severe and not confined to "old economy" jobs. Unlike in the early-1980s, when manufacturing was decimated, suddenly, white-collar work was under attack. The pressure was on to reduce costs, wherever possible, and the new work agenda was unceremoniously pushed to one side, where it would remain for nearly a decade as the focus of many real estate management teams shifted dramatically from a strategy of IT-enabled new patterns of work, such as that outlined by Stone and Luchetti, to a single-minded focus on reducing occupancy costs. This was a reasonable but narrowly focused reaction that had lasting effects because, while the short-term focus was on cost cutting, the long-term undercurrent of drivers that had been pushing the restructuring of the office economy continued their work.

The real estate managers and their colleagues in other corporate resource areas came under pressure from Boards whose broader agenda was simple: reduce the cost base and improve the competitive position. The chill winds of change gathered pace and jobs for company man were severely culled. And the whole ethos was underpinned by a plethora of management books, all in various ways proclaiming to have found an angle on the emerging economic landscape: the management guru reached "popular" status and, in some areas, possibly, cult status.

New-wave management theory and the names of Drucker, Hammer, Handy, Porter, Peters and Senge became very familiar to anyone with even a passing interest in what was happening to business culture. Each had their particular theses and approaches, but through the dense undergrowth of books and articles that emerged, the consistent messages were about downsizing, outsourcing, delayering, re-engineering, mobility and virtual work: in short, methods for becoming leaner, more efficient, more flexible and more competitive. Scientific management was dead: new-wave management had arrived.

Many commentators and advisors pursued the new-wave management agenda with an almost evangelical fervour, interweaving the cost-cutting agenda with theories about the nature of companies in the emerging office economy. We were told, for example, that as the efficiency measures took hold they would lead to horizontal networks replacing vertical hierarchies, and highly skilled, group-based knowledge workers replacing clerical, departmentalised information processors. Peter Drucker went so far as to suggest that knowledge had become the primary resource for individuals and the economy, and that the traditional factors of production favoured by economists — land, labour and capital — would not disappear, but would become secondary.[6] Robert Heller picked up the theme, arguing that since "horizontal business processes are all multi-functional and multi-disciplinary, the manager is being led in similar directions. Cross-functional, synergistic and inter-departmental working is unavoidable now: so are task-specific teams."[7] And *Business Week* argued that horizontal corporations should organise around processes rather than tasks; flatten hierarchies; use teams to manage everything; let customers drive performance; and reward team performance.[8]

Big business responded in kind. Outsourcing spread rapidly as companies sought to shrink to a newly defined core of activities, relieving themselves of the overhead burdens associated with support activities, such as catering, cleaning, building maintenance, security, IT and even accounting and personnel. Demergers multiplied as the fashion for breaking down the lumbering leviathans took hold: BAT, BTR, Courtaulds, Forte, Hanson, ICI, Racal and Thorn EMI all got in

---

6 Drucker P F (1992) The New Society Organisations *Harvard Business Review* September–October pp95–104.

7 Heller R (1994) The Managers' Dilemma *Management Today* January p44.

8 Cited in: The Horizontal Corporation *Business Week* 20 December 1993 pp44–49.

on the act. Others, such as AT&T, Eastman Kodak and General Electric delayered; while yet others underwent full-scale business process re-engineering, including Asea Brown Boveri (ABB), Rank Xerox and Shell. By the early-1990s, ABB was able to report that it had 215,000 employees worldwide, with a central staff of just 200; 5000 autonomous business units and only three layers of management.[9] In 1995, Europe's largest company, Shell announced the results of its own re-engineering process, the nub of which was redundancy for 1200 head office staff and the release of half its famous headquarters on the South Bank of the Thames in London.

To some extent, the early evangelists for the new economy oversold their case. The new-wave management theories of the 1990s exhibited that familiar trait of dramatically overestimating the short-term effects of innovation, while underestimating its medium- and long-term impacts. Their proclamations began to look a little fragile as the promised economic results failed to materialise. Doubts over aspects of new-wave management theory began to surface, and a growing body of evidence suggested that the slash and burn management fads had largely failed. For example, one study found that fewer than half the American firms that had downsized between 1990 and 1997 had seen any improvements in quality, profitability or productivity.[10] In another example, despite the fact that during the 1980s, North American and western European countries had invested heavily in new technology, the widely anticipated advances in output, or productivity, had not come about. Through the 1990s, manufacturing productivity in America rose at more than 3% per annum on average, but in services, annual gains averaged less than 1%. Productivity growth in America's business sector slowed from 2.6% in 1960–73 to 1% in more recent times. All this despite the fact that IT, as a percentage of American firms' total investment in equipment, rose from around 5% in 1960 to over 45% in 1997.[11] Then, in a dramatic *volte-face*, one of the leading exponents of downsizing — Stephen Roache from US investment bank Morgan Stanley — declared, "If you compete by building, you have a future. If you compete by cutting,

---

9 Peters T (1992) ABB's Prophet of Smallness Points Way to Profit in the Nineties *The Times* 11 November p25.

10 American Management Association, cited in: Instant Coffee Management Theory *The Economist* 25 January 1997 p83.

11 Cited in: Assembling the New Economy *The Economist* 13 September 1997 pp105–111.

you don't."[12] More subtly, it came to be recognised that accountancy practices that recorded assets such as plant and machinery failed to recognise the inherent value of the intellectual capital of the workforce. In other words, the slashing of wage bills, which pushed up earnings and share value in the short term, actually led to a reduction in shareholder value over the longer term. Downsizing quickly took on a new persona: dumbsizing.

But despite these tempering events, the fact of fundamental change in corporate life was becoming increasingly apparent. There was to be no return to the unwieldy corporate structures of earlier times. If for no other reason, the revolutionising impact of ICT would not allow that to happen. As real estate managers responded to the leaner times with cost cutting and efficiency measures (see chapter 8), so they also began to explore ways of using technology to support the more intensive occupation of property. The so-called *new ways of working* were employed with the aim of introducing changes to the way in which workers would engage with employers and colleagues by becoming more flexible and dynamic, and thereby reducing the amount of space that organisations required. In other words, the agenda was efficiency savings rather than the more positive technology enablement suggested by Stone and Luchetti.

As new ways of working spread, a new language in office design emerged. Group areas, encouraging interaction, co-operation, innovation and a higher density of use, replaced enclosed offices, which were seen to reinforce hierarchies and status, as well as consume valuable and expensive space. New approaches to space use, such as hot-desking, hotelling and virtual offices, became commonplace, giving rise to touch down areas, lagoons, oases and docking stations. Reception areas began to offer "concierge" services, where desks could be booked on an as-needed basis, and where personal belongings could be collected for the duration of the stay in the office. Workers' habits and routines were studied and classified, resulting in new typologies: nomads, guests, teleworkers and core/periphery workers were identified.

One of the earliest examples of new methods of working in the corporate sector was that introduced by IBM at Bedfont Lakes, near Heathrow in 1992. On moving in, IBM had 600 of what it referred to as

---

12 Carlin J (1996) Guru of Downsizing Admits he got it all Wrong Reported in the *Independent on Sunday* 12 May p20.

"smart" workers, who used the office as a base, but had no fixed, personal space. This was one of the earliest examples in the UK of free addressing, where personal space is given up and staff use those desks that are available. These people were expected to be away from the office for large parts of their time, and they made use of a pool of available desks when in the office. Each desk could be personalised to accept an individuals' telephone calls and to allow access to personal files. Each worker was equipped with a portable PC for use at home or in clients' premises.

Coopers and Lybrand (now PricewaterhouseCoopers) moved into its new headquarters at Embankment Place in London in 1992. Eager to maximise the use of the space and at the same time support the working needs of its highly mobile, professional staff, the firm introduced a radical approach to new ways of working, which it trade-marked as "Right Space", to house 1000 consultants. The objectives of the exercise were to provide consultants with appropriate types of workstation and work areas at the appropriate times; to reduce space use and costs as much as possible, and to bring about business advantage through co-location. The centre of the Right Space initiative was the service desk for booking space, providing administrative support and acting as a central information point. A net reduction of desks was accompanied by the introduction of areas for quiet working; team space, and formal and informal meeting areas. A few staff retained designated cellular offices, but even these were "bookable" so they could double up as meeting rooms. All staff were given a unique telephone number and issued with laptops. The change was introduced alongside extensive consultation and training, and a dedicated change management team was brought in.[13] Staff were issued with mobile phones, laptops, fax cards and home business lines (all quite novel at the time), and a system was introduced to allow all calls to be rerouted to wherever staff were located.

BT was one of the strongest advocates of new ways of working (some would say that was inevitable). It established a blueprint for its offices known as "Workstyle 2000" in 1995. The initiative was part of a programme to relocate office-based staff out of central London. The project differed to Right Space in that it did not seek to maximise free addressing, but to change the way that people worked and improve the quality of their working environment. The concept was first tried at

---

13 Barker L (1995) The Right Space Project *Flexible Working* November pp34–35.

Westside, near Hemel Hempstead. Around 1500 people were accommodated in the 16,500 sq m (180,000 sq ft) building, with 1100 using permanent desks; 200 hot-desking and 200 using the building as a base. The workspace was provided with touchdown centres, hot desks, project rooms and quiet rooms. The ground floor provided a restaurant, a cafe, a shop, conferencing facilities and general social space.[14]

Andersen Consulting in Paris moved from La Defense to Avenue George V in the centre of Paris. The move involved 1200 staff, into space that, on a metre-to-metre basis, was 30% more expensive. However, annual savings of £650,000 were achieved through a radical approach to space management. Each floor had an attendant looking after workspace bookings and ensuring that PCs, telephones and other services were available when required. Lounges on the first floor were designed to encourage a welcoming ambiance for staff to meet each other and talk to clients. Other floors were divided into quiet areas, desks for writing reports and spaces for group meetings. There were no private offices or desks. The firm destroyed 150 tonnes of documents when it left La Defense. In the new space, personal property, work in progress, portable computers and phones are moved around in small rolling cabinets and stored in docking banks until needed again.[15]

One of the most celebrated examples of new ways of working was that provided by British Airways in its purpose-built headquarters at Waterside, near Heathrow. The building was officially opened in summer 1998, and was designed specifically to help transform the way that people worked, to allow the business to streamline its processes and to increase efficiency. The architect for the building was Niels Torp, designer of the famous SAS Airways building in Stockholm. Waterside comprises six, four-storey buildings, all radiating from a central, enclosed "street". The street is 175m (575ft) long and includes cafes, a bank, a supermarket, a travel centre, a newsagent and such like. The project involved the consolidation of nearly 3000 people from a large number of disparate sites. Although the occupancy profile of the buildings has evolved somewhat since opening, the building was designed to accommodate a highly mobile workforce, with widespread hot-desking and over 650 of the staff having no fixed workstation. To enable this approach to work, BA opted for a radical telecoms system,

---

14 Cited in: Workstyle 2000: A New Flexibility *Flexible Working* February 1996 p32.

15 Lawson D (1996) Paris Commune *Property Week* 7 March pp40–41.

with each member of staff being given a single phone number with a PIN, allowing them to use any telephone extension in the building.

Just how radical new ways of working can be is influenced strongly by the scale and culture of the organisation. This is amply demonstrated by some of the more *avant-garde* advertising agencies and media companies. Where the company is relatively small and the business culture is one that embraces self-motivated, independently minded and innovative people, then the solution can be very radical indeed. For example, media consultants Michaelides and Bednash created a new work environment for its 11 staff in 1994. The focus of the office was a single table, over 20m (76ft) long, shared by all staff. Each day staff move around the table to meet and work with colleagues as necessary. Advertising agency Howell Henry Chaldicott Lury replanned its office to allow 120 staff to move from desk to desk, and from space to space; and St Luke's introduced a radical design that included a pool room, chill-out room and restaurant. Open spaces and bright colours completed the ambiance of a free-thinking and creative culture for its 100 staff. No one had a desk and anyone could sit and work anywhere. Each person was given a locker; there were no secretaries and no fixed hours.

Although the corporate world was driven in the early-1990s by the need to save money and introduce business efficiencies, the original impetus for new methods of working was to support changing management structures and technology-enabled business processes. This positive push towards new methods of work was championed by the public sector. Many county councils, including Surrey, Oxfordshire and Hertfordshire, built on their already well-established approaches to flexi-time with a mix of part-time working, job sharing and home-working with more radical uses of office space. One of the earliest and most significant projects was the relocation and consolidation of the Ministry of Defence's (MoD's) Procurement Agency at Abbey Wood, near Bristol in 1997.

The project challenged assumptions about how the Civil Service should occupy office buildings and how people should work within them. Traditionally, the Civil Service had worked in highly stratified structures with a high proportion of cellular offices, and space and furniture were allocated on a rigid status basis. Inter-departmental communication was typically poor and bureaucracy was rife. The Procurement Agency itself was scattered around London, the south coast and Bath. The geographical separation inhibited communications, militated against the flexible deployment of staff around projects, and led to wide duplication of functions. There was a mix of IT systems and many of the buildings were poorly designed and operationally inefficient. The new headquarters facility comprised 130,000 sq m (1.4m sq ft) of accommodation, in 13 buildings clustered around four neighbourhoods. Each neighbourhood had a central covered "street" with cafes, meeting areas and support services, such as reprographics. The site had a nursery, exhibition hall, conference suite, lecture theatre and training facility. The office space is virtually all open plan, with senior managers working among their teams.

The MoD provided a showcase example of how office space could be used to radically change the culture of an organisation, and bring about major changes to its processes and systems, and actually change the way an organisation thought about itself. The problem with a number of the new ways of working projects that were implemented during the 1990s was, however, that they were borne out of a compromise. While there were many positive aspects to the projects in establishing new patterns of work, and while there was much progress as each new project learned from the previous, the underlying cost-cutting agenda influenced and restricted their scope.

In some cases, approaches to flexible working were taken up with a kind of missionary zeal by managements who forgot the needs of individuals in their search for balance sheet savings. They saw hot-desking and telecommuting as panaceas for space and cost saving. But they ignored the significant cultural and social difficulties that people would experience. Some offices took on a closer resemblance to production lines: clinical, depersonalised spaces, where family photos were banned for their association with personal space, and the trappings of office life, such as stationery, files and "bits and pieces", were pulled around the office in portable pedestals to the pre-booked desk, before being returned on leaving the office. Personal filing was commonly limited to one linear metre, where before several metres might have been the norm. Instead of liberating workers and allowing them to structure a work-style that suited their needs, for some hot-desking often led to a feeling in which the lack of personal space created a sense of not belonging, of insecurity and a feeling of being a production unit rather than a valued member of staff. For some, the positive aspects of home-working (such as more control over hours worked, less travelling time and more family time) were outweighed by the practical disadvantages of structuring output, getting management input, missing opportunities for training, not feeling part of the corporate culture and a sense that not being seen in the office could be detrimental to career opportunities. Such issues underscore the importance of treating new ways of working initiatives as part of a broader change management process rather than simply a property initiative to reduce costs. This was alluded to in the conclusion to the previous chapter where integrated business resource management was discussed.

It was not long before the limitations of the exclusively cost-driven approach to flexible working were recognised. Evidence of unsuccessful projects is always more difficult to find than successful ones, and even when known about, the information can present certain publishing difficulties. However, anecdotal evidence suggests that there emerged in the later-1990s several projects where staff began to push back against some of the more draconian space-saving measures. A number of projects experienced serious problems as staff started to find ever-more ingenious ways around the new space regimes and as, in some cases, disillusioned staff defected to competitor companies. The lesson was that cause and effect had become confused: the mistake had been made to regard the general reorganisation of physical assets as the effect of an important, but narrow, short-term management focus — cost-reduction strategies — when in fact the cause, beyond the recession, was a more fundamental reorganisation of business.

The lesson was that design should recognise diversity, not slavishly follow a narrow, cost-based interpretation of space allocation. As companies increasingly focused on areas such as people issues, intellectual capital and key performance indicators, so design should respond with ever-more subtle and ever-more bespoke solutions to provide businesses with an occupancy profile that closely mirrored and supported the operational objectives of their diverse business plans. In other words, the real need is to recognise the diversity of management structures, work processes and people issues, and the changes that each is experiencing, and to devise a wide range of occupancy solutions that can respond to the growing complexity of the demands that each places on the work environment and the services needed to support them. Richard Donkin wrote that hot-desking could "no longer be looked on as a development in isolation" and that:

> Those companies which have pioneered the trend ... are discovering that what began as physical change often inspired by a desire to make cost savings, is demanding a change in thinking, particularly by managers.[16]

---

16 Donkin R (1995) Tales of the Office Nomad *Financial Times* 29 May p9.

As the 1990s drew to a close and the economy eased, so new ways of working began re-establish itself in a more strategic context, and its role in supporting a broader business change began to be realised: the new work agenda had been taken off hold and a more creative approach to new ways of working began to emerge. Design practice DEGW was one of the first to categorise different styles of work and the types of environment needed to support them. DEGW identified four generic work environments — den, club, hive and cell — to express both the physical and behavioural characteristics of different kinds of work (see figure 9.1). These four groups are characterised as follows:

- The den environment supported group work, where teamwork was high and autonomy low.
- The club environment supported creative and knowledge-based work, where concentration was important and where interaction and autonomy were important.
- The hive supported process work, where both interaction and autonomy were low.
- The cell described individual work, where interaction was low and autonomy high.

Figure 9.1 New environments for working

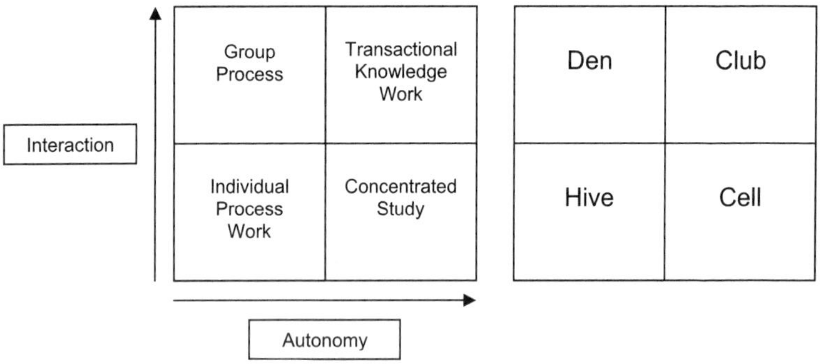

Source: Laing *et al*[17]

[17] Laing A, Duffy F, Jaunzens D and Willis S (1998) *New Environments for Working* Construction Research Communications Ltd, Watford.

This categorisation has stood the test of time and remains a useful way of gaining a rapid understanding of how an organisation's work processes translate into types of workspace.

DEGW had captured the essence of the strategy of IT-enabled new patterns of work, as had been outlined by Stone and Luchetti, and provided an intellectual underpinning for those organisations seeking to implement their own, specific projects. As the 21st century dawned, organisations were coming to be managed less as huge corporate machines and more as systems or networks in which work was increasingly about short-term assignments, communication, mobility and connectivity. In such organisations, knowledge becomes the currency of exchange, and traditional approaches to command and control structures break down. As these forces for change become stronger so, inevitably, the demand for office space will change.

The new office

In 1967, two futurologists, Herman Kahn and Anthony Weiner of the Hudson Institute in the US, published *The Year 2000: A Framework for Speculation on the Next Thirty Three Years*.[18] They took the then unusual approach of applying mathematical modelling, simulation techniques and qualitative assessments to a broad spectrum of technological and social trends in the hope of eliminating the subjectivity inherent in gathering the views of experts in particular fields. Many of their technological forecasts were incredibly prescient. They included: automation and cybernation in management and production; high-speed data processing; real-time credit, audit and banking systems; facsimile machines; high-quality reproduction; personal pagers and two-way pocket phones. All of these, and many others, have been central to the development of the office economy. Some of their other forecasts were less accurate. Personal flying platforms, such as interplanetary travel, have failed to materialise, and we still have cars with petrol engines and trains propelled by diesel. We do not have programmed dreams, chemical methods of improving the memory, cities lit by artificial moons, deep-sea mining or much influence over the

---

18 Kahn H and Weiner A J (1967) The Year 2000: A Framework for Speculation on the Next Thirty Three Years Macmillan, New York Cited in: John Kay: "The Future Is Not What It Used To Be" *Financial Times* 8 July 1998 p13.

weather. However, the work was hugely successful in anticipating some of the major changes that would touch everyone's lives, especially in the world of work, as the 20th century drew to a close.

Kahn and Weiner's work also raises an interesting dimension that is critical as we speculate on what the future office will look like. This is that the speed of technological change, and the possibilities opened up by it, far excels our own physiological and cultural abilities or aptitude to keep pace. We saw earlier in this chapter how the forecasts of the management gurus oversold the short-term impacts of technological developments on the way we work. As long ago as the 1970s, the paperless office was being anticipated, yet the annual usage of paper in offices has shown relentless year-on-year growth. The advent of the personal computer, and later the internet, led to claims that the era of the office was over and that the high street was redundant. This is technological determinism: because something is technologically possible, it will become a reality. Such hype reached its apotheosis in the dot.com boom of the late-1990s. Peter Drucker made the incisive observation that it is "the nature of knowledge that it changes fast and that today's certainties always become tomorrow's absurdities,"[19] but the claims for the dot.com market were by any measure fantastic.

Despite the enormous potential of technological advancement, our ability to absorb its implications and adapt rapidly is limited by behavioural traits that anchor us in the present. John Micklethwaite and Adrian Wooldridge[20] made the rather sobering comment that the most horrifying thing about the future of work may be just how similar it will be. Indeed, on one level, it might be argued that for the great majority of people the office of today is not very different to that of 20 or so years ago. While in a physical sense modern offices are generally of a higher quality than their predecessors of the 1960s and 1970s, the activity of office work is quite familiar. Many people have yet to be liberated from a fixed workstation; many are neither able nor permitted to structure their own work pattern; many remain task-oriented, and feel oppressed by the layers of seniority above them. Some employers do not allow or encourage internet access and home-working for fear that such "privileges" will be abused. And for large

---

19 Drucker P (1992) The New Society of Organizations *Harvard Business Review* September–October p96.

20 Micklethwaite J and Wooldridge A (1996) *The Witch Doctors* William Heinemann.

sections of the office workforce, the grim reality remains a daily commute to an office building and a workstation that, on a good day, just about allows them to do their job, in only minor discomfort.

Furthermore, the impact of much office technology has not been to liberate people and to lessen the hours they work and provide them with more leisure time. Laptops, faxes, mobile phones and home modems have all served to increase the time spent working (if not productivity) and increase the complexity of business relationships. The modern office environment, despite its technological advancement, has singularly "failed to address the growing bundle of problems that are arising from flattened organisations, greater numbers of mobile workers, information overload and time-based stress."[21] According to the Institute of Management, 41% of managers work over 50 hours a week and 13% work over 60 hours. Meanwhile, time off work for stress-related illness has increased by 500% since the 1950s.[22] The jobs might have changed dramatically, but the commitment to work remains just as high. For most people, Studs Terkel's plea from over 30 years ago will be uncomfortably applicable today:

> [work should be] about a search for daily meaning as well as daily bread, for recognition as well as cash, for astonishment rather than torpor, in short, for a sort of life rather than a Monday through Friday sort of dying.[23]

If BA's new headquarters and some of the more fashionable advertising agencies are models of the future, then they remain members of an exclusive club. The fact is that the great majority of office fit-outs are remarkably traditional. Even many of the case studies examined earlier disguise a tenacious grip on the past. This is partly explained by the fact that there remains huge inertia in the supply industry, which limits the opportunities for organisations to make truly radical changes to the way in which they organise themselves through space and time.

However, despite these cautious words, it would be foolish to deny that major changes are under way. Economic and technological change is relentless, and this is driving the office economy through an enormously turbulent time. This is bound to have major implications for the nature of the work that is conducted within offices and,

---

21 Cited in: Office of the Future *Financial Times Survey* 23 September 1998 ppi–iv.

22 Cited in: Toynbee P (1996) Is Work Good for You? *RSA Journal* March pp20–28.

23 Terkel S (1972) *Working* Avon Books, New York.

ultimately, for the type of office that is required, the amount of offices that will be required and on where they will be required.

As has been the theme throughout this book, to understand the nature of the new office, we must place our analysis in the context of the changing nature of demand, or the activities that are driving its changing profile. The service sector achieved its dominance of many western economies during the 1990s, with up to three-quarters of jobs being in the non-productive sectors. But the economy continues to evolve rapidly in response to competition and opportunities generated by commercial, social and technological pressures, often on a global scale. The nature of recent changes has led an increasing number of observers to argue that we are now witnessing the emergence of what is variously known as the quaternary, knowledge, or new economy. Table 9.1 is adapted from Diane Coyle and Danny Quah's work[24] and is, perhaps, one of the more useful summaries of the characteristics of the new economy.

The new economy is a vague term, and table 9.1 can be questioned in a number of areas. But it is clear that there are some significant trends within the economy that are leading to the re-organisation of jobs and the creation of new types of employment. Some of the more obvious outcomes of these changes within the office economy, and their impact on the demand for office space, are described below.

The Enron and WorldCom debacles and other recent examples of major failures in corporate governance have led the US Congress to introduce far-reaching measures to introduce transparency and accountability into public companies. The 2002 Sarbanes-Oxley Act (SOX) applies to all quoted US companies and puts in place CEO/CFO certification of accounts; improved financial disclosures; new roles for directors; more limited roles for accountants and attorneys, and defined criminal penalties. Given that real estate has a material impact on many companies' financial statements, new priorities will emerge. Corporate real estate executives will need to provide better, up-to-date information on their portfolios; they will need rigorous processes tracking acquisitions and disposals; they will need to normalise definitions, assumptions and metrics in transactions; they will need to document comprehensive real estate expenditure; and ensure accounting standards are applied to all excess space in the portfolio.

---

24 Coyle D and Quah D (2002) *Getting the Measure of the New Economy* The Work Foundation, London

Table 9.1 The new economy

Issues	*Old economy*	*New economy*
Economy-wide		
Markets	Stable	Dynamic
Scope of competition	National	Global
Organisational form	Hierarchical, bureaucratic	Networked
Structure	Manufacturing core	Services core
Sources of value	Raw materials, physical capital	Human and social
Business		
Organisation of production	Mass production	Flexible production
Key drivers of growth	Capital and labour	Innovation and knowledge
Key technology driver	Mechanisation	Digitisation
Competitive advantage	Lower costs	Innovation, quality, speed
Importance of research	Low-moderate	High
Relations with other firms	Go it alone	Alliances, outsourcing
Consumers		
Tastes	Stable	Changing rapidly
Skills	Job-specific	Broad and adaptable
Education needs	Craft or degree, one-off	Life-long learning
Workplace relations	Adversarial	Collaborative
Nature of employment	Stable	Risk and opportunity
Government		
Business relations	Impose regulations	Encourage growth
Regulation	Command and control	Market tools, flexibility
Government services	Nanny state	Enabling state

Source: adapted from Coyle and Quah[25]

A number of trends are likely to emerge as a result of these new demands. First, scrutiny of vendor relationships is likely to intensify as they themselves have to be SOX-compliant. Second, outsourcing of CRE might increase as companies seek to transfer risk. Third, best practice in management information systems (MIS) will become a

25 Coyle and Quah (2002) *op cit* p6.

priority. Finally, CRE decisions may become more centralised, reducing the opportunities for local decisions. All of this will lead to much tighter control of real estate assets, and probably to less willingness to lease real estate without a clear business case being prepared and approved.

Alongside new measures to improve corporate governance, there remains a perpetual search for cost savings. For example, the concept of core and periphery space is gathering ground, where a core of long-term property is held for planned headcount, complemented by shorter-term space to allow the organisation to respond flexibly to changes in business demand. Such approaches use sophisticated MIS systems that link space to financial performance measures, allowing constant review of the disposition and cost of space. The quality of benchmarking data has improved in recent years, and corporate occupiers are increasingly knowledgeable about the costs of their occupancy. Growing numbers of companies now relate their occupancy costs to some measure of business performance as a means of controlling their cost bases. One of the more common is the "affordability index", where the costs of occupancy as a proportion of turnover are used to control occupancy costs. In professional services firms, for example, an affordability ratio of between 10% and 12% is generally regarded as appropriate, while in banking, a lower figure of 7–8% might be a more realistic target.

The point about these apparently benign measures of corporate governance is that they act as a real brake on demand. As boardrooms accept more responsibility for decisions relating the property acquisition, capital projects and cost-reduction programmes, and as corporate real estate managers have better cost-containment tools at their disposal, so the acquisition of new space becomes a less reactive process. In short, occupiers are becoming more discerning about the quantum and quality of space they occupy and over the terms under which they do so.

There is growing evidence to suggest that the overall average density at which buildings are occupied is rising. In short, companies are "sweating" their assets to accommodate more people in less space. A decade or so ago, a density of 18–20 sq m of net lettable area (194–215 sq ft) was normal. The latest *Total Office Cost Survey* suggests that the overall average is now 14 sq m (150 sq ft) per person, and that the ICT sector is down to 12.5 sq m (134 sq ft) per person.[26] This phenomenon is

---

26 Actium Consult and Cass Business School (2004) *The Total Office Cost Survey Summary* March.

widely referred to as "spaceless growth" and there is increasing anecdotal evidence that the trend is permanent rather than simply a cyclical response to recessionary pressures. There are two principle ways of achieving higher occupancy densities.

First, allocations per person are reduced. Those companies that use corporate standards regularly review allocations and, in recent years, have adjusted them downwards. This strategy is effective, but has limitations due to building regulations on fire escapes, WCs and so on. For employees in open plan, there is simply less space around their workstations; while many of those organisations that have traditionally awarded enclosed offices to middle managers to mark their seniority are now shunning such extravagance in favour of sensitively designed open plan environments that can support higher densities. Support space budgets (including facilities such as meeting rooms, catering, storage and so on) are also more tightly managed to allow the overall density to increase. Historically, support space has regularly exceeded 25% of the total space budget, but is now more frequently around 20% and occasionally even as low as 15%.

Second, workspace is managed more dynamically, through the introduction of hot-desking, desk sharing and alternative work styles (discussed in more detail below). Such initiatives allow a building to support more people in the same amount of space. First introduced among mainly sales forces and consulting staff, such practices are now increasingly widespread and clearly a permanent feature rather than simply a knee-jerk response to cost pressure. Their impact on overall densities can be dramatic. Increasing numbers of companies are introducing alternative working strategies. Such regimes give individuals greater control over exactly where and when they carry out their work, with the *quid pro quo* that ownership of desks is surrendered. More importantly, such practices can reduce an organisation's demand for space by around 20–30%. Increasingly companies are introducing at least some element of alternative work styles.

The benefit of these strategies to reduce the amount of space per person and to maximise the utilisation of space through time is, of course, the achievement of reduced costs per head and therefore better bottom-line performance. When combined with initiatives that enable people to be "more productive" or "more effective", they can have a dramatic effect on an organisation's profile of demand for space.

Businesses operate within increasingly complex webs of relationships and rely on ever-more specialised input to their business processes. Much of this expertise is provided from outside of the organisation. The nature of the work that is undertaken, the processes used to support it, and the skills required, as well as when and where the work is undertaken are all changing. The consistent messages have been about mobility, virtual work, outsourcing, delayering and re-engineering, and the notion of the distributed workforce in dispersed workplaces to provide space for more agile business is gaining ground quickly.

Desktop PCs are already disappearing in many organisations, to be replaced by portable laptops, and this trend will spread much further. This will have an effect on workstation requirements and configurations. Broadband is having a dramatic impact on working patterns by giving individuals much more flexibility in their choice of workplace. Unified messaging is on its way, with combined e-mail, fax and voice messaging accessible from an Outlook-type interface on laptops and hand-held devices. Voice messages will be accessed either as attached recordings or will be transcribed into text by voice-recognition software. Voiceover IP will spell the death of the telephone. This technology transmits the voice over the internet, allowing companies in multiple locations to keep in contact for much-reduced costs. Abbey National has already gone live. Roving profiles and wireless networks with have further ramifications not only in enabling new work styles, but also in the nature of the buildings needed to support them.

Such technology is also reaching the domestic market. BT and Yahoo recently joined forces and have just launched a mass market voice over the internet product that allows consumers to manage all their home communications — phone calls, webcam, e-mails, texts and instant messaging — together in one place on their PC. Multi-way video will follow. This genuinely converged multi-media communications package will have ramifications far beyond the household. Vodafone and Microsoft have also announced an alliance that will integrate mobile phones and PCs. Developments such as these have already made communications between office and home very simple, and new products will push flexibility further. WiFi is set for explosive growth, further loosening the bonds to a fixed physical environment. WiFi enables companies to extend their networks to impractical or costly locations (homes, hotels, transport interchanges etc), allowing easy internet and network access to remote or mobile workers.

Because of all these trends, the office will increasingly be an enabler of communication, allowing people to interact with ease as the shift from process labour to knowledge labour gathers pace, and it will have to provide a much wider variety of settings in which individuals and groups can carry out their diverse activities. It will need to accommodate those individuals based permanently in the space, as well as the needs of those working part-time for the organisation and those visiting for work. The technology will have to cope with a multi-tasking, mobile and itinerant workforce. Increasingly, the office is becoming less a place to go to work, and more a place to visit and interact with colleagues and use support services. Frances Cairncross has argued that the office will become a place for the social aspects of work, such as celebrating, networking, lunching and gossiping.[27] Consequently, the range of environments within an office will become more diversified to allow for increasingly complex relationships to flourish. Table 9.2 shows a number of activities important in the new office, and for which settings will have to be provided. Clearly, our traditional approaches to providing open-plan floors, with some offices for managers, and a smattering of ill-sized formal meeting rooms will be inadequate to meet such a demand.

Table 9.2 The new office agenda

Communicate	Trade, meet, discuss, entertain, network and negotiate.
Analyse	Learn, create, research, design and forecast.
Share	Exchange, compare, co-operate, support and collaborate.

The technological developments outlined above are also having a major impact on traditional forms of employment. More and more people will be pulled (by quality of life factors) and pushed (by employers eager to save overhead costs) to work at least part-time or from home. There is also anecdotal evidence that the number of self-employed and smaller limited companies is increasing in key sectors, reflecting the ease with which individuals can now operate commercially outside the bounds of larger companies. The Institute for Employment Research has forecast that the growth of employment through to 2012 will be underpinned by female workers and part-time jobs.[28] Perhaps more significantly, they have also shown that the

27 Cairncross F (1997) *The Death of Distance* Orion Business Books.

28 Wilson R, Homenidou K and Dickerson A (2004) *Working Futures: New Projections of Occupational Structure by Sector and Region, 2002–2012* Vol 1 National Report Institute for Employment Research, University of Warwick.

number of self-employed is increasing significantly. Thus, self-employment increased by 282,000 (8.9%) in the year to September 2003, including 120,000 in financial and business services (the office economy).[29] Over a slightly longer timescale, the number of "sole directors of own limited companies" has risen from around 165,000 in 2001 to around 220,000 in 2003.[30] These are significant indicators of the liberating effect of technology and the consequently lower dependency of knowledge workers on the traditional office organisation.

The Institute for Employment Research has suggested a slowing-down of growth in the office economy, stating that while some parts of the service sector are set to grow at 4% per annum through to 2012, "banking and insurance are projected to grow at less than half this rate".[31] In further reference to the service sector, the report goes on: "this broad sector's share of all jobs is not expected to increase significantly between 2002 and 2012" and that "most of the projected employment growth [in the service sector] is accounted for by health and education services".[32]

Projections about the future impact of information technology on patterns of work during the 1990s tended to polarise between the Panglossian optimism of the technology apostles like Drucker, who believed that the changes taking place then were more profound than the Industrial Revolution, and the Armageddon merchants of doom like Norbert Weiner, who forecast that computer technology would destroy enough jobs to make the depression of the 1930s look like a picnic.[33] One forecast suggested, for example, that within 30 years, as little as 2% of all the world's current labour force would be needed to produce all the goods necessary for total demand.[34] The bulk of evidence suggests that something more subtle is happening. This is that as the effects of technology take hold, there will result a redistribution of employment and skills, and this redistribution will not necessarily mean continued demand for traditional forms of office accommodation. If the trends in the growth of self-employment and

---

29 Macaulay C (2003) Changes to Self-employment in the UK: 2002 to 2003 *Labour Market Trends* December pp623–628.

30 Lindsay C and Macaulay C (2004) Growth in Self-employment in the UK *Labour Market Trends* October pp399–404.

31 Wilson *et al* (2004) *op cit* p4.

32 Wilson *et al* (2004) *op cit* p5.

33 Cited in: A World Without Jobs? *The Economist* 11 February 1995 p23.

34 Toynbee (1996) *op cit*.

the forecasts of a slowing-down of the office economy are correct, then there are some clear signals for the office supply industry. We shall return to these in the concluding chapter.

It is becoming commonplace to find large numbers of people working within buildings who are not on the payroll of the occupying company. These are contract people, who will often not have a dedicated workstation — either in the host organisation or at their base organisation. They provide everything from secretarial support, audit and accounting functions, temp support, IT support to routine building maintenance tasks. Many are outsourced functions, and outsourcing changes the profile of demand as companies consider where to accommodate functions in core and periphery space. The outsourcing market is set to grow further and is likely to have a dampening effect on demand. Companies see the opportunity to reduce their commitment to real estate by accommodating fewer people.

By way of a real example, one company outsourced its entire IT, property and people functions. To enable this to happen, it established a "service centre", essentially a special purpose vehicle, responsible for delivering back into the business a comprehensive range of support services. The three outsourced organisations were all nationally-based organisations, with no employment or representation in the client's locality. The arrangement enabled the client to fix its overhead costs for a 10-year period, and secure a shared savings regime, whereby any savings made in the overhead costs would be shared between the service provider and the client. Most staff previously employed by the client in the relevant support areas were transferred to the outsourcing businesses. This involved nearly 300 people, or around 15% of the payroll. Discussions have now begun to relocate the outsourced staff away from the client buildings, allowing the client to surrender a whole building, representing around 25% of its property costs. Some space will be retained for sensitive areas, such as HR, but the remainder will be offsite.

In autumn 2004, the Director General of the Confederation of British Industry, the leading employers' organisation, told his annual conference that there would "be no jobs for unskilled workers in Britain within 10 years.[35] His was a dramatic message, made for dramatic effect. Nevertheless, he was at least in part alluding to a phenomenon that was having a growing impact on the office economy

---

35 Cited in: Unskilled Jobs to go in 10 Years *The Daily Telegraph* 8 November 2004 p1.

— offshoring. Much has been claimed in recent times about the offshoring of jobs to low-cost locations, principally in the Far East. Private consulting firm Forrester Research predicted that 3.3 million US jobs would be lost overseas by 2015.[36] In a follow-up report, Forrester Research predicted 1.2 million Eurozone jobs disappearing the same way, with 760,000 of them coming from the UK.[37] This latter report noted that India produces two million graduates each year, most fluent in English. And the potential threat is not limited to call centres. India has one of the most expansive software development industries in the world, and business consulting company McKinsey has a large proportion of its researchers based there.

The impact on office jobs is clear from table 9.3. A brief review of recent announcements counts over 49,000 jobs offshored — the equivalent of nearly six Canary Wharf towers. The key lesson is that many more jobs than hitherto have been considered are less obviously tied to the UK than was the case 10 years ago. One consequence of this offshoring of activity is to increase the pool of qualified workers, while suppressing the spiralling labour costs of three to four years ago. While some in the agency community feel that this will lead to a greater concentration of specialist, high-value jobs in the region, with a consequent increased demand for high-quality and responsive office space, overall the impact could be a net reduction in demand.

Table 9.3 emphasises that not all the jobs offshored are accounted for by call centre functions. They include back-office processing, administration, accounts, payroll and human resources. Also, in the US, companies such as GE and McKinsey have shown that high-end functions, from investment banking software development and medical research can all be offshored. With labour costs one-eighth of those in the UK, and occupational costs one-quarter, the contrast is stark and the choices obvious.

The property boom of the 1980s and early-1990s was caused partly because of the obsolescence of much of the office stock built during the 1960s and 1970s. Suddenly, the complexity of buildings and building services grew in order to accommodate the ever-more intense deployment of technological infrastructure used by occupiers.

---

36 McCarthy J C (2002) *3.3 Million US Services Jobs to Go Offshore* Forrester Research Institute, Cambridge, MA.

37 Parker A (2004) *Two Speed Europe: Why 1 Million Jobs will Move Offshore* Forrester Research Institute, Cambridge, MA.

Table 9.3 Offshoring from the UK

Company	*Function*	*Jobs*
Abbey National	IT development	100
ABN Amro	Credit risk management	2000
Accenture	Back office and software	3500
American Express	Various back office	4000
AOL	Customer support	1500
Aviva	Administration and IT	3550
Axa	Back office	100
Barclays	Business banking and credit	150
British Airways	Passenger accounting and other	2400
BT	Customer support	2200
Capital One	Customer services and risk operations	1200
Citibank	Banking products, billing and back office	3000
Dell	Customer support	3800
Fidelity Investments	Business process outsourcing	250
Goldman Sachs	Administration and IT	250
HSBC	Accounting and transactions	6000
JP Morgan Chase	Transaction processing services	3000
Lloyds TSB	Call centre	1000
Morgan Stanley	Transaction support	1600
National Rail Enquiries	Call centre	600
Prudential	Call centre	850
Standard Chartered	Various banking services	4500
Tesco	Call centre	350

However, recent trends suggest that the intensity of technology in buildings will reduce. Buildings will continue to have wired networks but they will increasingly use fibre optics rather than copper cable, and WiFi will have a growing significance within buildings. The former will be used where a totally reliable connection is needed and to carry bandwidth-hungry information, such as video-conferencing. The greater adoption of mobile working and plug-and-play devices linked via the internet will mean that the huge communications rooms in basements will become much smaller. Thus it is likely that, for most businesses, the demands that they place on their physical surroundings will diminish rather than intensify. Connectivity is now the single-most important criterion, and Wifi and Bluetooth technology, together with laptops, PDAs and computer tablets, will distribute demand and reduce the need, for example, for raised floors and expensive-to-maintain air-handling systems.

Technology, such as Motorola's ZigBee technology, enables the automation, control, monitoring and maintenance in buildings to take place in a wireless environment, thereby lessening the demand for huge risers packed with cabling. In short, buildings generally will need to be de-specified. The most likely impacts of such trends are that occupiers' needs will become more diverse, with implications for services infrastructure, while smaller units will become more important and space will become more commoditised. Greater mobility, increased demands for accessibility and workplace diversity will be critical.

As well as technological obsolescence, there is also the question of economic obsolescence. Occupiers have become much more adept in recent years at specifying their requirements and they have begun to question the whole life costs of buildings. It has become commonplace in PFI deals, for example, to specify the running costs of buildings. The outcome of these trends is a demand for certainty over cost and for the "de-specifying" of expensive features that increase running costs. Everything from air-handling systems to glazing systems to marble receptions are being reviewed for their cost implications. The significance for this report is that, as and when demand returns to the market, it will not necessarily be for the same highly specified buildings that were created on so many business parks during the 1980s and 1990s.

However it is defined, it is clear that the "new economy" is having some very significant impacts on the organisation of jobs and is leading to the creation of new types of employment. Because many of these changes are technology-driven, or technology-enabled, their impact on white-collar work, or the office, is and will continue to be profound. Some of the more obvious outcomes of these changes have been reviewed here, and it is clear that their effect on the demand for office space is likely to be far-reaching. Not only is the overall level of demand likely to change, but the profile of demand is likely to alter dramatically. New approaches to employment and career management; work-life balance issues; mobility, connectivity and ubiquitous access; distributed workforces and flexible working patterns are all converging at great speed to change the nature of demand for office space. These trends present the property-supply industry with a huge opportunity to re-think the supply model that has been in existence since the end of the last war, and to offer new products and services that meet the emerging demands of the contemporary office economy.

10 The Office of Tomorrow

A maturing office economy

We saw in earlier chapters how, during the 20th century, the office economy grew and matured into a fundamentally important and distinct facet of urban life. Five decades of almost continuous growth in the number of office workers after 1945 resulted in nearly half the working population being employed in offices. A process that began with the reorganisation of the US economy and the international expansion of European economies in the latter years of the 19th century, passing through white-collar factories and the rise of corporatism in the 1950s and 1960s, reached its apotheosis almost exactly 100 years later. Financial deregulation and globalisation during the 1980s, followed by the dramatic consequences of the revolution in information and communication technologies, helped to redefine the office economy. By the end of this process of change, office activities had become the dominant force in the economy and office buildings had become a defining feature of the urban landscape. This book has outlined a breathtaking pace of change in the nature of office work, the organisations at its heart and the buildings in which it is housed. How will it evolve over the next 20 years? Will there be more of the same? Or will the office economy begin a new phase of change, once again, testing our abilities to respond to its changing demands on the physical environment?

Economic turbulence, the impending millennium and rapid technological developments in the 1990s conspired to produce a crop of texts all with a similar ring to their titles, for example: *The End of History and the Last Man*;[1] *The End of Science*;[2] *The Death of Economics*;[3] *The End of Work*;[4] and *The Death of Distance*.[5] The common feature of these texts of course was the sense that society, or at least the rich, western, capitalist portion of it, was on the brink of fundamental change. And it was not long before observers of the office economy started to write in similar fashion. Many books and articles predicted fundamental change in office work and the traditional office environment. Radical corporate structures, emerging markets and new technologies were all implicated. They were heralded as harbingers of a new era in which our definition of white-collar work would be rewritten. The claims were reminiscent of the popular BBC TV programme *Tomorrow's World*. Launched in 1965 soon after Harold Wilson made his famous remarks about the white heat of the technological revolution, the programme dealt largely with new inventions and innovations. So fantastic did some of the products seem that rather than contemplate the ramifications, it was often easier to adopt the "not in my lifetime" stance.

In some ways, the office economy at the beginning of the 21st century is experiencing a similar syndrome. The potential changes are so great, and the implications so profound, that it is often easier — particularly from a supply-side perspective — to imagine that things will remain as they are. But just as *Tomorrow's World* had notable successes in predicting new technologies, such as computer banking, the pocket calculator, the digital watch and the personal stereo, so many of the projections for the office economy will become reality. The question is which and what will be the implications? One of the central themes of this book has been change, and we have seen, particularly during the past 20 years, immense change in the spatial and structural organisation of the office economy. The projection that there is more to come is undeniable. This concluding chapter examines some of the implications of continuing change within the office economy for office buildings, for the providers of office buildings and for the urban environment.

One of the continuing consequences of the transformation of the office economy is that growth has come to be taken almost as a given.

---

1 Fukuyama F (1993) *The End of History and the Last Man* Avon Books.
2 Horgan J (1997) *The End of Science* Little, Brown.
3 Ormerod P (1994) *The Death of Economics* Faber & Faber.
4 Rifkin J (1995) *The End of Work* G P Putnam & Sons.
5 Cairncross F (1997) *The Death of Distance* Orion Business Books.

With the exception of a small number of hiccups, the growth of the office economy since the end of the last war has been relentless. Employment in offices has grown generally, and more and more people have been employed to undertake increasingly specialised, knowledge-based work. As the office economy has grown, so too the demand for office space has expanded: more output, more people, more space. During the past two decades, this relationship between growth and demand has been fuelled further by the impact of ICT, which has had the dual effect of generating demand from a growing sector of the economy (ie technology- and media-based companies), and of creating secondary demand by rendering large swathes of building stock prematurely obsolete to the needs of organisations that had become dependent upon highly complex technology infrastructure. Between 1985 and 2005, and in round terms, the amount of office space in the UK nearly doubled, from 50m sq m (538m sq ft) to around 97m sq m (1050m sq ft)[6]. Our capital city, our metropolitan cities, county towns and suburban towns have almost without exception all shared in this huge change. But of course, such growth begs the question: will we need to double the amount of office space again over the next 20 years? It is difficult to see how this could be the case, and much of the material in this book provides the evidence for a rather different conclusion.

The situation in the London office market appears to reinforce the need for a more cautious interpretation. Viewed in the long term, the growth of the office economy during the post-war period can be seen as the latest in a long line of growth spurts that have shaped London's development over the past several centuries. Cubitt's generation had no less a dramatic impact on the shape and texture of the city when it created the great estates to house London's burgeoning and increasingly affluent population during the 19th century. As with most great cities, London has grown in fits and starts, as economic and social change has dictated. In this context, the growing office economy was absorbed into the fabric of the city and increasingly complex buildings were created to house its changing needs. But there is no innate reason to assume that its growth trajectory will continue.

---

6 Hillier Parker Research (1986) *Commercial and Industrial Floorspace Statistics England 1983–1986* Hillier Parker London, and Office of the Deputy Prime Minister (2003) *Commercial and Industrial Floorspace and Rateable Value Statistics 2002* ODPM, London.

At the start of 2005, around one-fifth of the office space in the City of London lies fallow. This amounts to no less than 1.4million sq m (15million sq ft). Beyond London, the Thames Valley and M25 office markets are awash with empty real estate — 1.1million sq m (12million sq ft) lies idle along the M4 corridor alone. Seasoned observers of the office market explain such oversupply in the context of cyclical trends and, indeed, recent historic experience broadly supports the view that gradually the space will be filled, and a new round of development will begin. But this short-term historical experience is not in fact a reliable guide to the future, and there are sufficient signals emanating from the office economy to suggest that something more structural is occurring, something that has major implications for all those involved in the supply, management and occupation of office buildings. Central to this structural change hypothesis is the notion that a number of drivers of change within the office economy are conspiring to create a situation in which it is no longer appropriate to assume that continued growth of output from the office economy means a correlating growth in the demand for additional office space. Organisations within the office economy have been working hard to remain competitive, and this has resulted in them taking a far more stringent view of their commitments to real estate.

It is clear that the relationship between occupiers and the space that they fill has changed as our understanding of the role of the office and its impact on organisational and individual performance has changed over the past two decades. The predominantly static, slow-moving organisations of the 1960s and 1970s have largely disappeared. Global competition, a changing economic landscape, emergent economies and the pervasive impact of ICT have all conspired to make the old model obsolete. Organisations are now structuring themselves to cope with uncertainty, to manage risk, and for responsiveness and flexibility. Whether large or small, public or private, and whether operating on the international stage or simply the domestic one, organisations are responding to pressures and forces of change that are pervasive through the office economy. They are also finding that their offices can act as a drag on their businesses and that it can be difficult to align the changing business landscape with the traditional form of property supply:

The accelerated business cycle ... has further stressed the relationships between organizations and their physical assets. Fixed physical assets cannot be reconfigured to meet changing business needs as quickly as organizational processes and structures may be modified .... Patterns of work and structures of organizations are evolving faster than the built environment can be transformed to meet their needs.[7]

Despite such tensions, many companies are adopting radical approaches to their use of space in response to the need for aggressive cost-containment measures, and they are finding that, by deploying their resources in new ways, they are able to achieve growth in output, or profits, without incurring the growth in headcount that has traditionally driven demand for space. As we saw in chapter 9, jobless growth leading to spaceless growth is already a reality, and is spreading as organisations introduce flexible working programmes. There is not only the possibility that long-awaited productivity gains from technology are beginning to emerge, but also the threat that new growth might not occur in the expensive office centres of Western Europe and North America but in the growing, lower-cost cities of the Asian economies.

It should also be remembered that the high vacancy rates mentioned above have occurred in the context of an economy that has enjoyed full employment for over three years. Unlike the high vacancy levels of the early 1990s, when the recession led to widespread, albeit quite short-term, reductions in office employment, today's vacancy levels have persisted during a period of office growth. If the high levels of vacancy in the office market are not fully explained by the business cycle, then they might be further evidence of a structural shift either in the relationship of office employment to economic growth, or the relationship of office space to office employment, or both. Such shifts are not easily captured by the statistical indicators that drive economic and property forecasts.

Just as organisations are constantly adapting in response to external pressures, so too are the people who work within them. Perhaps one of the most important features here is the trend towards choice and diversity. The traditional stereotype of the nine-to-five, white-collar office worker, with a job for life, and a highly structured work routine within a rigid command and control environment has been largely destroyed during the past 20 years. As organisations have responded to economic and technological change by becoming more flexible,

---

7 Harrison A, Wheeler P and Whitehead C (2004) *The Distributed Workplace* Spon Press, London p7.

adaptable and responsive to rapid shifts in their market environments, so the individuals within them have changed. "Knowledge workers" have emerged, whose value to the organisation lies in their unique contribution rather than in the output from a process that they manage. But workers generally have a different range of expectations and aspirations than was the case even 20 years ago. They are more mobile, more demanding, more discerning and increasingly willing and able to exercise choice over where and when they work. They are exercising choice, in part, to improve the quality of their lives, and they are increasingly introducing mixed mode working — part in the office, part at home and part elsewhere.

In a not unrelated signal of change from the office economy and its growing diversity, there is a rapidly growing number of small and medium-sized enterprises (SMEs). The liberating impact of technology, enabling SMEs to work in complex webs of relationships, is likely to see their number increase rapidly. Even for the larger organisations, their relationships with the people who work for them are undergoing important changes. For example, increasing numbers of people undertake contractually based work for limited time periods, while others work permanently for the organisation, but from outside. In these circumstances, and others, there is an overall net reduction in the number of people for whom the organisation needs to provide a permanent place of work, and a different style of workplace for those whom it does.

There are then a number of factors emanating from the office economy to suggest that a period of structural change is under way, and that the period of maximal growth is closing and a more mature phase of development is about to emerge. Such an interpretation fits with the longer-term perspective on the evolution of the office economy described in this book, in which the growth of the office economy can be seen to have a beginning (the late-19th century), a middle (perhaps the 1960s and 1970s) and an end (possibly beginning around now). It should be emphasised that it is the *growth* of the office econ-omy that is being questioned here, not the existence of the office economy itself.

If this prognosis for a new phase of development in the office economy proves to be correct, then the first and most obvious implication is that it seems unlikely that we will need to continue supplying offices at the phenomenal rate of the past, say, 20 years. This apparently simple, even naive conclusion, is in fact rather important. Of course, there will continue to be a need to replace obsolete stock, and opportunities will continue to be taken to create new stock. But if the relentless year-on-year growth in demand for offices that has characterised the past several decades ceases, and a period in which consolidation and re-organisation are more pervasive dynamics than growth, then some of the basic premises upon which the supply process is based must be questioned, and new approaches to the supply and management of office buildings will be called for.

New offices for new work

Within all this change, there are emerging a number of trends that provide insights into kinds of buildings that will be required to house an evolving office economy. Organisations are more permeable than in the past — they increasingly link into other organisations that provide specialist skills into others in their particular supply chain and into their customers. Working in partnership and collaboratively with other organisations is becoming more common. Some of the great corporate buildings built in London for the likes of Shell, Unilever and National Provincial Bank stood as edifices to corporate grandeur, but also they reflected isolationism. In the much more highly networked modern office economy, where connectivity is all-important, physical and cultural barriers are being dismantled within and between organisations. The "head office" is increasingly coming to be seen as the hub at the heart of a complex web of relationships, rather than a solid, physical representation of an organisation's strength and repute. Too many corporate ghosts lie in the accountants' cupboards to pretend any longer that a big building with all the marble and brass trimmings represents solidity and strength. The office will therefore increasingly perform a different kind of function — perhaps providing the cultural heart of an organisation into which employees, customers and other stakeholders connect as and when they need to do so. As organisations become more permeable, then so will the space that they occupy, suggesting different approaches to the design and provision of work environments.

While 20 years ago it was possible to accommodate monochrome-style organisations in equally monochrome space, today's more dynamic organisations require something more than a "one size fits all" style of accommodation. Increasingly, diverse working patterns require a more subtle approach to the provision of working environments and support services within the workplace. People who are able to exercise immense choice in their personal lives expect no less from their work environment. And organisations whose future prosperity depends upon highly skilled and expensive workers have to define themselves through the quality of work environments that they provide and the arrangements within which the work is conducted. The stark contrast that once existed between home and work is blurring, and the qualities that individuals have traditionally attached to their homes, such as comfort, choice, individualism and personal control, are creeping into the workplace. For example, there is a growing demand for more social space within office buildings. An increasingly itinerant workforce that exercises much greater choice than ever before about its work style is demanding more than simply a large, sedentary workstation or an enclosed office. Interaction with colleagues, distinctive settings for different kinds of work, instant and ubiquitous connectivity and support services are all critical and suggestive of the need to supply more than simply rented space on long leases. Growing numbers of forward-looking organisations have begun to tackle this new form of accommodation planning, and are finding increasingly innovative ways of utilising their offices as business enablers rather than as inert, costly drags on their businesses.

Andrew Harrison and colleagues succinctly summarised the pressures for change within the office economy and leading to a demand for alternative office models, with a focus on organisational change, shifting locational priorities and the impact of information technology:

- The changing nature of business organisations requiring greater flexibility in the use of space and time; allowing rapid responses to operational needs; and responding to higher expectations of employees for quality.
- The location of office work being far less constrained as a result of information technologies, enabling work to take place in a wide variety of locations both within and outside the conventional office building.
- The ubiquitous provision of information technology, which means that although workstation design will remain important, other shared working settings, meeting rooms, and other intelligent environments will become more significant.[8]

Each of these three factors is highly significant in creating a growing

8 Harrison *et al* (2004) *op cit* p11.

demand for a richer texture of office environments, supplied and managed in different ways to the established model. Whether for large companies seeking more flexible space for a part of their business process, or whether for SMEs seeking space on demand at a reasonable cost and with service provision added, there will clearly be opportunities for owners to consider a more demand-driven approach to offices.

While the supply process might have been slow to respond to these changes, there is no doubt that office organisations themselves have been developing increasingly sophisticated approaches to real estate management. Consequently, the office workplace has come to be regarded as something more than a physical shell within which economic activity is undertaken. A step change took place in the mid-1980s, as new thinking over product development and market research emerged to influence the nature of the space supplied, particularly in response to the growing influence of ICT and as approaches to building management became more professional. As a result, the role of the office in supporting and enabling organisational change has come to be understood more clearly. Organisations are increasingly managing their offices as an integral part of organisational planning and space is now expected to have a direct, positive impact on the performance of the business that it accommodates. Consequently, the management of the office is becoming more transparent, more performance-driven and more accountable. Ultimately, this will have a suppressing effect on demand as decisions over additional space come under increased scrutiny and as alternative ways of accommodating growth are implemented. Office space is also being organised to allow for flexibility. For example, larger organisations are increasingly organising around core (long term) and periphery (flexible and short term) offices to give themselves degrees of freedom in their forward planning. In another development, the critical interdependencies between accommodation, people and technology are being recognised, and integrated planning for all three resource areas is more common. Again, the impact on demand will be suppressing as the people and technology experts find more imaginative solutions to growth than simply taking more real estate.

The growing influence of integrated resource planning is also casting a spotlight on the traditional concept of the office building itself. This issue revolves around the apparently semantic difference between property and accommodation. The prevalent *upstairs-downstairs* approach to property and accommodation planning (referred to in chapter 8) led to chronic inefficiencies in its management and a focus on property issues, such as leases and values, to the detriment of service provision — a situation mirrored in the property-supply process. The term "property" comes with historical baggage: it has associations with ownership and title, it has major obligations, and it is associated with commitment. "Accommodation", on the other hand, is a resource, something to move in and out of; something to change and reconfigure as and when the business demands; something to take when needed and dispose of when not. Until recently, there has only been property, with space available on long leases to those organisations considered to be sufficiently financially robust. Serviced offices and other solutions have gone someway to addressing the balance, but there is emerging a growing need for the commoditisation of space, with offices being increasingly available as *accommodation* rather than as *property*. Of course, such a shift in mindset would require a wholesale change in the traditional property-supply process, and is therefore unlikely to occur in the short term.

A new agenda for property supply

The many signals of change from within the office economy raise a number of questions for those involved in the property-supply process. It is inconceivable that the demand for offices can continue to change without some significant implications for the structure and organisation of the supply chain. The transformation of the office economy over the past 50-plus years provided the office-supply industry with an extraordinary platform for growth. Although interrupted by periodic slumps, owners and developers enjoyed over five decades of expansion in their effort to keep pace with the almost insatiable appetite of the office economy to consume an ever-larger amount of real estate. Such was the growth of the office economy in the second half of the 20th century that the supply industry dictated the terms upon which the space was traded and occupied; and speculative development became the predominant form of supply because anticipated growth in demand could justify the necessary funding stream. Funding institutions emerged at the centre of the whole process, investing the insurance premiums and pension savings of their customers in commercial property, in the expectation that the value of real estate would continue to outstrip inflation.

Yet, as we saw in chapter 4, regular bouts of overdevelopment, followed by spectacular crashes, have featured strongly in the post-war history of the office market. The quality of the built stock, with some notable exceptions, was largely poor. And there has been an almost total disconnect with the real customer of the development process, the occupier. These are symptoms of structural weaknesses in the supply process. The availability of cheap money on soft terms, within the context of institutional lease arrangements that secured income streams for 25 years, contributed to a process in which speculative developers moved between phases of over and undersupply. And for several decades the office property-supply industry operated as a "one product industry". It supplied a standard product, built to a standard specification, let on standard terms. There was little product differentiation, and even less supplier differentiation. For a period of time, the industry mirrored the occupiers of its products. Large and clumsy with undifferentiated armies of clerical staff, corporate businesses between the 1950s and 1970s made fairly uniform demands on their space. Those who supplied space made little effort to be any different. But as we have seen, the nature of occupiers has changed fundamentally. The supply process has changed only marginally.

The demands of the institutional lease militated against competition in local markets, and they worked against the interests of very large numbers of small businesses whose covenant was not regarded as sufficiently robust. Institutions standardised the product in order to meet their requirements as an investment vehicle rather than as an operational asset for the companies that occupied the space. Attitudes have softened in recent times, and some companies in the supply chain have begun to contemplate the notion of service provision alongside their more traditional role. However, the "let and forget" philosophy has remained dominant, and there has been no incentive to add value through innovative approaches to management or design. In the US, where leases are for shorter periods, owners compete for occupiers, and in so doing seek to add service to their offer. The let and forget philosophy ultimately led to the most recent threat of one of the government's periodic interventions in the property market, this time apparently to save occupiers from the institutional inflation implicit in the FRI lease and from the need to sign up to long-term leases. The Government's climb-down over upward-only rents is not the end of the saga. The next phase could involve a Europe-wide debate.

Moreover, this particular battle is largely being fought in the wrong area, if a battle needs to be fought at all. The fact that rents in the City of London are lower today in real terms than they were 30 years ago is testament to the fact that lease reform is not the answer. Perhaps the debate should be about what kind of business the property-supply industry will be in, say, 20 years' time. The extent of change that is taking place within the office economy is little short of revolutionary. Reactionary measures by the supply side will do nothing to stop the inevitable. Perhaps what is required is a wholesale shift in attitude from a supply-led culture of fiefdom to a culture of service.

It is quite likely under this service scenario that the property-supply industry will divide. There will remain a role for specialist property development companies, taking advantage of local market knowledge to opportunistically build buildings as they have done in the past. But, increasingly, there will emerge a *wholesale* alternative to this *retail* model. This will involve property companies providing all-embracing property development and management services, either in tandem with specialist service providers or in their own right. We have already seen a glimpse of this approach with a number of property companies moving into outsourcing, but there is still a long way to go. As these *accommodation wholesalers* evolve, they are likely to develop more complex relationships with their customers. Why, for example, should occupier businesses have to become involved in the property industry through needing to procure everything from janitorial and maintenance services to partitions and lifts, when their wholesaler could provide such necessities for them?

The model also suggests more innovative approaches to management, such as charging for space on an as *used* basis rather than at a fixed rate, the provision of concierge-style services, providing help desks and service centres, and the procurement of facilities services with discounts passed on to occupiers. Such opportunities suggest that the era of the vanilla office building is coming to a close and that a wider range of commoditised products, with added services, will be available. As we have seen, some companies have begun to embrace this philosophy with their large outsourcing arrangements, and the serviced office market is now active. But there remains a long way to go before we move to a genuinely commoditised market in office space. However, if such a change in the supply process were to materialise, then there are likely to be ramifications for some of those businesses currently well established in the traditional supply chain. For example, such a model suggests a more complex relationship between supplier and customer. In this case, what is the role for intermediaries, such as surveyors? Will their role change as the need for third-party mediation lessens? It is not inconceivable that the dual role of brokering space and advising on space will split: after all, the same happened in the accountancy sector. What does the model mean for passive investors? For those whose business it has been to buy property, manage it remotely through a managing agent, and invest the income stream, the picture is perhaps rather different. They could take a share of the value emanating from a more intensive and innovative form of management. Already there is evidence of a lessening of direct involvement in the supply chain, with a number of developers providing specialist development management services to the institutions.

The changes taking place within the office economy and the organisations working within it are resulting in novel demands on the accommodation necessary for its operation, and these demand pressures will inevitably lead to changes in the organisation of the property-supply process. This dynamic between the emerging needs of the office economy and the response of the property-supply chain will find physical expression in the built environment. It will help to shape towns and cities as the nature of work and the nature of the places of work co-evolve. It is therefore imperative that policy frameworks that seek to guide the nature of development in urban areas are linked into the dynamics of this relationship. Such policy frameworks can be enabling, constraining or simply irrelevant, and past experience in the UK has been characterised at various times by all three. Although rooted in the economic expansion of the 19th century, for some reason our spatial and economic understanding of the role of the office economy lagged badly behind its development. Well into the 1970s there was in public policy only a primitive understanding of the internal dynamics of the office economy, and throughout the corporate years of the 1960s and 1970s, the government made various misguided attempts to control offices without truly getting to grips with the forces behind "the problem".

Going forward, if the tale of indifference and ineptitude in public policy is not to be repeated, then it will need to adopt a different approach to its treatment of offices. For example, planning policy has a critical supporting role in promoting London's economy and its world city status. To successfully plan, monitor and manage both the quantitative and qualitative profile of office provision, strategic and local planning authorities will need to integrate the changing structure of demand into policy frameworks. The overriding priority of policy makers must be for a clearer, activity-based approach to understanding the changing nature of the office economy and the implications for its demands on the built environment. The importance of this role is illustrated by reference to the current *London Plan*. In recent years, there has been a prolonged public debate over the merits, or otherwise, of tall buildings. Their exponents have prevailed, and a crop of such buildings is beginning to appear. One of the key arguments advanced for tall buildings was their ability to absorb expected growth in the office economy of central London by making significantly more intensive use of land. In a related move, the *London Plan* that was launched in the spring of 2004 argued that it was necessary for London to grow and become denser in its centre in order to maintain its competitive position.[9]

Both arguments rest on the basic premise that the office economy will continue to expand along its historic path. For example, the *London Plan* anticipates 636,000 new jobs by 2016, with 462,000 in the office economy. This represents growth of over 30%, and up to 8million sq m (around 90million sq ft) of additional office space between 2001 and 2016. How can such projections be squared with the evidence presented in this book about the nature of change within the office economy and its implications for the workplace? Tall buildings and an order of magnitude increase in the built capacity of London, assuming that there is sufficient transport infrastructure to move the increased numbers of people around, lie at the core of a policy framework that appears, in an echo from the past, to have no apparent contextual understanding of the current, internal dynamics of the office economy.

This chapter has painted a picture of continuing change in the office economy. The changes taking place are rapid and profound. And they are suggestive of a need to consider new and innovative ways in which to accommodate the office economy. Just as a new form of provision took hold in the early post-war period — large-scale speculative development — so perhaps now is the time for a new model to emerge. A key objective must be a more integrated approach to understanding the structure of demand and change in the office economy, and a shift in attitude that allows that the financial value of real estate is intrinsically related to its use value. This will require more sophisticated approaches to understanding how exogenous change impacts on the work environment, particularly the complex interrelationships of social, technological, economic, political and cultural forces. At a more practical level, there is a growing need to cater for choice and diversity, which presents enormous opportunities for the supply industry to find new ways of extracting value from the

---

9 Greater London Authority (2004) *The London Plan* GLA, London.

property-supply process. Such a change, however, requires the establishment of a new approach to the relationship between owners and occupiers. It might also require a quite radical rethink of the types of buildings and settings that will be required:

> the actual concentration in the centre of the city may grow smaller, there may no longer be a need for large office buildings, and businesses may be run from social gathering places such as restaurants or private houses or apartments in the city centre — a return to the coffee houses of the baroque city![10]

This apparently contemporary quote was in fact published 36 years ago! It is reproduced here not so much for its predictive accuracy, but for its sentiments about the potential for the office economy to metamorphose into a much richer texture of activities than has been the case for the past 60 years. It suggests that the trend towards gigantism is slowing and that there will emerge a need to cater for a far more diverse set of demands on the urban environment. The invisible "glue" of inter-company relationships and networks that holds the office economy together in city centres is likely to remain strong. But this does not mean that its requirements for physical space will remain unchanged: probably the contrary is true. The point about the social role of offices is beginning to become a reality. As a result, there is likely to emerge a growing demand for a greater variety of types of buildings to accommodate different kinds of organisations and activities, and the focus of developers and investors will increasingly need to turn to accommodating the needs of a diversifying office economy rather than an undifferentiated one. Such a conclusion sets down a new set of challenges for accommodating the office economy.

---

10 Cowan P, Fine D, Ireland J, Jordan C, Mercer D and Sears A (1969) *The Office: A Facet of Urban Growth* Heinemann Educational Books Ltd, London p44.

Index